Global Warming and Global Politics

Global warming has become established as the major environmental issue on the international political agenda. It is also commonly understood to be the most difficult problem to solve politically. The entrenched interests of powerful parts of industry as well as those of many states are threatened by attempts to reduce greenhouse gas emissions.

Global Warming and Global Politics is the first systematic study of the politics of global warming. Matthew Paterson looks closely at the major theories of international relations in order to establish what they have to offer in helping us understand global warming as a political issue. After discussing the dominant neorealist and neoliberal institutionalist models, Paterson concludes that both political economists and those developing more discursive approaches to international relations have much to offer to a study of the area. He goes on to suggest that the significant tensions between these two approaches provide rich ground for further analysis.

Global Warming and Global Politics makes a significant contribution to our understanding of international relations in general and international environmental politics in particular. Its combination of theory and empirical work will also make it a very useful text for students of international relations and of environmental politics.

Matthew Paterson is Lecturer in International Relations at Keele University.

Environmental Politics
Edited by Michael Waller, University of Keele, and
Stephen Young, University of Manchester

The fate of the planet is an issue of major concern to governments throughout the world and is likely to retain its hold on the agenda of national administrations due to international pressures. As an object of academic study, environmental politics is developing an increasingly high profile: there is a great need for definition of the field and for a more comprehensive coverage of its concerns. This new series will provide this definition and coverage, presenting books in three broad categories:

- new social movements and green parties;
- the making and implementation of environmental policy;
- green ideas.

Forthcoming titles:

Ecological Modernisation
Edited by Stephen C. Young and Jan van der Straaten

The Politics of Sustainable Development
Edited by Susan Baker, Maria Kousis, Dick Richardson and Stephen C. Young

Global Warming and Global Politics

Matthew Paterson

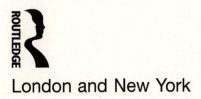

London and New York

First published 1996
by Routledge
11 New Fetter Lane, London EC4P 4EE

Simultaneously published in the USA and Canada
by Routledge
29 West 35th Street, New York, NY 10001

© 1996 Matthew Paterson

Typeset in Baskerville by Routledge
Printed and bound in Great Britain by
Redwood Books, Trowbridge, Wiltshire

British Library Cataloguing in Publication Data
A catalogue record for this book is available from the British Library

Library of Congress Cataloguing in Publication Data
Paterson, Matthew, 1967–
    Global warming and global politics/Matthew Paterson.
        p.   cm. – (Environmental politics)
    Includes bibliographical references and index.
    1. Global warming – Political aspects. 2. Environmental policy –
    International cooperation.   I. Title.   II. Series.
    QC981.8. G56P414   1996
    363.73'87–dc20   96–5372   CIP

ISBN 0–415–13871–x (hbk)
ISBN 0–415–13872–8 (pbk)

Well hello again! . . . and again seems to be the operative word here: same old faces, same old Palais, same old issues, and what could be more soothingly familiar than the first intervention, which, surprise surprise, came from a well-known major oil-producing state, followed by concurrence from an even more well-known major oil-consuming state. Some things never change, do they?

Though Léman's eagle-eyed spies report that the salad bar in the cafeteria has moved, and someone has even suggested that the head of delegation of the said oil-consuming state may have been replaced, but you'll have to excuse Léman if he can't tell the difference.

At any rate, the conference got off to a flying start today: with a rare display of unanimity every speaker expressed overwhelming delight at the continued presence of chairman Estrada, who, after stressing over and over again the extraordinary amount of business to be got through in such a short time, promptly adjourned the session after little more than an hour.

'Léman', *ECO*, 22 August 1995

Contents

Illustrations

FIGURES

TABLES

Series editors' preface

While concern for the human habitat and ideologies affirming the vital link between mother earth and the humans species have had a long history and a constant appeal, the past three decades have witnessed a surge in an awareness that humanity is inflicting on itself permanent and possibly irretrievable environmental damage. This series of books on the politics of the environment aims to provide the information and the perspective needed for an understanding of this predicament, of the anxieties to which it has given rise, and of the steps that are being taken at national and international level to address the problems that it poses.

The urgency of the environment predicament has already produced a substantial corpus of publications, and that corpus is constantly growing. The present series covers three broad areas. The first consists of the ideas and debates that the environmental movement has generated. There is room in the series for treatments of both speculative and practical contributions to those debates, the aim being to engage in analysis rather than advocacy. Second, the series contains analyses of the fortunes of the various political movements and organisations that have environmental goals. These range from inchoate and spontaneous collective action to the more organised and abiding political parties and non-governmental organisations. At the same time, the environmental policies that other political parties have been led to adopt are included, even in cases where those parties espouse ideological positions distant from those characteristic of green parties and movements. A third concern of the series is policy-making processes at national and international levels and, increasingly, the processes of trying to implement programmes to tackle existing environmental degradation in ways that do not simply worsen the problems and create new ones.

The emphasis, at least in the preliminary stages of the series, is on the advanced industrial countries. However, the series editors are fully aware of the interconnectedness of environmental issues and of the essentially international nature of environmental threats and of attempts to address them. While, therefore, it is not possible to include coverage of the environmental problems of individual developing countries, treatments of the broader international issues will be welcomed and, in particluar, those that highlight debates and developments concerning the global North–South issue.

The result is a comprehensive but manageable focus on the politics of the environment such as the series editors believe is needed as the twentieth century turns into the twenty-first century. As for the expected readership, the books in the series will carry the original research, but of an accessible kind. Many of the books will therefore have the character of a 'textbook plus'.

The work that we have chosen to lead the series illustrates a number of these considerations. Paterson's treatment on global wrming takes as its subject a topic that arouses widespread anxiety and has necessarily engaged both the scientific community and governments. It is truly international in its implications. As an authoritative treatment of a central aspect of environmental politics today, presented in an accessible form, it is eminently suited to introduce this series.

In conclusion, no scholarly endeavour should shy away from conveying a message of some sort if it is to catch imaginations and monitor the impact of change, as this series aims to do. While it is not the intention of the series editors to make any overt political statement, we are prepared to express a concern, based upon what we believe to be incontrovertible facts, from which everyone alive today must be prepared to draw the conclusions. Some of the resources on which we depend are finite and irreplaceable; the world we shall leave behind us will be, in many respects, worse than that which we inherited, and almost significantly worse; and the processes of discerning the signals of danger – framing responses to them, achieving agreement on the action to be taken to counter the danger and actually taking that action – are slow and difficult. Only one step of imagination is demanded of the reader beyond measuring these facts. This is to make the assumption that achieving the tasks imposed by the present environ-mental predicament is possible. Unfortunately, nothing at present could be less evident. What is evident is that we can escape the consequences of failing to cope with those tasks by returning to the earth from which we came, but that no-one escapes the responsibility for failure.

Michael Waller and Stephen Young

Acknowledgements

As do many first books, this book began life as a PhD thesis. There are, therefore, a great many people to whom I am indebted. Mike Clarke and Patrick Salmon in particular, at Newcastle University, gave me encouragement and the confidence to do a PhD in the first place. I am greatly indebted to my supervisor Hugh Ward, and to Rachel Walker who also supervised me for a year. Both were very enthusiastic about the project, and were always willing to give time and attention. Their contributions have undoubtedly improved my work considerably. In general, I am indebted to the excellent graduate community in the Government Department at Essex University, in particular to Toby Smith, Nikki Craske, Neil Robinson, Stephen Mew, Nick Presmeg, David Howarth and Aletta Norval, for providing both good friendship and a stimulating environment within which to work.

David Scrivener, Ted Benton, Hugh Ward, Hugh Dyer and David Sanders have all read particular incarnations of the text and gave useful comments. Dan Bodansky, John Barry, Mick Smith, John MacMillan, Richard Devetak, Albert Weale and Rachel Walker all read chapters and made useful comments, and members of the British International Studies Association's Global Environmental Change Group provided very useful comments on a draft of the conclusions presented to a meeting of the group.

For help with the research, four groups of people gave particular assistance. The Secretariat of the INC (see text for details), especially Stan Cornford and Michael Zammit Cutajar, were particularly helpful in letting me participate in their work and observe the negotiating process at first hand. Sally Cavanagh, at the Climate Action Network in London, was particularly helpful in sending me copies of *ECO* for each of the negotiations which I was unable to attend. The Economic and Social Research Council (Grant number R00429024884) funded the research, without which it would not have been possible. Claire Spencer put me up during my attendance at the fifth negotiating session in New York, in February 1992.

I also owe a substantial debt to the Energy and Environmental Programme at the Royal Institute of International Affairs, with whom I worked while working on the thesis. Thanks go especially to Michael Grubb, Nicola Steen and Matthew Tickle, whose contacts gave me access to a much greater base of information than I would otherwise have had, and whose friendship has also been important.

As someone who works best to music, many groups have helped me to concentrate as I ploughed through the swathe of UN Documents, and relieved the tedium of tidying up text. Orbital, Aphex Twin, The Nightingales, Dream Warriors, Le Mystère des Voix Bulgares and Portishead have all created an atmosphere conducive to working.

And finally, the mixture of friendship and critical awareness of Jo Van Every has been of invaluable importance throughout my time spent on this project.

Matthew Paterson

List of Abbreviations

AGGG	Advisory Group on Greenhouse Gases (WMO)
AOSIS	Alliance of Small Island States
CAN	Climate Action Network
CEQ	Council on Environmental Quality (US)
CFCs	Chlorofluorocarbons
CH_4	Methane
CO_2	Carbon dioxide
COP1	First Conference of the Parties to the United Nations Framework Convention on Climate Change
CPR	Common property resource
ECOSOC	United Nations Economic and Social Council
EPA	Environmental Protection Agency (US)
G77	Group of 77
GARP	Global Atmospheric Research Programme (WMO)
GCM	General Circulation Model
GEF	Global Environmental Facility (World Bank, UNEP and UNDP)
ghgs	Greenhouse gases
GISS	Goddard Institute for Space Studies (NASA)
ICSU	International Council of Scientific Unions
IEA	International Energy Agency
IGY	International Geophysical Year
IIASA	International Institute for Applied Systems Analysis
IMF	International Monetary Fund
IMO	International Meteorological Organisation
INC	Intergovernmental Negotiating Committee for a Framework Convention on Climate Change
IPCC	Intergovernmental Panel on Climate Change
IPE	International Political Economy

IPIECA	International Petroleum Industry Environmental Conservation Association
IR	International Relations (the discipline)
LDCs	Least Developed Countries
MedPlan	Mediterranean Action Plan (UNEP)
N_2O	Nitrous oxide
NAS	National Academy of Sciences (US)
NASA	National Aeronautic and Space Administration (US)
NGO	Non-governmental organisation
NICs	Newly industrialising countries
NIEO	New International Economic Order
NOAA	National Oceanic and Atmospheric Administration (US)
OECD	Organisation for Economic Cooperation and Development
OPEC	Organisation of Petroleum Exporting Countries
PD	Prisoner's dilemma
SCEP	Study of Critical Environmental Problems
SCOPE	Scientific Committee on Problems of the Environment (ICSU)
SEPP	Science and Environmental Policy Project
SMIC	Study of Man's Impact on Climate
SWCC	Second World Climate Conference
TNCs	Transnational corporations
UNCED	United Nations Conference on Environment and Development
UNCTAD	United Nations Conference on Trade and Development
UNCTC	United Nations Center on Transnational Corporations
UNEP	United Nations Environment Programme
UNGA	United Nations General Assembly
UNICE	Union of Industrial and Employers' Confederations of Europe
WCC	World Climate Conference
WCED	World Commission on Environment and Development
WCP	World Climate Programme (WMO)
WMO	World Meteorological Organisation
WWW	World Weather Watch (WMO)

Chapter 1

Introduction

Global warming emerged as a significant global political issue in 1988.[1] NASA scientist James Hansen's statement to the US Congress that 'it is time to stop waffling so much. We should say that the evidence is pretty strong that the greenhouse effect is here' (quoted in Pearce, 1989: 1) has often been taken as a defining moment. This came on the back of the biggest drought in the US since the 1930s, as well as freak weather patterns across the world, and the realisation that the six hottest years on record were in the 1980s. These events made claims by scientists such as Hansen about possible global warming increasingly plausible.

The events of 1988 stimulated a flurry of international conferences, and a major scientific assessment of the state of knowledge about global warming, in the Intergovernmental Panel on Climate Change (IPCC). As the momentum was maintained, climate politics 'matured', with formal negotiations to an international treaty starting in February 1991. These led to the signing of a 'Framework Convention on Climate Change' at the United Nations Conference on Environment and Development (UNCED) in Rio de Janeiro in June 1992 (United Nations, 1992).[2] At the same time, many industrialised states adopted unilateral targets to limit their own emissions of the gases believed to cause global warming. After 1992, states continued to negotiate between themselves how to respond to global warming, in particular how to build upon the Framework Convention. They also began to grapple with the practical problems of implementing the commitments they had unilaterally or multilaterally signed up to.

Popular interpretations of the politics of climate change quickly emerged. Some commentators advanced a variety of conspiracy theories. Warren Brookes, writing in *Forbes* magazine, suggested that 'just as Marxism is giving way to markets, the political "greens" seem determined to put the world economy back into the red, using the greenhouse effect to stop unfettered market-based expansion' (1989, cited in Athanasiou, 1991: 7). Similarly, although in less conspiratorial tones, Solow and Broadus asserted that it is a 'policy in search of a problem' (1990, cited in Hempel, 1993: 216). Another conspiracy theory has been that it is a case of 'environmental colonialism' (Agarwal and Narain, 1991), whereby the affluent West is trying to pull the ladder up behind it, using climate change as a political tool to stunt Southern development. In direct contrast, Singer suggested that it was a plot by 'Third World kleptocrats' to find new excuses to demand money from the West (Singer, 1992a). A final conspiracy theory is that the threat of global warming is manufactured by scientific elites to ensure continued funding for 'big science' (Boehmer-Christiansen, 1994a).

Others put forward interpretations not couched in the language of conspiracy. One is that global warming is a classic 'tragedy of the commons' (Hardin, 1968; Grubb, 1989: 22; Young, 1994: 20–1), where the lack of world government means that those resources on which all countries depend but none can control get overused. This of course has strong resonances with dominant realist and liberal traditions within International Relations (IR). Some Greens have seen it as a strategic tool for Western industry to shore up its power and usher in a new era of economic growth (Chatterjee and Finger, 1994). Others have seen it as a metaphor. Bill McKibben wrote eloquently of global warming as a metaphor for the 'end of nature', that industrial society has finally humanised nature, literally leaving no part of the biosphere untouched by human intervention:

> The temperature and rainfall are no longer to be entirely the work of some separate, uncivilisable force, but instead in part a product of our habits, our economies, our ways of life … By changing the weather, we make every spot on earth man-made [sic] and artificial. We have deprived nature of its independence, and that is fatal to its meaning. Nature's independence is its meaning; without it there is nothing but us.
>
> (McKibben, 1989: 47, 58)

In a not dissimilar vein, Paul Ehrlich saw it as an expression of global interconnectedness, stating on Earth Day 1990 that 'a cow breaks wind in Indonesia, and your grandchildren could die in food riots in the United States' (quoted in Ross, 1991: 198). Andrew Ross suggested that 'the crusade to claim the whole world as "free" for liberal capitalism is currently locked in step with the campaign to "free" the climate from human influence' (1991: 209). Oppenheimer and Boyle invoked religious imagery, suggesting that it was the 'wages of industrialisation' (1990: 18, quoted in Ross, 1991: 198). However, these interpretations have never been given any sustained examination.

POLICY DEBATES

To illustrate the lack of sustained explanations of climate politics, consider the following policy debates. One good example would be the debate over tradeable permits. This scheme would involve states being allocated permits to emit a particular quantity of CO_2 (and possibly other greenhouse gases [ghgs]) per year which would then be tradeable. The number of total permits distributed could decline over time to achieve overall global abatement targets. The point of the scheme would be that (for most allocation criteria) an industrialised country which emits more than it is given permits for would be able to buy permits from a developing country, should this be cheaper than reducing its own emissions domestically. This would be an economically optimal method of pollution control (by the standards adopted by neoclassical economists), and would facilitate North–South transfers, in the process possibly promoting development in the South which would not be based on fossil fuels. Much of the international policy debate has focused on the relative merits of tradeable permits over targets or carbon taxes, largely with a view to establishing which is the most economically efficient.[3] However, there is little in the way of discussion of the political context of the negotiations through which such schemes would have to be introduced. Grubb (1989) provides a notable exception, but even here it remains at a 'common sense' level.

Another example would be the debate about equity and North–South relations.[4] Some of this literature draws explicitly on traditions concerning justice; for example, the work of John Rawls figures prominently. Oran Young would be representative of many of these writers when he asserts that 'the availability of arrangements that all participants can accept as equitable ... is necessary for institutional bargaining to succeed' (1989a: 368). But as Grubb, Sebenius, Magalhaes and Subak (1992) point out, concerning global warming there are a number of viewpoints on this question. These positions include: 'polluter pays' rationales based either on current emissions or historically accumulated contributions to global warming; an equal entitlements approach, that all individuals have an equal right to use the atmospheric commons; a 'willingness-to-pay' justification derived from welfare economics; that each participant should shoulder a 'comparable' burden based on their situation; simply that the distributional implications of any agreement should be taken into account (a position which draws explicitly on John Rawls [1973]); and a conservative position that starts with the assumption that the status quo is legitimate in the sense that present emitters have established some common law right to use the atmosphere as they at present do (Grubb *et al.*, 1992: 312–13). However, it would again be reasonable to claim that this literature is underdeveloped regarding the political context into which such schemes would be placed (although it is politically more sophisticated than the debate over tradeable permits or institutional questions), and would benefit from a more detailed political analysis regarding that context.

A final example would be the debate over institutional questions. Many of those writing about global warming, and UNCED more generally, suggest that creating new international institutions with particular functions and powers would contribute significantly to ameliorating the problem (e.g. French, 1992; Gardner, 1992; Imber, 1993). But institutions are often conflated with organisations, and there is little analysis of the particular ways in which they can affect political outcomes. For example, Richard Gardner writes that 'A critical question throughout the UNCED process was what kind of new or improved institutions should be created to *assure* the implementation of the Agenda 21 program' (Gardner, 1992: 42, emphasis added), implying that institutional arrangements can in some simple fashion assure the implementation of such a huge programme. Hilary French (1992: 31–8) argues forcefully for the strengthening of UN institutions to improve the international response to environmental problems, but without any clear analysis of what strengthening means, or what institutions, such as an environmental dimension to the Security Council or a reformed UNEP, could achieve. And Mark Imber (1992) engages in a purely technical account of the changes involved in establishing the Sustainable Development Commission and the resultant changes in UNEP's role, assuming the importance of these changes without any explicit justification.

A SECOND SILENCE

Alongside the lack of a sustained attempt to explain the politics of global warming, there has been a similar paucity of efforts within International Relations to provide convincing and well developed explanations of the global environmental politics which emerged in the 1980s. The 1980s and the 1990s have seen a great amount of activity within International Relations theory. There have been (for the purposes of this discussion, at least) three major developments of concern here. First, following the publications of Kenneth Waltz's Theory of International Politics (1979), there has been significant debate of great relevance to any study whose focus is on interstate cooperation.[5] This has been a debate between neorealists on the one hand (such as Waltz), and neoliberal institutionalists (such as Robert Keohane) on the other, over the likelihood and extent of interstate cooperation, and the degree to which the emergence of international institutions mitigates the formal anarchy in the international sphere.[6]

Second, the 1980s witnessed a rise in theories which came from thoroughly different traditions to the essentially positivist approaches of both neorealism and neoliberal institutionalism. Feminism, critical theory, Gramscian thought and poststructuralism, all started to generate a literature specifically on International Relations, which, among other things, focused on a critique of the epistemological presumptions of much mainstream IR theory, and called into question many of the latter's central assumptions. The debate surrounding the rise of these theories has often been called the 'post-positivist debate' (Lapid, 1989; Vasquez, 1995).

Third, the 1980s, and even more so the 1990s, have also seen a resurgence of historical materialism. Variously termed transnational historical materialism, open Marxism or Gramscian International Political Economy,[7] this resurgence has been despite, or perhaps in part because of, the collapse of the Soviet bloc, which many interpreted as the death knell of Marxism. Much of its rise has been to do with the growing interest in questions of International Political Economy, for example increased concern with processes of globalisation.

However, in none of these debates have environmental problems been an important reference point for discussion. So discussion of global environmental problems has emerged largely without reference to the concurrent developments within IR theory. Almost all theoretical discussion of environmental problems within IR has been within liberal institutionalist frameworks. Within this tradition, there has clearly been some important work done in this area, notably Peter Haas's *Saving the Mediterranean*, Oran Young's *International Cooperation: Managing Natural Resources and the Environment* and *International Governance: Protecting the Environment in a Stateless Society*, and Haas, Keohane and Levy's edited volume *Institutions for the Earth* (Haas, 1990; Young, 1989b, 1994; Haas *et al.*, 1993).[8] Work on global warming which has tried to use IR theory has also largely been written from this perspective. The best of these is Ward (1993), who adopts a game-theoretic orientation and emphasises the importance of international institutions. Sebenius (1991) is one of the few others who have used IR theory material (in his case, negotiation analysis based largely on game theory, again broadly within an institutionalist framework), but he simply applies this model prescriptively to global warming, presuming both that the model holds for other areas of international cooperation (without demonstrating it) and that 'lessons' in other areas of international politics can be applied to global warming, largely without reflection on the political problems peculiar to global warming.

However, global warming is commonly seen to be such a challenging global environmental problem compared to others, that it is worth reinvestigating the claims made by these writers concerning it. In particular, the central claim of liberal institutionalists is that cooperation can often emerge within the states-system, despite formal anarchy. But if the claim that global warming presents by far the greatest challenge to humanity of all the major environmental problems is convincing, then this may make it more plausible that claims about the importance of institutions will fail to account for climate politics. Alternative explanations within IR will have therefore to be looked for.

A QUESTION OF QUESTIONS

This book tries to go some way to filling these silences. It attempts to do two things. The first is to explain the international politics of global warming, leading up to the First Conference of the Parties of the Framework Convention, which took place in March and April 1995. There are two basic questions involved in such an investigation, corresponding to two distinct processes which have been involved. First, huge scientific uncertainties remained about the timing, extent and likelihood of warming, when no empirical demonstration of a link between observed climatic changes and anthropogenic emissions of greenhouse gases had been observed. Given this, how and why did global warming become an issue on the international political agenda, which many states took seriously enough on the one hand to announce unilateral mitigating measures, and on the other hand to negotiate a multilateral agreement on the subject? The second question is, how did the processes of cooperation on the issue work, once formal negotiations had started?

The second purpose of the book is to look at strands of IR theory in the light of global warming, in order to see both how they would account for its politics, and whether these accounts are adequate. Such an investigation is needed in order to contribute to an explanation of the politics of global warming, but it is also intended that this will make it possible to say something about IR theory and some of its inadequacies.

Thus the book offers a set of interpretations of global climate politics within the frameworks provided by different strands of IR theory. I will offer an argument that two particular interpretations, those provided by historical materialism, and those by poststructuralist writers focusing on the notion of discourse, both provide convincing explanations. However, there is a clear tension between the two, and this tension and ways in which it could be resolved will be explored in the conclusion.

To a great extent, this argument turns on the questions which the perspectives ask, as much as the answers they give. The framework provided by historical materialism means that it asks more expansive questions, allowing us to cover more of the material of climate politics. Realists and liberal institutionalists restrict us by and large to interstate politics, to patterns of conflict and cooperation between states, to processes of negotiation within anarchy, to the relevance of international institutions. This leads us to questions merely about the content of formal treaties, to the question of which states got their way, whether international institutions mattered in generating these outcomes, and so on. The questions are furthermore positivist in their orientation, i.e. they act to obscure thorny normative issues (although some writers may be explicitly guided by normative concerns).

By contrast, historical materialist frameworks allow us to transcend a domestic–international division which obscures more than it reveals. They also allow normative questions, for example those of justice, to be more easily integrated into the analysis, focusing on the 'Who is theory for?' question (Cox, 1986: 207). Finally, they allow us to talk about capitalism, which helps us to place the politics of global warming in a context other than the abstracted formal anarchy of realists and liberal institutionalists. This allows us to see how state interests are constituted, and how global warming fits into broader developments within world politics.

In addition, the discourse-theoretic approach developed, for example, by Litfin (1994) – which is closely linked to the constructivist position developed by Wendt (1987) and others – has much to offer. Rather than abstractly assuming some instrumental rationality, as do realists and (most) liberal institutionalists, it suggests that the meaning which states and other actors confer on particular phenomena is crucial to their acting on these issues, and that these meanings are constituted intersubjectively between states rather than by those states separately. It emphasises that, rather than an international structure existing as a given, external to the existence of individual states and their practitioners, global political structures are things which are continually made and remade through the actions of states. This suggests that states have some room for manoeuvre in their dealings with others, but it also suggests (a point which is normatively important) that those international structures can be transformed.

The later chapters in this book develop this argument by examining the explanations of global climate politics which realists, liberals, those focusing on the politics of knowledge, and historical materialists, would in turn offer. The conclusion explores the creative tension between the latter two perspectives, both of which I am sympathetic towards. Before that, the book offers an historical account of climate politics to date. The first of these chapters deals with the history of climate science and international meteorological cooperation, and the emergence of global warming as a political issue. The second deals with the formal interstate negotiations leading up to the signing of the Framework Convention in 1992, and from then on to the first Conference of the Parties in 1995. The third discusses in detail some of the major political faultlines in the negotiations, and debates which dominated them.

This way of organising the chapters should not be taken to imply that history can be free of theory, but it is as much for convenience as anything. Some of the arguments in later chapters will be prefigured in these historical chapters. And the selection of material is designed so that each theoretical perspective can be adequately explored. For example, the interstate formal negotiations enable realism and liberal institutionalism to be explored. But the material in Chapter 2 is also necessary to explore adequately the importance of institutions in climate politics, for example with the history of international meteorological cooperation. Chapter 2 also enables a discussion of the politics of science, and the importance of science in agenda-setting. And Chapter 4 illustrates many of the themes which are necessary to explore some of the ideas bought up by historical materialism. So these historical chapters should give some sense of the plausibility of different accounts of climate politics.

POSTSCRIPT: AN INTRODUCTION TO GLOBAL WARMING

This section is provided mainly for those unfamiliar with some of the main features of climate change. For those who are familiar with those features, this section will be unnecessary. It does however emphasise how dealing with global warming is primarily a question of energy use, and how both the impacts of global warming, and the responses to mitigate it, have very significant distributional consequences, making it susceptible to high levels of political conflict. However, this introduction will only be brief; for fuller introductions to the scientific characteristics of the issue see Grubb (1990: ch. 1), Houghton *et al.* (1990), or Leggett (1990).

Science

Despite objections from some climate scientists, the most authoritative and widely accepted general viewpoint on global warming remains the report produced by the Intergovernmental Panel on Climate Change (IPCC) in 1990.[9] The IPCC, a body of the world's leading climatologists which was set up in 1988, felt able to state in that report that they were certain that some global warming would occur due to human activities, should existing emissions trends continue (Houghton *et al.*, 1990: xi). The basis for making such a claim was threefold: the naturally occurring greenhouse effect; the increases in concentrations associated with the greenhouse effect due to human activities; and an approximate correlation between increases in those concentrations and observed mean surface air temperature increases in the twentieth century.

The greenhouse effect is a natural phenomenon whereby certain gases in the atmosphere keep the earth's temperature significantly higher than it would otherwise be. It produces conditions at the earth's surface which are suitable for life. The main gases involved in the greenhouse effect are water vapour, carbon dioxide (CO_2), chlorofluorocarbons (CFCs), methane (CH_4) and nitrous oxide (N_2O).[10] These gases allow radiation to pass through from the sun, but they absorb the lower frequency, longer wavelength radiation from the earth's surface, thereby trapping heat in the atmosphere. It is estimated that without these gases, the earth's surface temperature would be 33 °C lower than at present (Nierenberg *et al.*, 1989; Leggett, 1990b).

With the exception of water vapour, both the emissions from human activities and the atmospheric concentrations of these gases have increased significantly during the twentieth century. The increases in concentrations are shown in Figure 1.1 (from Houghton *et al.*, 1990: xvi).

Lastly, the IPCC also produced figures which showed an increase in the global mean surface temperature over the previous one hundred years of between 0.3 and 0.6 °C (Houghton *et al.*, 1990: xii). Although the IPCC made clear their acceptance that this does not prove the global warming hypothesis, since it remains a warming within the natural variability of the climate system (1990: xxix), and in any case correlation does not prove causality, their inclusion of this (very) approximate correlation between increasing concentrations and observed warming indicates a belief that they may well be linked.

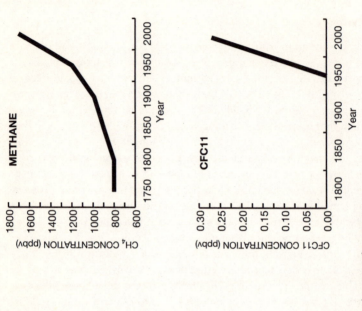

Figure 1.1 Increases in atmospheric concentrations of major greenhouse gases

Source: J.T. Houghton, G. J. Jenkins and J. J. Ephraums (1990) *Climate Change: The IPCC Scientific Assessment*, Cambridge: Cambridge University Press, xvi

Impacts

The implications of the IPCC's findings were then, and remain now, beset with uncertainties. They made projections of the likely rate of warming, and the implications of this, but the relevant point here is simply that the implications were sufficient to generate some action from the world's governments. Michael Grubb summarises the salient point well: 'all that can be usefully said is that the less the rate of atmospheric change, the less the risks and costs are likely to be' (Grubb, 1990: 12). The potential implications include: sea level rise (the IPCC projected a rise between 3 and 10 cm per decade on a 'business-as-usual' basis); drastically changed rainfall patterns (some parts of the world getting much more, others much less rainfall); agricultural migration as crops move towards the poles; changes in zones in which major diseases would be located; significant regional changes in potential agricultural yield; and potentially large numbers of environmental refugees.[11]

Politics

More important for the purposes of this discussion is a consideration of the political characteristics of global warming, in terms of how these flow from the causes of global warming, and therefore how responsibility can be allocated (or fought over). One politically extremely important question is how it may in the future affect various communities, countries and states differently through the impacts of global warming. I will not deal with this aspect, except in so far as it has clearly affected negotiating positions. Instead, I focus on the politics behind the negotiations, which have centred around negotiating ways to affect future emissions paths.

However, a brief consideration of these differential impacts is worthwhile here, if only to justify consideration of global warming as something worth studying. Global warming can be expected to intensify and alter existing disparities of power and wealth both between and within countries.

Between countries, impacts are likely to be differential, largely along the lines of pre-existing economic inequalities between North and South. This assertion is not largely based on climatological projections, since these are both very uncertain (especially at the regional level) and more disaggregated by region. It is simply that developing countries will be less able to compensate for impacts through adaptive changes, or to cope directly with climatic impacts, due primarily to lack of financial and technological resources. A brief comparison between the Netherlands and

Bangladesh will serve to illustrate this point. Both are in very similar, low-lying geographical situations, dependent on that low-lying land for agricultural production, but the Netherlands has a much greater capacity than Bangladesh to adapt, due primarily to techno-economic factors.

Within countries, it seems reasonable to mention three main likely differential impacts. The first is simply an income based one; that the impacts are likely to hit the poorest hardest. They will be least able to adapt to climatic changes by altering the crops they grow, or by moving, and they will be most likely to be further marginalised by governments who will be dealing with climatic impacts.[12] Second, in countries with strong ethnic, religious, or other divides, governments are likely to favour dominant groups in decisions, as resources such as agricultural land get scarcer, as they will in some countries. Third, some impacts may exacerbate existing gender-based inequalities. In particular, patriarchy in many developing countries means that women are predominantly made responsible for collecting wood and water, often travelling large distances daily to collect them (Sontheimer, 1991). Both of these resources may be adversely affected in some areas by global warming exacerbating the problems experienced by women in those situations. Also, the position of women in agriculture in many countries is likely to mean existing inequalities may be intensified. As agriculture in developing countries has been progressively capitalised during the twentieth century, women have largely been left responsible for subsistence agriculture outside the market in many countries, and left increasingly with more marginal land. They may thus be hit most by changes in agricultural zones. And in industrialised agriculture in developing countries, Cynthia Enloe has shown how those industries are heavily gendered (1989), and women can be expected to lose out, without strong struggles, from decisions made by male elites about investment as agricultural zones shift.

The bulk of this book deals, however, with the politics of allocating responsibility for reducing greenhouse gas emissions. The predominant gas involved in any anthropogenic global warming is undeniably carbon dioxide.[13] In 1990, the IPCC put its contribution at 55 per cent (Houghton *et al.*, 1990: xx). Furthermore, three factors increase the focus on CO_2. First, CFCs are already being phased out under the Montreal Protocol on Substances Which Deplete the Ozone Layer. Secondly, in the IPCC's 1992 Supplementary Report, the estimated contribution of CFCs themselves was reduced as the IPCC discovered an interaction between ozone depletion and global warming, thus increasing the relative importance of CO_2 (Houghton *et al.*, 1992: 14).

The third factor is that, when we look at the sources of the gases by

Table 1.1 Greenhouse gases and their main anthropogenic sources.

Carbon dioxide	Fossil fuel burning Deforestation and land use changes Cement manufacture
Methane	Rice paddy cultivation Ruminants (e.g. cows, sheep) Biomass burning and decay Releases from fossil fuel production
Chlorofluorocarbons	Manufactured for solvents, refrigerants, aerosol spray propellants, foam packaging, etc.
Nitrous Oxide	Fertilisers Fossil fuel burning Land conversion for agriculture
Precursor gases	(involved in ozone and methane chemistry)
Nitrogen oxides Non-methane hydrocarbons Carbon monoxide	Fossil fuel burning Evaporation of liquid fuels and solvents Fossil fuel and biomass burning

Source: Michael Grubb (1989) *The Greenhouse Effect: Negotiating Targets*, London: Royal Institute of International Affairs, 6.

activity, we note that many of the other gases involved also come from activities whose central pollutant product is CO_2. Thus, focusing on CO_2 will also reduce emissions of other ghgs. Table 1.1 illustrates this point (from Grubb, 1989: 6). The sources of some of the methane, some of the nitrous oxide, and most of the ozone precursors, all come from fossil fuel burning which accounts for approximately 80 per cent of the CO_2 emissions (a percentage which depends on assessments of rates of deforestation).

Thus the logic is to focus on fossil fuel energy production in addressing global warming, a logic which has informed the climate strategies of most states and environmental groups. And a brief consideration of the politics of energy, in particular in industrialised countries, reveals a clear idea as to why global warming becomes politically so problematic. The IPCC stated that CO_2 emissions would need to be reduced immediately by over 60 per cent if concentrations were to be stabilised at existing levels (Houghton *et al.*, 1990: xviii). In most industrialised countries, energy lobbies (in particular oil companies, coal producers and the road lobby) are politically very powerful, and in most countries a culture exists whereby the assumption is that energy use must grow in order to sustain economic growth, an assumption which is often built into Energy Department planning models (Baumgartner and Midttun, 1987). Thus, dealing with proposals to reduce energy use significantly (or proposals to transfer to non-fossil fuel sources), has produced large-scale political opposition from powerful groups, and presents politicians who are out to maximise their electoral advantage with potentially great problems.

A second dimension to the politically problematic nature of global warming is shown by looking at emissions across countries. Figures 1.2a and b (from Grubb, 1989) clearly demonstrate the huge inequalities involved.

Overall, industrialised countries (the US, the USSR, Japan, the EC, and the East European Six) account for over 60 per cent of the world's total fossil carbon emissions, but for just under 25 per cent of world population. There are great disparities in fossil carbon *per capita* emissions. The US emits approximately 5.7 tonnes of carbon per person per year, while India (for example) emits approximately 0.4 tonnes (Grubb, 1989: 16). This has increased North–South tensions during the negotiations, and it is clear how it has exacerbated problems in reaching an international agreement. Some of the implications of this division will be followed through and illustrated in later chapters, particularly in Chapter 4.

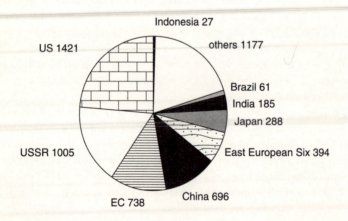

Figure 1.2a Fossil carbon emissions (commercial energy consumption only). Units: million tonnes of carbon
Source: Michael Grubb (1989) *The Greenhouse Effect: Negotiating Targets*, London: Royal Institute of International Affairs, 15.

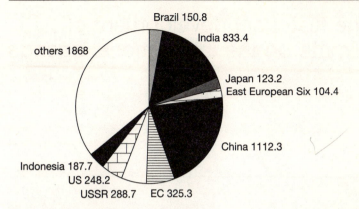

Figure 1.2b Population. Units: million
Source: Michael Grubb (1989) *The Greenhouse Effect: Negotiating Targets*, London: Royal Institute of International Affairs, 15.

Chapter 2

The historical development of climate on the international agenda

It is not difficult to understand that the problem of transforming the climate on a world or regional base scale is, by its very nature, an international one, requiring the united efforts and the coordination of the activities of all countries.

(Chief of USSR Hydrometeorological Service, 1967, quoted in Weiss, 1975: 812)

Oh Mother Earth, ocean-girdled and mountain-breasted, pardon me for trampling on you.

(Frontispiece, *Study of Man's Impact on the Climate* [Matthews *et al.*, 1971], quoted in Victor and Clark, 1991: 40)

This chapter outlines the emergence of climate as an issue in international politics. It looks at the emergence of the issue in four sections. These obviously overlap to a great extent, but they can be used to describe the developments as they have evolved.

The first section looks at the history of the science which led to theories about global warming, and at the origins of international cooperation on meteorological issues. The chapter then looks at the gradual emergence during the 1970s and 1980s of a scientific consensus that global warming was possible, and was increasingly held to be likely by many scientists within the relevant fields. One of the main conclusions to be drawn from these two sections is that both the early developments in the science and the early international meteorological cooperation were necessary preconditions for global warming to become a political issue during the 1980s. The development of the scientific theory of global warming provided the basis for consensus between (most) climate scientists which, in turn, acted as a context within which decision-makers acted. And the institutional network of meteorological cooperation which emerged and expanded continuously during the twentieth century, in particular after the Second World War, became self-perpetuating, as people within the institutions looked for ways to expand further those cooperative ventures.

The third section starts approximately at the Villach Conference in 1985 (see below for details), when climate scientists increasingly recognised a strong likelihood that global warming would become dangerous. Global warming underwent a transition from scientific to political issue, and a political response emerged in the form of pleas for action, initially by scientists, then by a few politicians and in the reports of international conferences. Finally, the chapter looks at the highly institutionalised scientific assessment of the problem which was embodied in the Intergovernmental Panel on Climate Change (IPCC), whose first Report precipitated the political negotiations which will be dealt with in the following chapter.

THE HISTORY OF THE SCIENCE AND OF INTERNATIONAL METEOROLOGICAL COOPERATION

Baron Jean Baptiste Joseph Fourier is generally recognised to have been the first person to have made an argument about the greenhouse-like properties of the atmosphere, and to suggest that the atmosphere was important in determining the temperature of the earth's surface.[1] He made this assertion in 1827, while studying the flow of heat as an application of his mathematical theorem. He called the effect the 'hothouse effect', through a (mistaken) analogy with how heat is trapped in a greenhouse (Fourier, 1827: 585).[2]

During the course of the nineteenth century, experiments and observations were undertaken to calculate the effect of the gases involved, and CO_2 and water vapour became recognised as the most important gases involved in the greenhouse effect (Boyle and Ardill, 1989: 12). Of particular importance was the measurement, by British scientist John Tyndall, of the absorption of heat radiation by water vapour. Tyndall measured the transmission of radiation through water vapour, and published a paper on the effects of water vapour as a greenhouse gas in 1863, entitled 'On Radiation Through the Earth's Atmosphere' (Tyndall, 1863). He estimated that water vapour holds about 16 000 times as much heat as does oxygen and nitrogen, the main constituents of the atmosphere.[3] Both Kellogg (1987: 115) and Gribbin (1990: 31) state that Tyndall was the first person to suggest that ice ages were caused by a decline in atmospheric carbon dioxide concentrations, and Victor and Clark (1991) suggest he also claimed that CO_2 rises would lead to temperature rises; these conclusions are not, however, in his 1863 article.

Meteorologists had already begun to cooperate across national boundaries, recognising that their measurements would be far more useful if they were pooled. Two early attempts to set up networks of atmospheric monitoring stations were made, one by the Academia del Cimento in Florence, between 1645 and 1667, both inside and outside Italy, and one by the Meteorological Society of Mannheim, in 1780. The network of stations based in Mannheim included one in the United States and one in Greenland (Van Miegham, 1968: 110). Both of these projects collapsed, however, the collapse of the one based in Mannheim being due to the French Revolutionary Wars.

Enduring cooperation began with the First International Meteorological Conference, held on 23 August 1853 in Brussels. This conference standardised meteorological observations to be taken from ships, by establishing a set of instructions for how to take measurements, and a standard form for recording them (Weiss, 1975: 809; Cain, 1983: 80; Soroos, 1991: 198). It was organised at the initiative of a naval officer, Lieutenant M. F. Maury of the United States Navy (Van Miegham, 1968: 111). The conference was attended by people from ten countries, with all the participants being naval officers, except Captain James of the British Army and Monsieur A. Quetelet, director of the Royal Belgian Observatory (Van Miegham, 1968: 112). James proposed to standardise land-based observations, but this proposal was not taken up.

Twenty years later, the cooperation was institutionalised. At the Leipzig Conference of Meteorologists in 1872, it was proposed that an International Meteorological Organisation (IMO) be established, and an official Congress be organised to establish the organisation, involving government officials (Van Miegham, 1968: 112). This conference also standardised land-based meteorological observations, following up James's earlier suggestion. The Leipzig Conference was attended primarily by meteorologists. Fifty-two directors of National Meteorological Services attended, along with other scientists (Van Miegham, 1968: 112). According to Weiss, the new developments were due to 'increasing interest in meteorological research, greater recognition of the economic importance of climatic data, and the development of the electric telegraph, which facilitated rapid collection and dissemination of observations' (Weiss, 1975: 809). There was also increasing recognition that meteorologists could not enhance their knowledge satisfactorily within national borders, but needed to cooperate across countries. As John Ruskin stated at the time:

> The meteorologist is impotent if alone; his observations are useless; for they are made upon a point, while the speculations to be derived from

them must be on space.... The Meteorological Society, therefore, has been formed not for a city, nor for a kingdom, but for the world....

(Daniel, 1973: 8, quoted in Weiss, 1975: 809)

By the time the First International Meteorological Congress was held in September 1873 in Vienna, governments had become sufficiently interested that attendance was by government representatives rather than by meteorologists in their private capacity. The Vienna Congress formally established the IMO, which was then set up as an organisation over the following six years, through a series of meetings of the Permanent Committee established at Vienna. These meetings drew up a charter for the organisation, which was finalised at Utrecht in 1878, when the IMO was formally founded (Van Miegham, 1968: 113). Following Swoboda (1950), Van Miegham outlines five main stages of the IMO's existence (Van Miegham, 1968: 111–20). The first of these included the preliminary conferences of Brussels and Leipzig. The second was the 'preparatory phase', from 1873–1878, when the organisation was set up. The last three periods lasted from 1879–1914, 1919–1939, and 1946–1950 respectively.

During Van Miegham's third period, the IMO coordinated the standardisation of measurements, and also organised a system of exchanging weather information between countries (Cain, 1983: 80). Occasionally, the IMO also coordinated pieces of research on meteorological issues. The most prominent of these was in the International Polar Year in 1882–3, when twelve states cooperated to establish and operate fourteen stations round the North Pole, observing various phenomena, including those of a meteorological nature (Maunder, 1990: 56).

During this period, a committee of nine non-governmental experts was set up (the International Meteorological Committee) and cooperation on meteorological issues became largely non-governmental again until the inter-war period (Weiss, 1975: 809–10). Van Miegham refers to the IMO as a 'federation of directors of national networks of observing stations' (Van Miegham, 1968: 111). The other development during this period was the establishment of a number of Technical Commissions (some of which still exist) to look at, and standardise measurement procedures for, various aspects of meteorology (Van Miegham, 1968: 114–15).

At the end of the nineteenth century the next development in greenhouse science occurred. Following up work such as that of Tyndall, and based on the theory proposed by Fourier, Swedish scientist Svante Arrhenius published a paper entitled 'On the influence of carbonic air upon the temperature of the ground' in the Philosophical Magazine in 1896 (Arrhenius, 1896; Lunde, 1991: 58). In this article, Arrhenius calculated that if the concentration of CO_2 in the atmosphere was doubled, the temperature of the planet would increase by between 5 and 6 °C (Arrhenius, 1896: 268). These calculations were based on 'measurements of infra-red radiation from the moon at different angles above the horizon, carried out by an American astronomer, Samuel Pierpoint Langley' (Gribbin, 1990: 32; Lunde, 1991: 58). It was possible to measure the absorbent effects of carbon dioxide because radiation coming in at different angles would pass through different thicknesses of air (Arrhenius, 1896). Arrhenius is generally credited with having taken a crucial step in greenhouse science, by calculating the effect of changing the CO_2 concentration in the earth's temperature. However, it is clear from his article that his work was related to, and based on, the work of a number of other scientists. In particular, his only reference in the 1896 article to coal in relation to carbon is in a quote from another Swedish scientist, a Professor Hogbom.[4]

Later, in his book *Worlds in the Making* (1908), Arrhenius made the first claim that human industrial activities might significantly affect climate. He wrote there that:

> The actual percentage of carbonic acid [CO_2] in the air is so insignificant that the annual combustion of coal, which has now (1904) [1908 was the publication date] risen to about 900 million tons and is rapidly increasing, carries about one-seven-hundredth part of its percentage of carbon dioxide to the atmosphere. Although the sea, by absorbing carbonic acid, acts as a regulator of huge capacity, which takes up about five-sixths of the produced carbonic acid, we may yet recognise that the slight percentage of carbonic acid in the atmosphere may by the advances of industry be changed to a noticeable degree in the course of a few centuries.
>
> (Arrhenius, 1908: 54)[5]

He also sounds an optimistic note on this question, countering the 'lamentations' which he says were often heard 'that the coal stored up in the earth is wasted by the present generation without any thought for the future', stating that:

> By the influence of the increasing percentage of carbonic acid in the atmosphere, we may hope to enjoy ages with more equable and better climates, especially as regards the colder regions of the earth; ages

when the earth will bring forth much more abundant crops than at present, for the benefit of rapidly propagating mankind.

(Arrhenius, 1908: 63)

The arguments of Arrhenius went unnoticed for much of the next sixty years. The only major exception to this was the suggestion by a British scientist, G. D. Callendar, that human emissions of trace gases were sufficient to lead to significant climate change (Pearce, 1989: 97; Lyman, 1990: 11; Lunde, 1991: 58–9; Rowlands, 1994: 82). In a presentation to the Royal Society in 1938, he compared the measured growth of atmospheric CO_2 and the temperature records from 200 meteorological stations, and argued that this evidence supported Arrhenius's thesis about the relationship between CO_2 and temperature (Callendar, 1938). Callendar remained convinced despite the scepticism of the Royal Society, and, like Arrhenius, was optimistic about the implications, suggesting that the extra CO_2 would be good for agriculture in northern temperate zones, and that the warming would be protection against the 'return of the deadly glaciers' (Lyman, 1990: 11).

Meanwhile, technological advances such as the development of radio and aviation had made gathering meteorological data much easier, and had made governments more aware of the importance of such data for their economies (Weiss, 1975: 810). As a result of this, the IMO became once more an intergovernmental body. The Conference of Directors of the IMO decided in 1935 that future meetings of the IMO would involve governmental representatives and requested governments to send representatives from national meteorological offices (Weiss, 1975: 810).

After the war, this process became more formalised when the IMO was turned into the World Meteorological Organisation (WMO). The newly formed United Nations had the effect of providing a new framework for international cooperation in various scientific and technical fields (Cain, 1983: 80). In 1947, the World Meteorological Convention was adopted, which established the WMO. The WMO began operating in 1951, and officially replaced the IMO.

In the years immediately after the Second World War, two technological advances led to greatly increased cooperation on meteorological issues. These were the development of jet aviation, which created new demands for meteorological data, especially at high altitudes, and the development of satellites, computers and improved radio communications, which together enabled meteorologists to meet this demand (Weiss, 1975: 810; Cain, 1983: 80–1). Another technological development, the nuclear bomb, also led to increased research on climate, in particular in the US, where the potential climatic effects of the bomb were seen to be important (Hart and Victor, 1993: 647–8).

These developments led to the International Geophysical Year (IGY), held between 1 July 1957 and 31 December 1958. The year was sponsored jointly by WMO and the International Council for Scientific Unions (ICSU),[6] and 30 000 scientists from more than 1 000 research stations in sixty-six countries participated (Boyle and Ardill, 1989: 24; Soroos, 1991: 201). It had as its precedents the International Polar Years of 1882–3 and 1932–3, but the fifty-year interval was halved to twenty-five years (Atwood, 1959: 682). It was held to conduct studies of the earth and upper atmosphere, and was timed to coincide with a period of strong solar activity and the first satellite launches by the Soviet Union and the United States (Weiss, 1975: 810; Soroos, 1991: 201). Among other things, it resulted in the first daily weather maps of the earth, the beginning of the British Antarctic Survey's monitoring of stratospheric ozone at the South Pole, the first comprehensive look at Antarctic weather, and the discovery of three counter-currents in the oceans (Weiss, 1975: 810; Boyle and Ardill, 1989: 24).[7]

Perhaps the most important of the outcomes of the IGY for the purposes of this discussion was the establishment of the first permanent CO_2 monitoring station at Mauna Loa in Hawaii. The origins of this lie in another reason why 1957 is an important year in 'greenhouse' history.

Prior to 1957, the prevailing view was that any extra CO_2 emitted by humans would be absorbed by the oceans, which was the main reason why Callendar's views had been rejected. Consequently there appeared to be no reason to worry about emissions from fossil fuel burning. In an article in *Tellus* in 1957, Revelle and Suess first gave good reasons to believe that this would not be the case (Revelle and Suess, 1957).[8] They suggested that about half the CO_2 emitted would remain in the atmosphere, and that humanity was thus conducting a 'large-scale geophysical experiment' (Revelle and Suess, 1957: 19; Pearce, 1989: 97). They estimated that the atmospheric CO_2 concentration would probably increase by 20–40 per cent 'in coming decades' (Revelle and Suess, 1957: 26).

The importance of this argument was that it enabled Revelle to persuade others that it was important to begin collecting systematic data about how much CO_2 was in the atmosphere. Before this time only sporadic measurements had been taken. Callendar had only had small numbers of CO_2 measurements on which to base his claims. Revelle persuaded one of his graduate students, Charles David Keeling, to begin regular measurements of CO_2 concentrations at Mauna Loa, as part of the IGY. These measurements have continued since 1958 and produced a direct refutation of the arguments of those who believed that the CO_2 would be absorbed by the oceans.

According to Soroos, the success of the IGY led to much greater cooperation on meteorology (Soroos, 1991: 201). This led WMO and ICSU to follow up a suggestion by the UN General Assembly (UNGA) to develop the World Weather Watch (WWW – not to be confused with the World Wide Web) and the Global Atmospheric Research Programme (GARP). The WWW was established in 1968, and was an extension and expansion of existing cooperative arrangements between countries to collect and distribute weather information. The WWW organises the systematic observation, processing and transmission of meteorological data between countries, which in turn make modern weather forecasting possible.

In 1975, 130 of the then 135 UN member states were participating in WWW (Weiss, 1975: 812). There are approximately 9 500 land-based observer stations and 7 000 merchant ships, which collect readings every six hours, and over 100 000 stations which make more simple observations on a daily basis, as part of WWW (Davies, 1972: 330; Bruce, 1990: 28). There are also satellites from the US, the (ex-)USSR, Japan, and the European Space Agency which are involved in WWW (Cain, 1983: 81). There are both geostationary and polar satellites involved, and all points on the earth come under surveillance at least twice daily (Bruce, 1990: 28). It was, according to Davies (then Secretary-General of WMO), the development of satellites which made the extensiveness of WWW possible (Davies, 1972: 330; Bruce, 1990: 28).

GARP was created in 1967 by WMO and ICSU jointly, and is a coordinated research effort to understand the global weather system as a whole, and 'to develop the underlying scientific knowledge as a base for improving the services to be provided by WWW and the scientific understanding of climate' (Cain, 1983: 81). It has conducted several large-scale experiments, the most prominent of which has been the First GARP Global Experiment, which became known as the Global Weather Experiment (Weiss, 1975: 812; Cain, 1983: 81).

The developments in greenhouse science by the beginning of the 1970s were such that sufficient information was being gathered to make rigorous assessments of the state of knowledge about climate and any potential climate changes possible. Simultaneously, the institutional developments, in particular within WMO and ICSU, laid the foundations for the organisation and coordination of further research which would facilitate the development of a scientific consensus on global warming during the 1970s and 1980s. It is to the emergence of that consensus that we now turn.

THE EMERGENCE OF A SCIENTIFIC CONSENSUS ON GLOBAL WARMING

During this period there was a broad discursive shift in the general understanding of climate as a problem. There was a rather rapid change from the mid–late 1960s, when climate research was viewed as a precursor to humans consciously changing climate to make it more favourable, towards research into how humans may be changing climate inadvertently. The quote from Federov, Chief of the USSR Hydro-meteorological Service in 1967, at the beginning of this chapter is one example. US President Kennedy proposed to the UN General Assembly in 1961 'further cooperative efforts between all nations in weather prediction and eventually in *weather control*' (Weiss, 1975: 811, emphasis added). Revelle, while heading a White House team in the mid-1960s to evaluate the potential threat of a CO_2-induced global warming, wrote in the team's report that, should such changes become likely, humanity could try to effect 'countervailing climate change' (Rowlands, 1994: 67). The director of the National Center for Atmospheric Research in Boulder, Colorado, stated to Congress that he wanted 'maximum possible mastery of the atmospheric environment' (quoted in Hart and Victor, 1993: 663). However, from the late 1960s, as the first wave of modern environment-alism emerged, this technocratic image of climate as something to be controlled by humans fades towards an image where humans are more dependent on climate for their welfare, and are unable to manipulate it for their own ends (Hart and Victor, 1993: 666–9). By 1971, the participants in the Study on Man's Impact on Climate (see more below) included a Sanskrit prayer as a frontispiece to their report, also cited at the beginning of this chapter.

According to Cain, the 'turning point' in relation to awareness of climate issues and to the development of greenhouse science were two studies undertaken in 1970 and 1971, the Study of Critical Environmental Problems (SCEP), and the Study on Man's Impact on Climate (SMIC) (MIT, 1970; Matthews *et al.*, 1971; Cain, 1983: 91). These studies highlighted the importance of the CO_2 question and, according to Cain, caused this problem to be included on the environmental agendas of national and international institutions (Cain, 1983: 91). SCEP was a month-long workshop held during July 1970 in Williamstown, Massa-chusetts. William Kellogg, chair of the Work Group on Climatic Effects, later wrote 'I think it is fair to say that virtually every member of the Work Group came away with a heightened awareness of the subject with which we were dealing' (Kellogg, 1987: 120).

The SCEP report pointed out several possible implications of the rise in CO_2 levels which had occurred since the Industrial Revolution. The Work Group concluded that, although 'the probability of direct climate change in this century resulting from CO_2 is small, we stress that the long-term potential consequences of CO_2 effects on the climate or of social reaction to such threats are so serious that much more must be learned about future trends of climate change' (MIT, 1970: 12).

SMIC was organised as a conference by MIT and Swedish scientific bodies in July 1971 in Wijk near Stockholm, at which thirty leading scientists from fourteen countries attended (Lunde, 1991: 64). Kellogg states that Carroll Wilson, the organiser (he was also the organiser of SCEP), intended SMIC to be explicitly international (Kellogg, 1987: 120). The 300-page report from this conference went into greater detail about the possible climatic effects, and was used as the major background paper on climate change issues at the 1972 UN Conference on the Human Environment (Kellogg, 1987: 121; Lunde, 1991: 64).

The state of knowledge at this point was, however, still considerably undeveloped. The report from SMIC stated bluntly on the question of whether CO_2 rises would lead to climatic changes: 'We do not know yet' (quoted in Lunde, 1991: 67). The theory that industrial and agricultural aerosols would lead to a cooling of the atmosphere was also widespread, and no agreement could be reached between the participants as to which tendency would be most important (Kellogg, 1987: 121–2; see also Ross, 1991: 200–6 on the cooling debate). Its main recommendations were, therefore, that what was needed was 'more measurements and more theory!' (Lunde, 1991: 67).

According to Cain, the 1972 Stockholm Conference on the Human Environment, which led to the founding of UNEP (Cain, 1983: 81), represented a major shift in the priority given to climatic issues by international organisations. Climate impacts were 'central concerns', she suggests (Cain, 1983: 82). This change led to two developments. First, there was a series of UN-sponsored conferences during the 1970s on climate-related problems. These included the UN World Food Conference in 1974, the UN Water Conference in 1976, and the UN Desertification Conference in 1977. These conferences highlighted various aspects of severe problems associated with different climatic variations, and made clear the possible consequences of significant human-induced climate change. During the 1960s and early 1970s there were several extreme climatic events, including the Sahel five-year drought, the 1962 drought in the then Soviet Union, the monsoon failure in India in 1974, and the drought in Europe in 1976. These made clear human dependence on climate and provided a rationale for stepping up research into climate in general.

The second development, related to the first, was a change in the character of meteorological research. Prior to this, scientific research had been largely into the general understanding of weather. After 1972–3 the research programmes expanded into the field of long-term climatic trends and conditions, rather than short-term weather patterns. This change was stimulated both by the SMIC report and by the events outlined above. Davies stated in 1972 that WMO had already considered possible climatic changes due to increased CO_2, and had begun collecting and studying the necessary data (Davies, 1972: 335).

Substantial cooperative research on potential climate changes began with a Conference in Stockholm in July 1974, on the 'physical basis of climate and climate modelling'. This conference, organised by GARP, gathered together about seventy climate scientists from a wide range of countries (GARP, 1975; Lunde, 1991: 64).

The GARP 1974 Conference largely repeated the SMIC statement that the state of knowledge was too uncertain to make any strong statements about any potential global warming. It recognised that some specialists believed that 'the cooling trend which began in the 1940s [would] continue for several decades' (GARP, 1975: 1), and stated that, while some have claimed to be able to make climatological forecasts, the view more widely accepted by specialists was 'that our understanding of climate and climatic variability is far too meagre to warrant pronouncements of this sort' (GARP, 1975: 1). The important aspect of the conference was that it was aimed at developing a consensus about how best to model the climate system, thus providing a basis on which the future growth in confidence about potential global warming could develop.

Also in 1974, WMO's Executive Committee recommended that a Panel of Experts on Climate Change be established, which happened the following year. In 1976, WMO's Executive Committee suggested that a workshop be convened to develop a comprehensive model of the atmosphere to estimate the effects of increased CO_2 on climate. The first model of the atmosphere had been developed in 1956 (White, 1990: 19; Lunde, 1991: 62). However, models existing up to the mid-1970s remained rudimentary. The workshop was held at the offices of the US National Oceanic and Atmospheric Administration (NOAA) from 28 November to 3 December 1976 (Cain, 1983: 82), and its report constituted a full account of the state of knowledge at the time, and included recommendations to improve predictions of future atmospheric CO_2 concentrations (Cain, 1983: 82).

Other influential studies were published in this period which indicate that the possibility of climate change due to increased CO_2 was being taken increasingly seriously by climate scientists. In 1975, the International Symposium on Long-Term Climate fluctuations was held in Norwich, organised by WMO. The importance of this meeting was that it established that industrial aerosols and smoke particles and agricultural slash and burn practices, previously thought to cool the troposphere, do not do this, thus clearing the way for CO_2 to be the main candidate for affecting temperature (Kellogg, 1987: 122). Also of particular note were three assessments made by the US National Academy of Sciences (NAS) in 1975, 1977 and 1979 (Lunde, 1991: 71; White, 1990: 20; Rowlands, 1994: 69). The 1979 report was based on a study group which met during the summer of 1979 to determine whether the models being used to calculate global warming had a scientific basis and were sufficiently credible. Its conclusion stated that there was no good reason to doubt the calculations that a doubling of CO_2 concentrations would lead to a warming of 1.5–4.5 °C, and that, on present trends, such a warming would occur during the twenty-first century (NAS, 1979; Kellogg, 1987: 123).

The recommendation of the WMO Executive Committee for an increased monitoring of CO_2 was followed up at its session in June 1977, where it set up a research and monitoring project to expand existing monitoring of CO_2 (Cain, 1983: 82). The 1977 meeting also discussed a broader climate research programme, and an outline of such a programme was developed at an ad hoc group of expert members meeting in Cairo in January 1978 (Cain, 1983: 83). The initiation of a World Climate Programme had been endorsed by the UN Economic and Social Council (ECOSOC) and the UN Desertification Conference in 1977 (Cain, 1983: 82). In May 1978, the WMO Executive Committee's Thirtieth Session approved the programme outlined by the group which met in Cairo (Cain, 1983: 83).

These developments culminated in February 1979, when WMO, in conjunction with other UN bodies and the International Council of Scientific Unions (ICSU), organised the first World Climate Conference (WCC) in Geneva. Greater concern about possible effects of increased CO_2 on climate was one of the major reasons for convening this conference (White, 1979: 4; Lunde, 1991: 71). The conference was attended by approximately 400 'scientists and other specialists from fifty different countries representing many scientific and other disciplines' (WMO, 1979a: Preface). Its purpose, decided at the twenty-ninth session of the WMO Executive Committee during May–June 1977, was '(a) To review knowledge of climatic change and variability, due both to natural and anthropogenic causes; and (b) To assess possible future climatic changes and variability and their implications for human activities' (Davies, 1979: vii).

By the time of the World Climate Conference, its participants were prepared to state that:

> ... we can say with some confidence that the burning of fossil fuels, deforestation, and changes of land use have increased the amount of carbon dioxide in the atmosphere by about 15 per cent during the last century and it is at present increasing by about 0.4 per cent per year. It is likely that an increase will continue in the future. Carbon dioxide plays a fundamental role in determining the temperature of the earth's atmosphere, and it appears plausible that an increased amount of carbon dioxide in the atmosphere can contribute to a gradual warming of the lower atmosphere, especially at high latitudes. Patterns of change would be likely to affect the distribution of temperature, rainfall and other meteorological parameters, but the details of the changes are still poorly understood.
>
> (WMO, 1979b: 714)

The Declaration also appealed to nations to 'foresee and to prevent potential man-made [sic] changes in climate that might be adverse to the well-being of humanity' (WMO, 1979b: 713). While this appeal did not have a significant direct impact, the conference did publicise the climate issue, and gave extra legitimacy and profile to the activities of the soon-to-be-formed World Climate Programme. Many of the supporting documents to the Conference Declaration were concerned with the prospective aims of the Programme and how it should be supported by scientists and governments. Lunde states that the conference 'marked a new important threshold in the international efforts at improving our knowledge of man's [sic] impact on global climate' (Lunde, 1991: 14).

Later, in June 1979, the Eighth WMO Congress formally established the World Climate Programme (WCP), following the outline developed by the WMO Ad Hoc group, the ECOSOC endorsement, and the World Climate Conference recommendations. The WCP was the first internationally coordinated programme of research into the world's climate system (WWW and GARP focused on weather). It works generally on understanding climate more fully, as well as on specific issues of climatic change such as global warming, ozone depletion and acid rain.

The WCP has four main components; the World Climate Data Programme, concerned with 'the assembly and availability of climate data sets'; the World Climate Application Programme, which deals with 'the use of knowledge about climate to increase the safety and economy of human activities'; the World Climate Research Programme, concerned with the influence of changes in the composition of the atmosphere on climate; and the World Climate Impact Studies Programme, which deals with the 'effect of climate change on ecosystems and human activities' (Cain, 1983: 83).

The WCP provided the organisational framework within which much climate change research has operated. Possibly more importantly, it organised the Villach conference of 1985, which began the process through which global warming became politicised (Bruce, 1991: 152).

A scientific consensus on global warming appeared to be emerging for the first time at the 'International Conference on the Assessment of the role of carbon dioxide and other greenhouse gases in climate variations and associated impacts', held in Villach, Austria, during 9–15 October 1985 under WCP auspices. This conference aimed to examine the state of knowledge on climate and climate change, and to establish some sort of scientific consensus on the degree of responsibility for global warming of each gas, and on a preliminary prediction of what sort of warming the world was likely to see. There were also some generalised reports on what might happen to different specific parts of the world. In Lunde's words the conference was 'probably the most important greenhouse event between 1979 and the convening of IPCC in October 1988' (Lunde, 1991: 77).

The statement and conclusions of the Villach conference were significantly more confident than that of the WCC. It stated that the current consensus was that:

> The most advanced experiments . . . show increases of the global mean surface temperature for a doubling of the atmospheric CO_2 concentration or equivalent, of between 1.5 and 4.5 °C.
>
> (WMO, 1986: 2).[9]

The confidence expressed at Villach was based on a significant growth in both the scope and the complexity of climate research during the 1980s. The most important of these developments included much more realistic models of the atmosphere, and the consolidation of the realisation that other anthropogenic gases (CFCs, methane, nitrous oxide, tropospheric ozone) are radiatively important (Malone, 1986: 30).[10] This had been realised in the mid-1970s by some scientists (Ramanathan, 1975) but it was only by the 1980s that it was widely incorporated into models, or that its policy significance was realised (Victor and Clark, 1991: 21, 54–8; Jaeger, 1996).

GLOBAL WARMING BECOMES POLITICISED

As scientific knowledge increased concerning the likelihood of global warming, the types of gas involved and their anthropogenic sources, and about the severity of the possible changes, the activities of the scientists involved in the WCP and in national programmes became inherently more political because of the implications of the responses they envisaged. As early as 1978, the International Institute for Applied Systems Analysis (IIASA), WMO, UNEP and ICSU's Scientific Committee On Problems of the Environment (SCOPE) had organised a workshop which looked at energy strategies in relation to a possible global warming (Williams, 1978).[11] Several individuals had also written books on the necessity of a political response: for example, Crispin Tickell's *Climatic Change and World Affairs*, Stephen Schneider's *The Genesis Strategy*, and Amory Lovins's *Least-Cost Energy: Solving the CO_2 Problem* (Tickell, 1977; Schneider, 1976; Lovins et al., 1981).[12]

There was a small rise in public interest in global warming in the early 1980s, stimulated in particular by press coverage in 1984 of reports by James Hansen and Stephen Schneider (Mazur and Lee, 1993: 695–6). This then died off until 1988, when global warming exploded on to the political agenda. However, scientists had started to call on politicians to act. During the period 1985–8, many more scientists also became convinced of the need, not only for some framework convention analogous to that developed for ozone depletion (the Vienna Convention), but for strong preventive action on global warming. This process occurred as they became more convinced that the human-enhanced greenhouse effect was responsible for the global warming experienced in the 1980s. For example, Kenneth Hare, Chair of the Climatic Board of Canada, and of the Advisory Group on Greenhouse Gases (see below), wrote in 1988:

> Until a short while ago, my own position was . . . that the evidence was too equivocal to do more than give a yellow alert to governments . . . I was an announced wait-and-see conservative . . . It was the paper by Jones *et al.* [1986] published in *Nature* that began to sway me to the above position [that temperature rises in the 1980s can reasonably strongly be attributed to ghg concentration increases] . . . I can and do tell them [governments] that they should base their environmental planning on the assumption that the greenhouse warming will continue and accelerate.
>
> (Hare, 1988: 646)

This process of politicisation started at the Villach Conference. A major part of the conference's report involved detailed description of what the priorities for further research should be. This was not, however, purely to do with natural science research, which had previously been the case. The Villach Conference made recommendations which emphasised the need for economic, social and technological research into policy options for responding to any potential climate change. 'Support for the analysis of policy and economic options should be increased by governments and funding agencies. In these assessments the widest possible range of social responses aimed at preventing or adapting to climate change should be identified, analysed, and evaluated.' (WMO, 1986: 3). The last recommendation was that a small task force set up by UNEP, WMO and ICSU should 'initiate, if deemed necessary, consideration of a global convention' (WMO, 1986: para. 5). One of the speakers at the conference reveals the change in attitude which was occurring: 'As a reversal of a position I held a year or so ago, I believe it is timely to start on the long, tedious and sensitive task of framing a CONVENTION on greenhouse gases, climate change and energy' (Malone, 1986: 33). A shift of emphasis away from solely the need for more research, towards including assertions of the need for political action, had started.

To ensure that the recommendations of the Villach Conference were followed up, WMO, UNEP, and ICSU established the Advisory Group on Greenhouse Gases (AGGG) (Maunder, 1990: 9). The AGGG set up four working groups which examined various policy aspects of reducing greenhouse gases, each of which produced reports in 1990 (Clark, 1990; Fisher, 1990; Jaeger, 1990; Rijsbern and Swart, 1990).

WCP also followed up the Villach Conference with two workshops entitled 'Developing Policies for Responding to Climatic Change' held in Villach and in Bellagio, Italy, in 1987. These workshops came to similar, but stronger, conclusions, stating that 'a prudent response to climatic change would consider limitation *and* adaptation strategies' (Jaeger, 1988: iv). They called for the 'examination . . . of the need for an agreement on a law of the atmosphere as a global commons or the need to move towards a convention along the lines of that developed for ozone' (Jaeger, 1988: v). They also called for intensified development of non-fossil fuel energy systems, support for measures to reduce deforestation, and implementation of measures to limit the growth of non-CO_2 ghgs in the atmosphere (Jaeger, 1988).

Alongside these developments, the World Commission on Environment and Development (WCED) presented its report *Our Common Future* (also known as the 'Brundtland Report' after the Norwegian Prime Minister Gro Harlem Brundtland, who chaired the commission), on 27

April 1987. This was a general report on environmental degradation and how it related to development issues. The commission had been set up by the UN in 1983. Regarding climate, its report reproduced the recommendations of the 1985 Villach Conference, and in particular emphasised the 'urgent' necessity of increasing energy efficiency and shifting the fuel mix towards renewables (WCED, 1987: 176–7).

Among state decision-makers, however, there was still considerable inertia about the issue, and the idea of a convention or any sort of political agreement on greenhouse gases was not being addressed. During 1985–7 the environmental issue being given priority by political leaders was ozone depletion, with the adoption of the Vienna Convention in 1985, and the Montreal Protocol in 1987. The ozone depletion issue was obviously related, as CFCs are both ozone destroyers and ghgs. However, at this stage ozone depletion was being treated more urgently.

The political discussion of global warming had developed gradually during the mid-1980s. However, it gained much momentum in 1988. A combination of factors produced this rapid rise. Of particular importance was the US drought in 1988. This drought was reported to be the worst since the dustbowls of the 1930s (Idso, 1989: 41; Gribbin, 1990: 2). Over half the counties in the US were officially listed as suffering from drought and, in some places, water levels were 10 metres below normal (Pearce, 1989: 1). *Time* Magazine, among others, highlighted the problems experienced by US farmers facing baked-hard soil and extensive forest fires (Boyle and Ardill, 1989: 47–8). Temperatures in the US were also at an all-time high; in Death Valley, for example, a record high of 53 °C (127 °F) was recorded on 18 July, and the day before, San Francisco had its highest ever temperature for that day by nearly 11 °C (Idso, 1989: 41).

The US drought combined with the perception that freak weather patterns were being experienced throughout the world during the 1980s. Boyle and Ardill note that, in 1988 alone,

> There was also drought in the USSR; continued drought and unexpected floods in Africa and India; floods and drought simultaneously in China; floods in Brazil, and Bangladesh; hurricanes in the Caribbean; a cyclone in New Zealand and a typhoon in the Philippines.
>
> (Boyle and Ardill, 1989: 48)

The hurricanes, Gilbert and Joan, were hugely destructive. Gilbert left a fifth of the people of Jamaica homeless. Joan 'brought a similar trail of death and devastation' (Boyle and Ardill, 1989: 49).

The point of these references to the natural disasters during that period is merely to show that they provided a backdrop for the increased confidence with which scientists made claims about a potential global warming. The fact that publics, in particular in the industrialised countries, had already been sensitised to environmental issues in the 1980s, because of ozone depletion, acid rain and other problems, contributed to the rapidity with which global warming moved up the political agenda. Faced with the freak weather conditions alluded to above, and the realisation that the 1980s was clearly the hottest decade on record, including the six hottest years ever recorded (Houghton and Woodwell, 1989), publics were 'softened up' for the increasingly confident assertions by some climate scientists that anthropogenic global warming was the most likely explanation for the climatic variations experienced. The most clear of these views, and perhaps more importantly, the most widely hyped by the media (Mazur and Lee, 1993: 697–8), was given in the statement by James Hansen, chief climate scientist at NASA's Goddard Institute for Space Studies (GISS), at a hearing of the US Senate's Energy and Natural Resources Committee, on 23 June 1988 (Hansen, 1989). Hansen's most widely reported statement was that 'it is time to stop waffling so much. We should say that the evidence is pretty strong that the greenhouse effect is here' (quoted in Pearce, 1989: 1). Hansen's team at GISS had undertaken much of the research which showed the 1980s to be the hottest decade on record. In his formal statement, while recognising that 'it is not possible to blame a specific heat wave/drought on the greenhouse effect', he emphasised that 'global warming has reached a level such that we can ascribe with a high degree of confidence a cause and effect relationship between the greenhouse effect and the observed warming' (Hansen, 1989: 40–2). According to Gribbin, Hansen's statement was all the more important because he 'had a reputation for caution and was a proponent of the "wait and see" approach' (Gribbin, 1990: 3–4).

The freak weather conditions, especially the US drought, the general importance of environmental issues in the mid- to late 1980s, and Hansen's testimony, combined to cause global warming to emerge rapidly onto the international political agenda.[13] The Toronto Conference on 'The Changing Atmosphere: Implications for Global Security', held during 27–30 June 1988 in Toronto, and hosted by the Canadian government as a response to the WCED Report (Maunder, 1990: 9), was where global warming was first dealt with as a major political issue. 'More than 300 scientists and policy makers from forty-eight countries, United Nations organisations, other international bodies and non-governmental organisations participated in the sessions' (Toronto

Conference, 1988: 46). The Toronto Conference was the meeting at which ideas about the sort of international response needed came to be expressed more strongly. Howard Ferguson, the conference's Director, stated in his address that 'the time to act on the problems is now' (Toronto Conference, 1988: 45).

Like the WCED Report, the Toronto Conference repeated the Villach Conference assessment of the degree of likely warming under a 'business-as-usual' scenario, and what sort of impacts were likely to result from this warming. It graphically outlined the possible consequences of global warming by suggesting that 'humanity is conducting an uncontrolled globally pervasive experiment whose ultimate consequences could be second only to a global nuclear war' (Toronto Conference, 1988: 46).

However, it also innovated in making detailed recommendations for action. It called upon governments 'to work with urgency towards an Action Plan for the Protection of the Atmosphere. This should include an international framework convention . . . The Conference also called upon governments to establish a World Atmosphere Fund financed in part by a levy on the fossil fuel consumption of industrialised countries . . .' (Toronto Conference, 1988: 47). The conference outlined an ambitious aim with respect to reducing CO_2 emissions. It stated that governments and industry should 'reduce CO_2 emissions by approximately 20 per cent of 1988 levels by the year 2005 as an initial global goal' (Toronto Conference, 1988: 53). This was the first international conference to call for such radical action.[14] Other actions recommended included revising the Montreal Protocol, making sure energy R&D budgets were directed at options which would reduce or eliminate CO_2 emissions, setting targets for energy efficiency improvements, switching to lower CO_2 emitting fuels, and reviewing strategies for both renewables and nuclear energy (Toronto Conference, 1988: 52–3).

Following the Toronto Conference, global warming moved rapidly up the international agenda. Many world leaders made statements on the need for a response to global warming. In the UK, the then Prime Minister Margaret Thatcher stated in a speech echoing the words of Revelle and Suess that humanity had 'unwittingly begun a massive experiment with the system of this planet itself' (Thatcher, 1988: 2). She noted some of the potential impacts of global warming, in particular the effect on low-lying islands which had been 'brought home' to her at the Commonwealth Conference in Vancouver the previous year by the President of the Maldives (Thatcher, 1988: 2). Thatcher's speech was widely viewed as a 'conversion' (McCormick, 1991: 62). According to McCormick, James Hansen was one of the people credited with causing this change. Hansen had made a presentation to her during 1988 (McCormick, 1991: 63) and, according to Gribbin, she had read his Congressional testimony (Gribbin, 1990: 5). Crispin Tickell, then UK Ambassador to the United Nations, and author of *Climatic Change and World Affairs* as far back as 1977, was however most widely accredited with influencing her (apart from the general effect of the rise of environmental issues in general and global warming in particular, and the resulting electoral pressure).

Other prominent politicians also made important statements. Eduard Schevardnadze, then Soviet Foreign Minister, made a stronger speech to the UNGA on 27 September 1988 (Schevardnadze, 1988), where he proposed that UNEP should be transformed into 'an environmental council capable of taking effective decisions to ensure ecological security' (quoted in Boyle and Ardill, 1989: 99–100). George Bush made global warming an issue in the US Presidential election of 1988. 'Those who think we're powerless to do anything about the greenhouse effect are forgetting about the White House effect' was his famous line on the issue (Boyle and Ardill, 1989: 100). He pledged to convene a global conference on the subject at the White House in his first year in office (see below).

The Toronto Conference also led to a series of international and intergovernmental conferences about global warming. These continued through to late 1990, and provided a great deal of the pressure and momentum which led to the formal negotiations which started in 1991. In September 1988, the issue first reached the UN General Assembly, with Malta proposing that climate become part of the 'common heritage of mankind [sic]' (Bodansky, 1993: 465). By December of that year, the General Assembly had passed a resolution, endorsing the establishment of the IPCC and urging that the issue become a priority one, but withdrawing from the 'common heritage' concept towards an assertion that climate change was merely a 'common concern' of humanity (Bodansky, 1993: 465).

In November 1988 a World Congress on Climate and Development was held in Hamburg. This called for carbon dioxide emissions to be reduced by '30 per cent by the year 2000 and 50 per cent by 2015. It argued for unilateral action from the industrialised nations to start the process of change; a global ban on the production and use of CFCs covered by the Montreal Protocol by 1995, ... and urgent strategies for reversing deforestation and beginning afforestation programmes' (Boyle and Ardill, 1989: 158). This was despite some, notably the Soviet climatologist Mikhail Budyko, claiming that global warming would be beneficial to agriculture, and emissions should possibly even be deliberately increased (Boyle and Ardill, 1989: 130).

During 20–22 February 1989 the Canadian government hosted an 'International Meeting of Legal and Policy Experts on the Protection of the Atmosphere' in Ottawa. This produced a statement which comprised a series of elements to be included in a framework convention on the protection of the atmosphere (Ottawa Meeting, 1989). It included the provision that 'States should consider the possibility of establishing a World Atmosphere Trust Fund' (Ottawa Meeting, 1989: 7). At the same time, the first conference on perspectives on global warming from developing countries was held in New Delhi (New Delhi Conference, 1989). While the New Delhi Conference did not propose a new body like an Atmosphere Fund, it did highlight the need for global warming to be addressed in a North–South context, focusing on the primary responsibility of the industrialised countries to limit emissions and to help developing countries reduce emissions while developing (New Delhi Conference, 1989: 5).

In London in March 1989, the UK Government hosted a conference to get new signatures to the Montreal Protocol and plan for a conference to be held in May in Helsinki to update that protocol. However, many of the discussions elaborated on what should be done about global warming. In London, Margaret Thatcher, the UK Prime Minister, argued that 'no new international bodies were needed to protect the world from a thinning ozone layer or the greenhouse effect' (*New Scientist*, 18 March 1989: 33). In a similar vein, at the Helsinki conference, the 'First Meeting of the Parties to the Montreal Protocol on Substances that Deplete the Ozone Layer', Nicholas Ridley, the then UK Secretary of State for the Environment, said that a climate fund 'implies a degree of sovereignty over sovereign nations that can never really be there' (*Guardian*, 4 May 1989). The Helsinki Conference agreed to a drastic revision of the Montreal Protocol to be signed in 1990 in London, but no decision was reached concerning ideas about a climate fund.

Many of those present at Helsinki wished to set up a climate fund, following the call of the Toronto Conference. They included Mostafa Tolba, UNEP's director, as well as the delegates from Norway and many developing countries. Tolba saw a fund as an 'essential mechanism for assisting the Third World' (*Guardian*, 6 May 1989). This view was preceded by that of a meeting at the International Court of Justice in the Hague in March 1989, only a week after the London Conference. This was organised by the governments of France, the Netherlands and Norway and attended by representatives, most of whom were heads of state, of twenty-four countries. Its declaration called for the development within the UN framework of a 'new institutional authority, either by strengthening existing institutions or creating a new institution', with responsibility for combatting global warming, and with 'power to monitor governments' performance ... and to enforce compliance through the International Court of Justice', and also for an Atmospheric fund to assist developing countries (*Declaration of the Hague*, 11 March 1989).

The Ottawa meeting in February 1989 was followed up with proposals for a draft convention prepared by the UK government and presented to a meeting of UNEP's governing council in Nairobi in May 1989 by Lord Caithness, UK Minister of State for the Environment (House of Commons Energy Committee, 1989: para. 25). According to the UK House of Commons Energy Committee, following the UNEP meeting, the British, Canadian and Maltese governments were made responsible for preparing a convention (House of Commons Energy Committee, 1989: para. 25). It was always intended that such a convention should be ready for signing at UNCED in 1992.

In July 1989 the Group of Seven major industrial democracies' annual summit was held in Paris, and was widely dubbed the 'green summit' (*Economist* 15 July 1989: 14–15; *Scientific American* September 1989: 10). The statement of the summit called for 'common efforts to limit emissions of carbon dioxide', and stated that a 'framework or umbrella convention' was 'urgently required' (*Scientific American* September 1989: 10; *Keesings Record of World Events*, 1989: 36802–3). The Meeting of Non-Aligned Countries in Belgrade in September 1989 called on the industrialised countries to 'fundamentally change their attitude to world development, particularly in the protection of the planet' (*Keesings Record of World Events*, 1989: 36907). The Commonwealth Heads of Government Meeting of October 1989 stated that one of the major problems facing the world was global warming. The statement resolved that Commonwealth members would take 'immediate and positive' action, both 'collectively and individually', on the issue, and it called for 'the early conclusion of an international convention to protect and conserve the global climate' (Commonwealth Heads of Government, 1989: 9).

Later, in November, a large 'Ministerial Conference on Atmospheric Pollution and Climatic Change' was held at Noordwijk in the Netherlands, attended by representatives from seventy-two States. This conference's declaration committed its signatories to stabilising CO_2 emissions at levels to be set by the IPCC in its preliminary report to the second World Climate Conference in 1990, 'at the latest by the year 2000' (Noordwijk Declaration, 1989: para. 16). It also reiterated the previous timescale proposed for the preparation of a 'climate change convention', and contained a large section on funding, recognising that this is a vital part of the success of a convention. Bodansky suggests that Noordwijk was the most significant meeting in 1989 (1993: 467), because it was the first to involve large numbers of high level political representatives. It was also the case, as he notes (1993: 462–3), that after Toronto few meetings made as radical proposals on limiting emissions, because they became increasingly intergovernmental. Proposals for 20 per cent cuts in emissions gave way to ones for stabilisation.

Also in November 1989, representatives from some of the Small Island States (Kiribati, the Maldives, Malta, Mauritius, and Trinidad and Tobago) met in Male in the Maldives to discuss global warming from their perspective (Faulks, 1991). This produced the 'Male Declaration' (reproduced in Churchill and Freestone, 1991: 341–3), and later led to the establishment of the Alliance of Small Island States (AOSIS) at the Second World Climate Conference (see Chapter 4).

During 17–21 December, the World Conference on Preparing for Climate Change was held in Cairo, Egypt. At the opening address, Suzanne Mubarak from Egypt referred to the 'grim irony' of the fact that, while the 'primary responsibility' for global warming lay with the industrialised countries, the effects would be experienced 'mostly in the countries of the South, where the capacity to cope [was] weaker'. The declaration argued that it was in industrialised countries' own interests to 'develop, bilaterally and multilaterally, funding mechanisms for the transfer of additional financial and technological resources to poorer nations' (*Keesings Record of World Events*, 1989: 37138).

In 1990, the political meetings continued. During 17–18 April, President Bush hosted a conference at the White House as he had pledged to do during his election campaign. The conference was attended by government delegates from seventeen countries. The gulf between the positions of the US and other industrialised countries began to become clear at this point. Bush stated at the conference that no action should be taken until more research had been completed and the science was more certain (*Keesings Record of World Events*, 1990: 37394). Journalists commented that, for the White House, the purpose of the conference was to emphasise both the scientific uncertainties of global warming, and the costs of reducing emissions (*Economist*, 14 April 1990: 46; *Guardian*, 18 April 1990: 8, 23). Bush argued that 'what we need are facts, the stuff that science is made of' (White House, 1990; Rowlands, 1994: 76-7). In contrast, the West German Environment Minister, Klaus Topfer, argued that 'gaps in knowledge must not be used as an excuse for worldwide inaction' (*Keesings Record of World Events*, 1990: 37394).

Throughout 1990 and 1991, the Woods Hole Research Center in the US organised a series of regional conferences in developing countries, along with organisations in those countries. The first of these was held in May 1990 in Nairobi to discuss African perspectives on global warming. The Nairobi meeting was organised with the African Centre for Technology Studies, and was attended mainly by people from non-governmental bodies. The second was in June in Sao Paolo, co-organised by the University of Sao Paolo. The third, in South-East Asia, was held in 1991. These conferences helped raise the political profile of global warming in developing countries, and highlighted how the perspectives of industrialised and developing countries differed. There is, however, a considerable difference between the statements of the Nairobi and Sao Paolo meetings. The African Declaration places more emphasis on what African governments can and should do about global warming, while the focus of the Sao Paolo Declaration is firmly on the primary responsibility of the industrialised countries with respect to causing global warming, and the conditionality of any actions taken by developing countries on finance and technology from the North (African Centre for Technology Studies, 1990; Universidade de Sao Paolo, 1990).

Also in May 1990, the UN Economic Commission for Europe held a large conference on Sustainable Development in Bergen, Norway. This was intended as a regional follow-up to the WCED report. The Ministerial Session of the conference was attended by 303 delegates from thirty-four governments (UNECE, 1990: 12). The Ministerial Declaration stated that 'we [the ECE region governments] assume a major responsibility to limit or reduce greenhouse gases' (UNECE, 1990: 17). It pledged their support for completing a framework convention, and noted:

> ... with appreciation that some countries have already committed themselves in advance to stabilize CO_2 emissions at present levels or to reduce them by the year 2000 ... [and urged] ... all ECE countries to take action now, and we agree to commit [sic] to establish national strategies and/or targets and schedules ... to limit or reduce CO_2 emissions and other greenhouse gases as much as possible and to stabilize them. In the view of most ECE countries, such stabilization at the latest by the year 2000 and at present levels must be the first step.
> (UNECE, 1990: 17)

However, beneath this apparently strong consensus for action, the US, and to a lesser extent the UK, was emerging as the country to be vilified for lagging. The US had refused to commit itself to a quantified target for limiting its CO_2 emissions, citing scientific uncertainty and the costs of reducing emissions as the main reason. The UK was at this point preparing to commit itself to a CO_2 target. However, it too was emphasising the cost of action. 'We will have to make it clear to our electorate how much pain and anguish they will have to suffer in order to save the planet', said David Trippier, UK Environment Minister (quoted in the *Guardian*, 17 May 1990).[15]

In other forums, the importance of global warming as an issue declined relative to 1989. In particular, at the G7 summit in 1990 in Houston, the environment was sidelined to make room for the row between the EC and the US over agricultural subsidies, and the collapse of the USSR and Eastern Europe (*Guardian*, 7 July 1990). The summit did agree that negotiations towards a framework should start after the Second World Climate Conference in November 1990. However, the priority given to the issue was significantly lower than in the previous year.

The other development during 1990 was that many industrialised states began to undertake unilateral commitments to limit their greenhouse gas emissions. The status of these commitments at the time the convention was signed (June 1992) is given in Table 2.1. Some of these states undertook their commitments earlier than 1990. Sweden was the first, in 1988, when it undertook to stabilise CO_2 emissions at 1988 levels by 2000. Sweden later retreated from this undertaking in January 1991, to the commitment outlined in Table 2.1. In 1989, both Norway and the Netherlands committed themselves to their targets. Then, in 1990, the following states set targets: Denmark, Italy, and the UK, in May; Austria, Canada, Germany, and the Netherlands (an updated target), in June; New Zealand in July; France in September, Australia, the EC, and Japan, in October; and Iceland and Switzerland in November. In 1991, Belgium announced its target, Sweden revised its, and the United States announced its 'Climate Change: An Action Agenda' policy document, timed to coincide with the start of negotiations (see Chapter 3) (Schmidt, 1991; Fish and South, 1994).

THE IPCC

While global warming developed into a contentious political issue during this period, the Intergovernmental Panel on Climate Change (IPCC) was also established in 1988, by UNEP and WMO. Nitze and Bodansky both suggest it was at the instigation of the United States government (Nitze, 1989: 44; Bodansky, 1993: 464).[16] The IPCC was established in order to

Table 2.1 Status of commitments of OECD countries on global climate change.

Country	Type of commitment	Gases included	Action	Commitment year
Australia	Target	NMP GHG	Stabilisation	2000
			20% reduction	2005
Austria	Target	CO_2	20% reduction	2005
Belgium	EC agreement	CO_2	(see footnote)	
Canada	Target	CO_2 and other GHG	Stabilisation	2000
Denmark	Target	CO_2	20% reduction	2005
Finland	Target	CO_2	Stabilisation	2000
France	Target	CO_2	Stabilisation	2000[1]
Germany	Target	CO_2	25–30% reduction	2005
Greece	EC agreement	CO_2	(see footnote)	
Iceland	EFTA agreement	CO_2	(see footnote)	
Ireland	EC agreement	CO_2	(see footnote)	
Italy	Target	CO_2	Stabilisation	2000
			20% reduction	2005
Japan	Target	CO_2	Stabilisation	2000[2]
Luxembourg	Target	CO_2	Stabilisation	2000
			20% reduction	2005
Netherlands	Target	CO_2	Stabilisation	1995
	Target		3–5% reduction	2000
	Target	All GHG	20–25% reduction	2000

New Zealand	Target	CO_2	20% reduction	2000
Norway	Target	CO_2	Stabilisation	2000
Portugal	EC agreement	CO_2	(see footnote)	
Spain	Target	CO_2	25% growth only	2000
Sweden	EFTA agreement	CO_2	(see footnote)	
Switzerland	Target	CO_2	At least stabilisation	2000
UK	Target	CO_2	Stabilisation	2000
US	Commitment to set of policies	All GHG	Stabilisation	2000
EC	Target	CO_2	Stabilisation	2000

Notes:
1 This is a *per capita* per year target of less than 2 metric tons of carbon.
2 This is stabilisation on a *per capita* basis.
NMP = Non-Montreal Protocol (gases covered by the 1987 Montreal Protocol on Substances which Deplete the Ozone Layer)
GHG = Greenhouse gases
EC Agreement means that the country falls under EC-wide Target but has not yet developed its own target; EFTA agreement means that the country falls under the agreement between EFTA and the EC.

Source: IEA (1992) *Climate Change Policy Initiatives*, Paris: International Energy Agency, 24–5.

make the fullest assessment of the state of scientific knowledge and potential impacts of global warming, and to examine potential response options. Its purpose, as outlined by WMO and UNEP, was:

(i)   assessing the scientific information that is related to the various components of the climate change issue, such as emissions of major greenhouse gases and modification of the Earth's radiation balance resulting therefrom, and that needed to enable the environmental and socio-economic consequences of climate change to be evaluated;

(ii) formulating realistic response strategies for the management of the climate change issue.

(IPCC, 1988: 4)

It was regarded by many as the primary forum for coordinating policy research related to climate change and as a forerunner to establishing formal negotiations towards an international treaty (UK Government, 1989: 1; Nitze, 1990: 2). It presented its First Assessment Report to the second World Climate Conference in November 1990 (Houghton *et al.*, 1990; IPCC, 1990b; McTegart *et al.*, 1990).

The IPCC first met on November 9–11 1988, in WMO offices in Geneva. At this meeting it agreed its work programme, and what its main tasks were. These were decided to be:

(i)   assessment of available scientific information on climate change;

(ii) assessment of environmental and socio-economic impacts of climate change;

(iii) formulation of response strategies.

(IPCC, 1988: 4)

The panel decided to organise this work through three Working Groups. At this meeting it also elected Bert Bolin as Chair of the panel (IPCC, 1988: Annex V).[17]

In January 1989, the IPCC working groups started meeting. Each of the working groups had a fair amount of autonomy with respect to how it would operate. Working Group I (Science) organised itself by commissioning lead authors to cover different aspects of the scientific problems of global warming and having other members review the work, while Working Groups II (Impacts) and III (Responses) worked through sub-groups which looked at particular aspects of the problem and reported collectively.[18]

Most attention was focused on the developments within Working Group I of the IPCC. This was because the central message the outside world expected to hear from the IPCC deliberations was the extent to which global warming was a threat to be taken seriously. In this, the expectation of many – that global warming was a serious threat – was confirmed. Schneider argues that 'the least scientifically original product of IPCC, the Working Group I report, has proved to be the most useful. . . . it contains few fundamental ideas or results that were not already noted in previous assessments of global warming' (Schneider, 1991: 26). However, two features of the IPCC Report make it stand out from previous assessments. The first is its representativeness. The Working Group I Policy-makers Summary (drawn from the conclusions of the sections written) was a negotiated consensus document; it represented, or aimed to represent, the consensus among the world's leading climate scientists. John Houghton, Chair of Working Group I, claimed that 'virtually every scientist in the world who has made significant contributions to the science of global climate change had a part in the generation of the assessment (WGI), and a wide range of other scientists were involved in its approval.' (Houghton, 1990). The political importance of representativeness was underlined by the establishment by the IPCC at its Second Session of a 'Special Committee on the Participation of Developing Countries' (IPCC, 1989: 19–20), to try to make sure that developing countries' scepticism of scientific assessments made purely in the North would be circumvented. In Bolin's words, 'right now (1987/8), many countries, particularly developing countries, simply don't trust assessments in which their scientists and policy-makers have not participated' (quoted in Schneider, 1991: 25). The unprecedented representativeness achieved by the IPCC (although it fell short of hopes regarding geographical representativeness) made the political status of its findings different from studies undertaken by small research teams.

The second important feature of the IPCC Working Group I Report was that it made the statement, which had not been made as forcefully in any previous consensus document such as the report from the Villach Conference, that the scientists involved were *certain* that 'These increases [in greenhouse gas emissions] will enhance the greenhouse effect, resulting on average in an additional warming of the Earth's surface' (IPCC, 1990a: xi). This certainty marked out the IPCC Report as unique, as well as fuelling a considerable debate as to whether it was justified in such a statement.

As Schneider noted, however, the IPCC report was not significantly different in its conclusions from previous assessments, such as that expressed at the Villach Conference. It was, however, more detailed and quantitative in presenting its findings. The main findings were to give a range of 1–3 °C warming resulting from a 'business-as-usual' scenario (where no ameliorative action was taken to reduce ghg emissions). The Villach report had this range as 1.5–4.5 °C. The IPCC also calculated the reductions in emissions of CO_2 and other ghgs which would be needed to stabilise atmospheric concentrations at current levels. For CO_2, it estimated this reduction to be over 60 per cent.

The IPCC was careful to include statements acknowledging that the uncertainties in greenhouse science were great. It stated that the warming experienced during the twentieth century could not be definitively attributed to ghg emissions. 'The size of this warming is broadly consistent with predictions of climate models, but it is also of the same magnitude as natural climate variability', it stated (IPCC, 1990a: xii).

The IPCC Working Group I Report did not, however, prevent dissenters from continuing to criticise its findings. In particular, a fierce debate has continued regarding both the scientific and political/organisational aspects of the IPCC. There were claims that the IPCC organisers had deliberately excluded strong dissenters, such as Richard Lindzen, Hugh Elsaesser and Fred Singer, from participating in the IPCC. One unnamed scientist went so far as to claim that the supporters of the greenhouse theory 'behave like Hitler' by conspiring to prevent critics from publishing their conclusions in leading scientific journals (quoted in Thomas, 1990).[19]

There were also claims that they had ignored 'valid scientific objections to computer models that predict a significant global warming' (Singer, 1990). The US-based Science and Environmental Policy Project (SEPP), directed by Singer, Professor of Environmental Sciences at the University of Virginia, produced a report based on a survey of 126 climate scientists, some involved in the IPCC, others not, to judge the level of acceptance of the IPCC conclusions (Singer, 1991a).[20] The SEPP Report stated that 50 per cent of the respondents believed that the IPCC WGI summary 'did not represent the report fairly and could be misleading to non-scientists' (Singer, 1992a: 35). An 'overwhelming majority' agreed with 'the key IPCC conclusion, buried on page 254 of the report, that "it is not possible to attribute all, or even a large part, of the observed global-mean warming [of 0.5 °C since 1890] to the enhanced greenhouse effect on the basis of observational data currently available"' (Singer, 1991). Similarly, 'nearly all respondents expressed scepticism about the adequacy of the global climate models (GCMs) used to predict future climate warming' (Singer, 1992a: 35). Singer (1992a: 36) also reports other surveys of scientists which suggest the consensus was not as strong as leading IPCC members liked to suggest. In particular, he cites a Greenpeace survey which states that 47 per cent of climate scientists believed a 'runaway greenhouse' was impossible.

There are two main problems with Singer's survey and arguments. First, the figures reproduced above are highly misleading in themselves, primarily because of the way the questions are posed. It is not particularly relevant that 47 per cent of scientists believe a runaway greenhouse to be impossible, since this was never the basis on which mainstream scientific worries about a potential warming were based. It would arguably be more meaningful to have stated that 53 per cent believed a runaway greenhouse *was* possible. Similarly, the statement that almost all the scientists surveyed agreed that the warming observed this century could not be attributed to the enhanced greenhouse effect is not particularly meaningful as a critique of the IPCC Report. The summary of that report stated merely that the warming was consistent with model predictions, but was also consistent with natural variability.

The second problem with Singer's survey is Singer himself. He was recognised as a long-time, politicised opponent of global warming theories, and had the clear intention of delegitimising global warming proponents. He was not reticent about his political views. Elsewhere, he referred to global warming, and the UNCED process in general, as a political issue driven by 'Third World kleptocrats' trying to revive the political agenda of the New International Economic Order (Singer, 1992b). He thus generates little confidence in his willingness to conduct detached surveys of scientists.

There were also (arguably inevitable) suggestions that the fact that the IPCC process represented 'soft' or 'negotiated' science should delegitimise its findings. The IPCC recognised that its purpose, at least in the Policymakers' Summaries, was to present the information which was relevant to policymakers. Hence some scientists, such as Singer, objected to the inclusion of some material which was, for them, too 'political'; the 60 per cent reductions required for CO_2 atmospheric stabilisation would be one example of this. Singer objected in particular to the inclusion of the statement at the head of the summary that referred to the natural greenhouse effect, saying that it was like 'revealing, in hushed tones, that the Earth is round' (Singer, 1991). Yet it was always intended that the audience for the summaries would be politicians and the public, not scientific experts.

Many of the delegations were at least quasi-political in their appointments, being represented in some cases by Foreign Office diplomats as much as by scientists. However, Lunde, in his detailed examination of the IPCC consensus, looking at 'pure scientific' factors, and 'non-epistemic' (i.e. explicitly political) factors which were involved in the production of the IPCC report, concluded that (most of) the scientists involved managed to prevent themselves from being significantly swayed by political pressures. According to Lunde, they managed to make sure that non-scientists remained confined largely to Working Group III, and appointments within Working Group I remained based on scientific rather than political criteria (Lunde, 1991: 88). Industry lobbyists (as well as environmentalists) were present at IPCC meetings, and, in particular at the final meeting in Sundsvall, were vociferous in their lobbying to get the IPCC scientists to emphasise the uncertainties of the science more than the latter appeared willing (Lunde, 1991: 100–10). Greenpeace and others alleged that the US delegation consistently tried to weaken Working Group I's conclusions (Greenpeace International, 1992: 2). Lunde cites a *New Scientist* editorial accrediting John Houghton – 'a man not known for his radical views' – with standing up to pressures from the US delegation to water down the Working Group I Policymakers' Summary in line with US political wishes (*New Scientist*, 8 September 1990: 25; Lunde 1991: 88–9).

To a great extent, the politicisation of the IPCC process remained confined in particular to Working Group III. The disparity between the conclusions of WGI and WGIII were widely commented on by environmentalists and pro-environmentalist climatologists such as Stephen Schneider (see Schneider, 1991). Schneider states clearly his view of the inadequacy of the WGII report given the expectations generated by the outcome of WGI's deliberations (see also Grubb, 1990: 7–10).

In general, the IPCC did manage to convey the message that the overwhelming majority of the world's scientists involved in climate research believed that the likelihood of a significant and potentially highly damaging global warming was sufficiently strong to warrant a high-level political response. It made sure that the Second World Climate Conference (SWCC), scheduled originally for May–June 1990 but moved back to November to accommodate itself to the IPCC's timetable, became a high-level political affair, attended by heads of governments from around the world.

CONCLUSIONS

The IPCC Report set the stage for the Second World Climate Conference, held in Geneva from 29 October to 7 November 1990. The primary goals of the conference were 'to formulate recommendations for the continuing World Climate Programme', and 'to provide an opportunity for Ministers' to consider actions in the light of the IPCC Report, consider the special needs of developing countries with respect to climate data, and to consider goals for enhancing intergovernmental cooperation in monitoring climate change (Obasi *et al.*, 1991). The conference was split into a Scientific and Technical Session, and a Ministerial Session.

The scientists involved sent a clear message to politicians that they believed the latter should act to reduce the threat of global warming. The Conference Statement from the Scientific and Technical Sessions urged countries to 'take steps towards reducing sources and increasing sinks of greenhouse gases through national and regional actions, and negotiations of a global convention on climate change and related legal instruments' (Jaeger and Ferguson, 1991: 497). It argued that 'technically feasible and cost-effective opportunities exist to reduce CO_2 emissions in all countries. Such opportunities for emissions reductions are sufficient to allow many industrialised countries . . . to reduce these emissions by at least 20 per cent by 2005' (Jaeger and Ferguson, 1991: 498).

The Ministerial Declaration had a less strongly worded section on CO_2 emissions, 'welcoming' the individual targets adopted by many industrialised countries, and 'acknowledging' the initiatives of other industrialised countries which would limit emissions. At a surface level the following sentence seems as strong as in the Scientific Session Statement. It urges 'all developed countries to establish targets and/or national programmes or strategies which will have significant effects on limiting emissions of greenhouse gases not controlled by the Montreal Protocol' (Jaeger and Ferguson, 1991: 536–7). However, 'national programmes and strategies' was the US alternative to an approach based on targets, and was (at the time) widely perceived to represent a weaker commitment than targets. Also, 'limiting' was widely understood as not necessarily meaning reducing, or even stabilising, emissions. It could simply involve reducing the rate of emissions growth, relative to projections.

By the end of 1990, the political momentum built up by the series of intergovernmental conferences, and unilateral commitments by many states on the one hand, and the IPCC Report published in the summer of 1990 and the calls for action by scientists at the SWCC in November on the other hand, was such that negotiations towards an international convention were virtually unavoidable.[21] The Ministerial Declaration of the SWCC called for the UNGA to establish a negotiating forum for such a convention (Jaeger and Ferguson, 1991: 539). The negotiations were formally established by the UNGA in Resolution 45/212 (UN General Assembly, 1990). It is to these negotiations that we now turn.

Chapter 3

Before and after Rio
Interstate negotiations

No doubt some sort of international agreement on fossil fuels will be reached, and no doubt it will be too timid and too often broken to make a great difference.

(Stewart, 1990: 39)

INTRODUCTION

At the Second World Climate Conference, in November 1990, the UN General Assembly was urged to establish formal negotiations towards a Framework Convention on Climate Change. Prior to this, in September 1990, UNEP and WMO convened an ad hoc working group of government representatives to prepare for negotiations and discuss possible structures, rules of procedure, and so on, for a negotiating forum (INC, 8 March 1991; Bodansky, 1992). The General Assembly discussed this issue on 21 December 1990, and established the Intergovernmental Negotiating Committee for a Framework Convention on Climate Change (INC), in Resolution 45/212, entitled 'Protection of global climate for present and future generations' (UN General Assembly, 1990). The committee was charged with the task of negotiating a Framework Convention and any associated protocols designed to counter climate change.

This chapter discusses the interstate negotiations concerning climate change. These led initially to the signing of the United Nations Framework Convention on Climate Change at the United Nations Conference on Environment and Development (UNCED) in Rio de Janeiro in June 1992. The negotiations have continued after Rio, and still continue. However, this chapter finishes with the first Conference of the Parties in Berlin in March–April 1995 (COP1). Like the previous chapter, its primary purpose is descriptive; to outline the course of the negotiations in broadly chronological fashion.[1]

The focus of the discussion is largely on two sections of the convention; those dealing with the commitments made by industrialised countries to limit greenhouse gas emissions, and those dealing with questions about the transfer of finance and technology to developing countries. This is not to say that the other issues dealt with in the convention are not important. These other issues are addressed when they illustrate particular points. However, if we had to identify where the main controversy in the negotiations lay, it would be over what ended up as Articles 4.2 (a) and (b), 4.3, 4.5, and 11. For reference, the substantive parts of the final version of those texts are given here. Firstly, concerning industrialised countries' commitments:

> The developed country Parties . . . commit themselves specifically as provided for in the following:
>
> (a) Each of these Parties shall adopt national policies and take corresponding measures on the mitigation of climate change, by limiting its anthropogenic emissions of greenhouse gases and protecting and enhancing its greenhouse gas sinks and reservoirs. [followed by qualifications about taking into account level of development, resource bases, etc]
>
> (b) In order to promote progress to this end, each of these Parties shall communicate . . . detailed information on its policies and measures referred to in subparagraph (a) above, as well as on its resulting projected anthropogenic emissions by sources and removals by sinks of greenhouse gases not controlled by the Montreal Protocol . . . with the aim of returning individually or jointly to their 1990 levels these anthropogenic emissions of carbon dioxide and other greenhouse gases not controlled by the Montreal Protocol.
>
> (United Nations, 1992: Article 4.2)

And on North–South transfers:

> The developed country Parties . . . shall provide new and additional financial resources to meet the agreed full costs incurred by developing country Parties in complying with the obligations under Article 12, paragraph 1 [reporting of greenhouse gas inventories and measures to limit them]. They shall also provide such financial resources, including for the transfer of technology, needed by the developing country Parties to meet the agreed full incremental costs of implementing measures that are covered by paragraph 1 of this Article [establishing green-

house gas inventories and drawing up programmes containing measures to limit emissions] . . .

(United Nations, 1992: Article 4.3)

The developed country Parties shall take all practicable steps to promote, facilitate and finance, as appropriate, the transfer of, or access to, environmentally sound technologies and know-how to other Parties, particularly developing country Parties, to enable them to implement the provisions of the Convention.

(United Nations 1992: Article 4.5)

Article 11 defines a 'financial mechanism', whose functions are to be to provide 'financial resources on a grant or concessional basis, including for the transfer of technology' (United Nations, 1992: Article 11.1). It will have an 'equitable and balanced representation of all Parties within a transparent system of governance' (Article 11.2). The interim arrangements stated that in the intervening period until the Conference of Parties had organised the specifics of how the mechanism would operate and where it would be located, the Global Environmental Facility (GEF) of the World Bank, UNEP and the UN Development Programme would administer it (United Nations, 1992: Article 21.3).

Following Rio, the main contentious issues were of a similar character. One which pervaded was whether or not the commitments contained in Articles 4.2 (a) and (b) were adequate to meeting the objective of the Convention (Article 2). North–South issues were also still to the fore – focusing again on whether the financial mechanism should be based in the GEF, and on the concept of 'Joint Implementation' (on which more below).

PROCEDURAL WRANGLING

Session One: Chantilly

The US Government hosted the first session of the negotiations, at the Westfields International Conference Center in Chantilly near Washington DC, in February 1991, as they had previously offered to do (Jaeger and Ferguson, 1991). It became clear from the first meeting in Chantilly that the negotiations were going to be highly conflictual. Despite the publication of its 'Climate Change: An Action Agenda', the perception by environmental non-governmental organisations (NGOs) and other states, that the US was dragging its feet on the issue, was quickly consolidated.

However, at the formal level, much time was spent at both of the first two sessions on organisational and procedural questions, such as electing officers, and deciding how to proceed, as is usual for UN negotiations. The activities of the first meeting consisted of organising the Committee's work. It elected a Chair and Vice-Chairs,[2] decided to organise itself into two Working Groups to deal with different aspects of the negotiations, and established the rules of procedure for the committee (INC, 11 February 1991). Political speeches within the formal sessions were essentially reserved for the opening addresses by Antoine Blanca, Director-General for Development and International Economic Co-operation (of the UN), Michael Deland of the US President's Council on Environmental Quality, Mostafa Tolba, Executive Secretary of UNEP, and G. O. P. Obasi, Secretary-General of WMO. Statements of national positions were also made by many countries, but these did not form part of any formal negotiations.[3]

The roles of working groups were as follows. Working Group I, co-chaired by Nobutoshi Akao of Japan, and E. de Albe-Alcaraz of Mexico, with M. M. Ould El Ghaouth of Mauretania as Vice-Chair,[4] would deal with the question of what commitments states were to make. Its charge, according to the first decision of the Committee (Decision 1/1), was to prepare a text related to:

(a) Appropriate commitments, beyond those required for existing agreements, for limiting and reducing net emissions of carbon dioxide and other greenhouse gases, on the protection, enhancement and increase of sinks and reservoirs, and in support of measures to counter the adverse effects of climate change, taking into account that contributions should be equitably differentiated according to countries' responsibilities and their level of development;

(b) Appropriate commitments on adequate and additional financial resources to enable developing countries to meet incremental costs required to fulfil the commitments referred to above and to facilitate the transfer of technology expeditiously on a fair and most favourable basis;

(c) Commitments addressing the special situation of developing countries, taking into account their development needs, including, *inter alia*, the problems of small island developing countries, low-lying coastal areas and areas threatened by erosion, flooding, desertification and high urban atmospheric pollution; also taking into account the problems of economies in transition.

(INC, 8 March 1991: Annex II)

Working Group II, co-chaired by Elizabeth Dowdeswell of Canada and

Robert Van Lierop of Vanuatu, with M. Sadowski of Poland as Vice-Chair, would address the questions of what institutions and mechanisms would be set up by the convention, preparing a text related to:

(a) Legal and institutional mechanisms, including, *inter alia*, entry into force, withdrawal, compliance and assessment and review;
(b) Legal and institutional mechanisms related to scientific co-operation, monitoring and information;
(c) Legal and institutional mechanisms related to adequate and additional financial resources and technological needs and co-operation, and technology transfer to developing countries corresponding to the commitments agreed to in Working Group I.

(INC, 8 March 1991: Annex II)

Perhaps not surprisingly, then, the first meeting was widely criticised as failing to address what NGOs perceived to be the urgency of the global warming problem. It was suggested that the universality of the UN General Assembly approach was a hindrance to an effective climate treaty. The pages of *ECO*, the daily magazine produced by environmental NGOs at the negotiations, are filled with criticisms of the slowness of the pace. The headline of *ECO* on the last day of the Chantilly negotiations was 'Global Warming "Overtakes Talks"' (*ECO*, 14 February 1991). Another NGO representative, Dan Becker of the Sierra Club, complained at the end of the session, 'We've just spent two weeks arguing over the shape of the table' (quoted in Charles, 1991).[5] However, as Borione and Ripert (1994: 85) point out, the debates over the remits of the working groups were 'tantamount to defining the scope and content of the Convention'.

Much of the problem was that behind the apparently technical question of the allocation of responsibility was the politics of what precisely went into the remit of the committee as a whole and of each of the working groups, and of who would be chairing each working group. The chair of Working Group I was heavily fought for. Most Asian countries were keen to promote Japan, in order to increase their chances of receiving Japanese aid (*ECO*, 21 June 1991: 2). *ECO* reports that the US had opposed including a mention of 'limiting and reducing' greenhouse gas emissions within the remit of Working Group I since it was opposed to such reductions. Similarly, the EC had opposed combining sources and sinks in Working Group I, on the basis that this would lessen pressure to agree a text on limiting emissions. Developing countries had in general preferred to split the groups into Working Group I for commitments on sources and sinks and implementation mechanisms, and Working Group II for financial assistance and technology transfer (Bodansky, 1991: 3).

Some delegations had also hoped for more working groups to be established to speed up the work; the reason why there were only two was that most developing countries only had one or sometimes two delegates present, and would otherwise be excluded from much of the debate (*ECO*, 14 February 1991: 16).

Informally there was much debate about what the nature and content of the convention should be. Several informal draft convention texts were circulating at the session although, since negotiations had not formally started, none of these were official documents. In particular, the focus was immediately put on whether or not specific quantitative commitments on greenhouse gas emissions should be imposed on industrialised countries within the convention.[6]

Much of the debate was driven by the publication by the US Administration of its 'America's Climate Change Strategy: An Action Agenda', timed to coincide with the opening of the negotiations. Criticised by many as 'an inaction plan',[7] it established clearly the US opposition to quantified targets as a viable way of approaching the issue. Instead, it outlined a set of policies which the US Administration claimed to be implementing for climate reasons, which would have the effect of returning their overall greenhouse gas emissions to their 1987 levels by 2000. However, this generated huge controversy, as it relied on the US's Comprehensive Approach, which looked at all greenhouse gases together and allowed trade-offs of reductions in one gas for increases in another. Since CFCs were already being controlled and ultimately eliminated under the Montreal Protocol, this gave the US huge leeway. The planned CFC reductions actually gave the US the ability to increase CO_2 emissions by 15 per cent by the year 2000 within the plan, as widely noted and criticised (Mott, 1991).

The approaches of most other industrialised countries contrasted strongly with that of the US. The Europeans in particular were highly critical of the US's approach, and preferred a strict quantified target to be included within the convention.

The North–South conflict within the negotiations also emerged strongly at the start. Within the debates on the remit of the working groups, 'delegations from the US, Europe and Japan were expressing frustration at the insistence of the Group of 77, led by India, that specific reference should be made in a set of "Guidelines for Negotiation" to the need for "new and additional funding" to help developing countries implement measures to help combat global warming' (*ECO*, 14 February 1991: 16).[8]

Session Two: Geneva

In Geneva in June, procedural questions still dominated. The Chairs and Vice-chairs of the working groups were elected (this took three days, according to *ECO*), and the working groups started to meet. Proposals had been previously submitted by delegations to the secretariat and these had been circulated, and the secretariat had also compiled the presentations into a single document. There was, however, little more than a formal presentation of, and statements about, these proposals by delegations, with little actual debate on the substantive issues (INC, 19 August 1991). The formal result was that a new text would be prepared for each of the working groups, based on the submitted proposals and on the interventions made during the debate (INC, 19 August 1991: 10, 12).

There were therefore, similar complaints at the slowness of progress in the negotiations. At the start of the Geneva session, a German delegate complained that 'during the last round of negotiations we used up a great deal of time discussing procedural questions and we were still unable to find answers to all of them' (quoted in *ECO*, 20 June 1991). *ECO* noted that the climate negotiations finally started on 23 June, four days after the session opened (*ECO*, 24 June 1991).

Of course, official reports conceal great disagreements and developments. The most the report of the Geneva meeting could say on the subject of commitments on greenhouse gas emissions was: 'There was a divergence of views concerning the nature of commitments to be included in the framework convention. Several delegations considered that specific commitments should be included; others felt that commitments of this nature should not be sought at the present stage'.[9] The continuing controversy is more easily grasped in the contemporary commentaries. Debora Mackenzie, writing in the *New Scientist*, stated that the negotiations looked 'likely to end in deadlock, as the US continues to reject the idea of targets for the reduction of greenhouse gas emissions' (Mackenzie, 1991: 16).

Already, the US was identified as the chief obstacle to agreement on quantified commitments on carbon dioxide and other gases. The UK government had proposed to the US a compromise on their comprehensive approach, to try to break the deadlock. Michael Heseltine, then UK Secretary of State for the Environment, had travelled personally to Washington two weeks before the Geneva Session, to try to persuade chief US officials, including John Sununu, White House Chief of Staff, White House Counsel Boyden Gray, and Richard Darman of the Office of Budget and Management, of the merits of his proposed compromise. This would disallow counting reductions in CFCs made under the Montreal Protocol, and would drop wording which specified by how much gases were to be reduced, but would identify carbon dioxide and methane as priority gases to address (*ECO*, 19 June 1991; Mackenzie, 1991).

Another approach developed by the UK and Japanese governments at the Geneva Session to try to appease the US was the 'pledge and review' proposal. This would commit industrialised countries to set unilateral targets within one year of entry into force of the convention, and then to have their performance in relation to those pledges monitored internationally (see *ECO*, 27 June 1991). This was widely regarded in NGO circles as a backward step.[10] They frequently made the claim that, in the words of Richard Mott of the Worldwide Fund for Nature, 'Selling out the climate treaty just to have the US on board is a great mistake' (quoted in Hunt, 1991). The 'pledge and review' idea did, however, dominate a good deal of the debate on commitments on greenhouse gases during the summer of 1991, including a high-level seminar in London involving delegates from many countries, organised by the Royal Institute of International Affairs and funded by the UK Department of the Environment (Grubb and Steen, 1991), before effectively dying during the Nairobi Session in September (personal notes; *Network 92*, August 1991: 4).

SUBSTANTIVE NEGOTIATIONS START

Session Three: Nairobi

The negotiations began to develop significantly during the Third Session in Nairobi in September 1991. It was here that the most salient issues began to crystallise and find themselves presented in texts which dominated not just the informal debate, but also the formal work of the Working Group. By the end of this session the negotiators were left with something approaching a single text on which it was agreed that they were all negotiating; prior to that there was great disagreement, within Working Group I in particular, about what text should be used as the base negotiating text. The formal submissions made by states during the earlier session still remained as formal negotiating texts, and delegates would frequently intervene to complain that a point in their text had been missed out from the consolidated text produced in between the sessions by the Bureau.[11]

However, it should be stressed that, at least in the formal arena, the negotiating was at a fairly primitive level. Little of the sophisticated bargaining described in much of the literature on negotiations was present. Much of the process of establishing a single text simply involved a repeated process whereby a text was used, a series of interventions was made, and then the secretariat was asked to go off and prepare another text on the basis of those interventions. The secretariat was given little leeway to try to produce texts which represented compromise wordings; every viewpoint which had been expressed had to be reproduced, in the attempt to produce one text which had all the possible options contained within it, so that the text could then be discussed again. While this may have been a laudable goal, it produced a virtually unreadable piece of English (and, presumably, French, Spanish, Russian, Arabic and Chinese also), where there were frequently two or three sets of square brackets round almost every word (square brackets representing text objected to by any state).

Gradually, then, the negotiations developed a text on which delegations agreed they could negotiate formally. However, the apparent snail's pace continued to be criticised. Jeremy Leggett, of Greenpeace International, stated that 'A real sense of urgency is missing from these negotiations' (quoted in the Nairobi *Daily Nation*, 21 September 1991). Another NGO commentator argued that 'Nairobi was supposed to be a turning point, but they've just been going round in circles with countries restating their positions but not getting anywhere' (Alden Meyer of the Union of Concerned Scientists, quoted in the Nairobi *Daily Nation*, 21 September 1991). On the other hand, another commentator did express the view that, despite the fact that there was 'no derth [sic] of skeptic opinion, one should not underestimate the achievement made in such a short span of time' (AALCC, 1991).

The slow progress was again attributed by observers largely to the intransigence of the US over emissions targets. It was of course true that the slow pace could be due to the unwieldy number of countries and to the complexity of the issues involved. However, it seems that, had there been greater agreement on substantive issues, at least between the major actors, the formal, procedural issues would probably have fallen into place. The isolation of the US became even more clear during the Nairobi Session. The 'pledge and review' concept all but collapsed. The British delegation handed out copies of the report of the London Workshop mentioned above at the opening plenary, there was a brief discussion, and the idea was hardly heard of again. The Japanese made it clear that, in their view, pledges had always involved multilaterally negotiated and imposed targets, reflecting a linguistic difference from the English in which the concept was initially introduced. The EC and the Japanese then agreed that, if 'pledge and review' was to be used at all, it was to back up commitments already contained in the convention (Pool, 1991). The Japanese then reinforced their own commitment to quantified targets in the convention, albeit in slightly less strong language than the EC's preferred wording, favouring that which would commit industrialised countries to 'make the best effort aimed at stabilising emissions' (quoted in *ECO*, 9 September 1991). The effect of this was to leave the US even more out on a limb from other industrialised countries.

Session Four: Geneva revisited

At Geneva in December, the pace continued to be slow. Arguably, the negotiations went backwards. Examining the text on commitments, it is clear that the negotiators left Geneva with a substantially longer text than the one they started the session with (INC, 25 October 1991; INC, 19 December 1991). However, the oral report of the Co-Chairs of Working Group I clearly indicated increasing consensus on many issues, reflected in the decline of square brackets in the text. But on the major issues, principally the nature of industrialised countries' commitments on emissions, and finance and technology transfer to developing countries, no agreement emerged (INC, 29 January 1992: 9–10). The report notes that one positive development leading to a speeding up of proceedings was that 'delegations were keener to meet in informal groups to sort out their differences and come up with compromise texts' (INC, 29 January 1992: 10).

An important development at Geneva was the breakdown of the G77. Developing countries began to meet in their traditional forum at the beginning of the session, but the G77 meetings quickly revealed sharp disagreements within the group. Notably, AOSIS states wanted to propose stronger CO_2 targets than others would accept. A rump group (called the G24 but including forty-four states) proposed their own text (which left the question of industrialised countries' commitments on emissions blank), and AOSIS followed this up with a proposal of their own advocating stricter emissions targets (INC, 18 December 1991).[12]

Commentators on the negotiations remained largely critical. The NGO statement at the end of the session, delivered by Michael Oppenheimer of the Environmental Defense Fund, lamented that 'We remain confident that the texts of a Convention will emerge. However, we are not at all confident it will be an effective Convention. Those square brackets exist for the purpose of defending the supposed interests of countries. But in so doing they may yet commit us to global catastrophe' (quoted in *ECO*, 19 December 1991). *ECO* referred to it as 'Death By

1,000 Brackets' (10 December 1991: 2). Others, however, did express a certain optimism. Pier Vellinga, delegate from the Netherlands (widely regarded as one of the most 'progressive' countries), remained confident that the convention text would 'include the words "stabilization of CO_2 emissions by industrialised countries at 1990 levels by 2000", but I can't guarantee what words will go in front of that or behind!'. He was confident that it would be possible to persuade the US of the political feasibility of committing itself to such an objective (interviewed in *ECO*, 20 December 1991: 4–5).

FINALISING THE CONVENTION

Session Five: New York

By the beginning of the New York Session in February 1992, considerable frustration had developed among many delegations about the inability of the countries collectively to move forward. However, there was a general perception that a treaty would be ready for signing by UNCED in June. On the one hand, the process was now a laborious one of removing the square brackets from each piece of text, solving the problems some states may have had with those bits of text by negotiation or rewording. On the other hand, sharp divergences remained on several of the main issues of industrialised countries' commitments and on North–South transfers. The states which felt most strongly on these issues had been engaged in tactics designed to maximise the likelihood of getting their preferred text across (for example, see below on the attempts by European countries to get the US to change its position). Or, in the case of the oil-producing states (in particular Saudi Arabia and Kuwait), they were deliberately trying to slow down the process in order to make sure that the outcome was a lowest common denominator agreement, with no controls on CO_2.

However, by February, it was clear that significant compromises would have to be made in order to produce a text in time. Consequently, the process of negotiation became significantly more flexible. Large numbers of smaller meetings, known as 'informals', or even 'informal–informals'[13] began to take place outside the formal negotiating rooms, at lunchtime and in the evenings, where select groups of delegates would thrash out their disagreements on various issues. These resulted in a host of in-session single-page documents which outlined the status of negotiations on each piece of text, updated daily – or, in some cases, twice a day.

The main controversial issues were resolved either during the New York meeting, between that meeting and its resumption on 30 April, or during its resumed session. The pace and sense of urgency in the negotiations increased significantly during this period.

Formally, the INC achieved a significant amount at the New York meeting in February. While the major political disagreements remained, the text which emerged at the end of the session had significantly fewer brackets. The committee agreed at the beginning that the purpose of that session should be to 'produce a clean text, with only a few brackets indicating major political choices still to be made. Major substantive differences should be reduced to essentials, clearing the way for political intervention' (INC, 28 February 1992: 7). To an extent, this was achieved.

Nevertheless, as the draft report just cited shows, the major political disagreements remained. One commentator claimed that 'The text is hardly in better shape than at the start of the Session' (*Network 92*, March 1992: 3). The Alliance of Small Island States suggested that, despite developments in some areas of the text,

> these relatively modest advances are overshadowed by the lack of consensus on key issues, notably commitments by industrialised countries on the stabilisation and reduction of emissions of carbon dioxide and other greenhouse gases, as well as commitments on the provision of financial resources and technology.
>
> (AOSIS, 1992).

The strategy of those industrialised countries trying to deal with the problem posed by the United States had changed since Nairobi. Instead of trying to accommodate the US, the focus was on criticising the US's stance on emissions control. It was generally believed that the position of the US might change. This was for a number of reasons. It was partly because John Sununu, the White House Chief of Staff who was highly hostile to quantified commitments on greenhouse gases, had resigned in December 1991. Another reason was the impending US election and the Democratic candidates' proclaimed commitments to controls on CO_2. Finally, there were a number of economic studies which were increasingly giving the impression that the costs of reducing emissions might be lower than the US claimed (see, for example, Doniger, 1992: 4). Under the new White House Chief of Staff, Samuel K. Skinner, the US Administration organised a high-level committee to implement and develop environmental policies, including William Reilly, Environmental Protection Agency (EPA) Administrator, and Michael Deland, Chair of the White House Council on Environmental Quality (CEQ) (Nusser, 1992). Thus, the Europeans felt that putting on pressure by expressing intransigence might be effective. Within the formal negotiations, however, the debates on the commitments section were effectively in stalemate, with almost all countries expressing a belief that there should be wording which legally bound industrialised countries to stabilise their emissions, but the US steadfastly opposing any such wording.

At home, US President Bush was under pressure to change policy. All five potential Democratic Presidential candidates criticised Bush for refusing to accept stabilisation as a target to which the US should commit itself. Criticism also came from other quarters. Bert Bolin, Chair of the Intergovernmental Panel on Climate Change (IPCC), made a statement to the INC Plenary during the session, introducing the update to the 1992 IPCC Report which had recently been published (Houghton *et al.*, 1992). In his speech – which also emphasised that limitations then being contemplated by industrialised states on carbon emissions were inadequate even to reduce significantly the rate of rise of carbon dioxide concentrations in the atmosphere – he made a thinly veiled reference to the dangers of letting the US off the hook, stating that he was worried 'that even a very modest achievement to reduce the rate of increase of carbon dioxide in the atmosphere as aimed for by some OECD countries might be compromised by special allowance among the OECD countries' (quoted in *ECO*, 21 February 1992: 1).

The US, possibly in response, worked hard to give the impression that its attitude to global warming, while it did not believe in the efficacy of targets as a mechanism, was a committed one. In the US statement on commitments, Robert Reinstein, US Chief negotiator, outlined $25 million of new aid to developing countries to draw up national inventories of greenhouse gas sources and sinks, and an extra $50 million into the core fund of the GEF. He also outlined the series of measures introduced in the US to mitigate global warming (Reinstein, 1992). However, he reiterated the US position that 'We do not see targets as a goal . . . We see actions, not targets, as a goal, and the actions we've announced today are intended to help all parties join hands in a kind of partnership' (quoted in *Earth Summit Times*, 28 February 1992: 1).

However, the US statement was not perceived as a significant change in the US position. While one NGO representative (David Doniger of the Natural Resources Defense Council) did consider that it was 'a sign of flexibility in the post-Sununu White House', he still suggested that 'the climate talks will fail unless the Bush Administration agrees at least to emission stabilization as the EC is demanding' (quoted in *ECO*, 28 February 1992). Others went further, and suggested that the US remained a 'potential treaty-buster' (Michael Oppenheimer, quoted in *ECO*, 28 February 1992).

The US administration was able to ride out the criticisms of its position. By the time of the resumed Fifth Session in New York in April–May, other states, in particular the UK, as well as Jean Ripert, the INC Chair, had lost hope that they could change the Administration's mind, and reverted to the strategy of trying to produce a compromise text. Michael Howard, the then UK Secretary of State for the Environment, was widely credited with/lambasted for securing the compromise with the US. The text which was finally agreed during this session, formally presented by Ripert (and reproduced at the head of this chapter) was 'widely regarded as an American/British text' (*ECO*, 4 May 1992: 1). Ripert himself stated his belief that the text should go further, but added: 'The reason we have an ambiguous text here is because there is a lack of agreement among the industrialised countries. The United States has not changed its position, and is not going to change its position in the next four days. Neither is it going to change by Rio' (quoted in *ECO*, 5 May 1992: 1)[14]

The US strategy of holding out on its position had therefore, to a great extent, succeeded. The text which the negotiators ended up with was significantly closer to its preferred option than to that of the other industrialised countries. However, when we look closely, the US had moved substantially since the start of the negotiations in February 1991.[15] At that point, it had not only been opposed to quantitative targets on greenhouse gas emissions, it had also objected both to the mention of target dates, which were finally included (although rather obliquely), and to the specific singling out of carbon dioxide as the major greenhouse gas, which they did finally accept. In February 1991 it had wanted a full-blown comprehensive approach, which simply mentioned sources and sinks of all gases (including CFCs) in one bundle. It quickly dropped the insistence on including CFCs, but maintained opposition to specific mention of carbon dioxide. Eventually it accepted the formulation 'carbon dioxide and other greenhouse gases not controlled by the Montreal Protocol'. This represents a significant shift. It had also moved significantly with respect to the issue of 'financial resources and technology transfer' (Dasgupta, 1994: 141). Of course, these shifts can be interpreted in several ways. The US could have genuinely changed its position, accepting the problems associated with the comprehensive approach (see Grubb, Victor and Hope, 1991); it could have changed its position because of changing political pressures within the US; or it could have submitted to pressure from other industrialised countries in order to extract concessions from them elsewhere within the negotiations. It would be very difficult to establish which of these factors was dominant.

During the resumed Fifth Session, the remaining difficulties were rapidly ironed out.[16] The process became one where Ripert would propose compromise texts to the plenary, based on informal negotiations with what were regarded as crucial delegations.[17] By the end of the February Session, Ripert had clearly resolved to get the most important delegations together to draw up a final text.[18] He had organised to this effect what was known as the 'extended Bureau', consisting of the formal Bureau members alongside other delegations individually invited by Ripert. This met during the last 2–3 days of the February Session in a room in the Secretariat's offices[19] and then had an inter-session meeting in Paris in between the two New York Sessions. During the resumed session, the negotiations were held primarily through the clusters of delegations mentioned above. There were three main clusters, with Vice-Chair Djoghlaf of Algeria coordinating the one on the Preamble, Principles and Objective, Ripert coordinating the one on Commitments, the Financial Mechanism and on Communication of Information to the Conference of Parties, and Vice-Chair Estrada-Oyuela of Argentina coordinating the one on Institutional Provisions and Final Clauses. These clusters met throughout the session, interspersed only with a plenary on Monday 4 May. There were no formal meetings between 4 and 8 May. Nevertheless, this method succeeded in producing a clean text. By 8 May, Ripert was able to present to the plenary a revised text from the one he had produced at the beginning of the resumed session. After another day of informal discussion, a final text was presented on 9 May, which – with a few small amendments from the floor – was adopted by consensus (INC, 16 October 1992).[20]

This is not to say that the resumed Fifth Session was devoid of controversy. Many observers felt that the fact that the US remained adamant in its objection to a commitment to stabilise its emissions was highly ironic, when its estimations of the impact of its revised policies pointed increasingly to the assessment that it was in fact going to stabilise its CO_2 emissions anyway by the year 2000 (see 'New US Policy Points to Stabilization', *ECO*, 30 April 1992: 1). As John Adams of the Natural Resources Defense Council stated, 'The US had completely undermined its own reasons for opposing a meaningful treaty' (quoted in *ECO*, 30 April 1992: 1). Many states, and Ripert himself, Chair of the Committee, and head of the French delegation, kept up the pressure on the US, hoping for a last-minute change of opinion. *ECO* reports that, at the Paris inter-sessional meeting, the US had remained isolated in its opposition to targets (30 April 1992). The US House of Representatives joined in the pressure on the US Administration, sponsoring an amendment to the National Energy Bill which would require the Administration to join other industrialised countries in committing the US to stabilisation by 2000 (*ECO*, 30 April 1992). The European Environment Commissioner, Carlo Ripa de Meana, declared that the proposed compromise text was 'completely unacceptable. I hope that our people in New York will continue to resist such a sell-out' (quoted in *ECO*, 6 May 1992: 1).

By the end of the resumed Fifth Session, the main substantive issues had finally been agreed upon, and a clean text (i.e. one without square brackets) was produced which was ready for signing (INC, 27 May 1992). The Rio Conference was therefore, at least as far as the Climate Convention was concerned, largely a rubber stamp. Very little needs to be said here about the actual conference with regard to the Climate Convention. The text had already been finalised, and what happened in Rio was the fanfare of signing it.

THE FRAMEWORK CONVENTION

Commentaries on the Climate Convention abound.[21] The general assessment has been that while, from an environmental point of view, it is clearly inadequate, it is possibly as good a political compromise as could be reached given the constraints. These constraints were various, some structural/procedural, and some merely dependent on the position of one state, the United States of America.

By the structural constraints, I mean here the constraints imposed by what realists term the structure of anarchy in international relations; the fact the world is composed of sovereign states, and thus any international policy which emerges effectively needs to go through some consensual process.[22] This gives greater power to those wishing to block or delay proposals than would other forms of decision-making, such as majority voting. In fact, the INC's rules of procedure did allow for majority voting, although this could only be used if attempts to reach consensus failed. The primary mode of operation was dependent on Rule 27.1 of the INC, which states that 'The Committee shall make its best endeavours to ensure that the work of the Committee is accomplished by general agreement' (INC, 11 February 1991: 7). Other than in adopting Reports of Meetings, in practice votes were not used, except in the resumed Fifth Session of the INC.[23]

Thus the structural factor of anarchy was able to exert a significant slowing effect on the negotiations, by allowing states (such as the oil producing states) which wished to see no agreement emerge to disrupt the proceedings. It is quite probable that the Saudis made more interventions on the floor of Working Groups I's meetings than any other delegation.[24]

The constraint imposed by the position of the United States has been outlined throughout this chapter. Here it is simply worth emphasising that the text finally agreed upon arguably represents a significant political achievement for the negotiators trying to work round the US position in order to achieve as strongly worded a Convention as possible. The interpretation of David Fisk, chief negotiator for the UK, that the final text's commitment to enact policies with an aim of stabilising emissions was 'indistinguishable' from an absolute guarantee (quoted in the *Guardian*, 12 May 1992) is probably overoptimistic, but it still remains a significant advance on what would have been achieved if other countries had simply capitulated to the US.

This assessment points to an interesting set of questions which will be followed up later in this book. If the US was forced to move through purely international pressures (i.e. without domestic politics playing a significant role), what does this tell us either about US power in the international system, or about the significance of anarchy in the international system? Does it imply that states cannot meaningfully be thought of as self-regarding units, since they can be brought to change their behaviour and even identity, however slowly, through the development of international norms? Also, why did the negotiations only produce a lowest common denominator outcome, in spite of the wide literature on how to avoid such outcomes in negotiations? Some of these questions will be followed up in later chapters. Now we turn to the negotiations after Rio.

DETAIL OF IMPLEMENTATION

The convention provided for the INC to continue meeting before the convention itself came into force, and this decision was ratified by the UN General Assembly (UN General Assembly, 1992). The purpose of this was both to prepare for the first Conference of the Parties (COP1), and to prepare possible amendments to the convention, or protocols to it. The INC met twice a year from the signing of the convention until the first Conference of the Parties met in Berlin between 28 March and 7 April 1995.

The focus of the first three sessions, INCs 6–8, was primarily on technical issues related to the implementation of the convention's various features. These questions included: how the Subsidiary Bodies on Implementation and on Scientific and Technological Advice would work in practice; what methodologies countries should use to prepare their inventories of greenhouse gas sources and sinks, or their climate plans; and what criteria would be used for disbursing funds under the Financial Mechanism.

Two main themes dominated the negotiations at this point. One was the Financial Mechanism. The debate from before Rio about whether it should be housed in the GEF had moved on to the question of the relationship between the GEF and the COP of the convention. Most industrialised countries maintained that the GEF should remain independent from the convention in its operations, while cooperating with the bodies set up by the convention. By contrast, developing countries argued it should be, in effect, a subsidiary body of the convention, subject to direction on operational questions. The issue was the same one of governance, the COP being under the one-member-one-vote system, while the GEF, through the World Bank, is dominated by the industrialised countries.

The second was the question of Joint Implementation. This debate had been present before Rio, but intensified after it. The convention had agreed that industrialised countries could implement their commitments 'individually or jointly' (Article 4.2 (a)). This became a big North–South question. Partly because it was (deliberately) ambiguous in the convention itself, and partly because some industrialised countries, such as Norway, wished to widen the scope of JI, developing countries suspected that it would become a new way of entrenching an 'eco-colonial' division of the world's resources, with high consumption in the North compensated by investments in the South in forests, energy efficiency projects, and so on. Southern countries were therefore sceptical in general of JI, but in particular tried to make sure that it would only apply between industrialised countries, rather than among any parties, and also that no credits under the convention could be gained for action implemented jointly.

During 7–10 December 1992, the INC met for the first time since Rio, this time in Geneva. This was a short procedural meeting, where the main items discussed were a plan of work for the committee until the convention came into force and then the first COP, and, following this, revising the roles of the two working groups of the INC (INC, 6 January 1993; *ECO*, December 10 1992: 2). The Secretariat produced with the meetings agenda a list of the parts of the convention which required work to be undertaken before the first COP, and this was adopted by the Committee (INC, 24 August 1992; 30 October 1992; 6 January 1993: 9). These tasks were split into three clusters. Cluster A dealt with commitments, covering methodologies for calculating emissions inventories, criteria for joint implementation, reviewing information submitted by industrialised countries, and reviewing the adequacy of commitments. Cluster B dealt with the financial mechanism of the convention, and Cluster C dealt with the rules of procedure for the COP, the organising of a permanent secretariat, and institutional questions concerning implementation of the convention (INC 6 January 1993: 10). Working Groups I and II were reorganised so that Working Group I now dealt with Cluster A, and Working Group II with the other clusters.[25]

In March 1993, the INC held its seventh meeting, this time in New York. It was here that the impact of the new US Administration came to be felt. Madeleine Albright, the Permanent Representative of the US to the United Nations, addressed the meeting, implicitly criticising the previous Administration by stating that 'we are well aware of the disappointment in many quarters that the Convention did not go further' (*ECO*, 16 March 1993: 1). NGOs, such as the Environmental Defense Fund's Michael Oppenheimer, stated that the speech 'sent a strong signal of the Clinton Administration's intention to move rapidly forward on climate change' (*ECO*, 16 March 1993).

However, the formal sessions still concentrated on two technical and procedural issues. First, many of the INC's previous officers had stepped down – Jean Ripert retiring, and Liz Dowdeswell taking over from Mostapha Tolba as Executive Director of UNEP.[26] Second, the December session had decided that only Working Group II would meet at this session, and that it would focus on the financial mechanism. The INC discussed this, but made no substantial decisions.

Again in Geneva, during 16–27 August, the INC continued on these technical issues. This was the first meeting at which the whole range of issues in the INC's list was discussed (INC, 20 October 1993). It focused, for example, on the structure of the subsidiary bodies on implementation and on scientific and technical assessment (*ECO*, 19 August 1993: 2); on the criteria of eligibility for funds; and on who should control the financial mechanism. There were also the first tentative but informal discussions of the adequacy of the commitments contained in articles 4.2 (a) and (b) of the convention, in a meeting organised by the Climate Action Network (CAN) at which a number of delegations argued that these articles were too weak (*ECO*, 26 August 1993: 1).

THE ADEQUACY OF COMMITMENTS

During February 7–18 1994, a month before the convention came into force on 21 March, the INC again met and started to produce concrete proposals on many of the technical issues it had been discussing, for example by adopting the IPCC's draft guidelines on National Green-house Gas Inventories as its methodology for inventories (INC, 15 February 1994: 2). However, it also began to think seriously about whether the commitments on limiting emissions in the convention were adequate to meeting the convention's objectives. The INC Secretariat produced a background document highlighting relevant issues, and outlined some of the options available to the INC (INC, 16 December 1993). The issue was discussed at length, and the Working Group Co-Chairs were able to report that the Committee, in general, thought that the commitments contained in Articles 4.2 (a) and (b) were inadequate to meet the objective of the convention (INC, 16 February 1994; *ECO*, 16 February 1994: 6). However, at this point no industrialised countries were prepared to propose reductions in CO_2 or other greenhouse gas emissions (*ECO*, 18 February 1994: 2).[27]

This discussion continued and intensified in the meeting from 22 August to 2 September. Here, again in Geneva, the German delegation tabled a formal proposal for a protocol on CO_2 emissions. This had been anticipated (*ECO*, 22 August 1994: 1), and the final text proved a significant disappointment for environmental NGOs. They had been expecting a proposal to reduce CO_2 emissions by 20 per cent by 2005, but instead the text read: 'At COP1 ... the Annex 1 Parties [industrialised countries] should commit themselves to reducing their CO_2 emissions by the year (x) individually or jointly by (y) per cent' (quoted in *ECO*, 24 August 1994: 1). Despite the introduction of a formal text into the proceedings which proposed CO_2 reductions,[28] the session remained deadlocked on the introduction of a protocol such as that proposed by the Germans (*ECO*, 2 September 1994: 1). Despite the fact that it was Germany which had proposed it, the EU rapidly said it was not prepared to consider a protocol for COP1, and many developing countries were also opposed, believing it might be a pretext for commitments to be imposed on them (*ECO*, 2 September 1994), or in some cases even that OECD action itself would hurt their interests (Grubb, 1995: 3). Oil-producing countries often presented their own interests in this way, suggesting OECD action would harm developing countries as a whole (e.g. see Al-Sabban, 1991).

In the end, the report of the meeting suggests that fewer countries believed that the existing commitments were inadequate than had done so in February. It simply says that some states felt there was no rationale for changing the commitments until new science emerged or until the implementation of existing commitments had occurred, and that others were in favour of making the commitments more stringent (INC, 10

October 1994: 14–17). However, the major industrialised countries were all agreed that the commitments were inadequate (Pearce, 1994c).

During this period it was becoming clear that, while industrialised countries were agreeing that existing commitments needed to be strengthened, many were also accepting publicly that they were going to fail to meet their existing commitments. The Norwegian government was the first to do this (*Acid News*, February 1995: 11). Of the major ten emitters of CO_2, only the UK, Germany and Russia (the last because of economic collapse) were likely to meet their stabilisation commitment, with the emissions of France, Japan, the US, Canada and Italy all likely to rise, as were those of the EU as a whole (China and India had no commitments under the convention) (*Environment Digest*, 1995, 2: 9; Pearce, 1995: 4; USCAN/CNE, 1995).

The final meeting of the INC before the COP in Berlin was held between 6 and 17 February 1995, in New York. It was here that the first discussions of AOSIS's proposed protocol took place. Trinidad and Tobago, on behalf of AOSIS, had formally submitted a draft protocol in September 1994, the deadline required if a proposed change to the convention could be taken at COP1. The AOSIS proposal added to the German proposals by stating that, by 2005, emissions should be reduced by 20 per cent from 1990 levels (INC, 27 September 1994). NGOs and Germany applauded the text (*Global Environmental Change Report* VI, 19, 4 October 1994: 3). The INC prepared recommendations for the first COP to consider on all the issues it had been discussing. Concerning the adequacy of the commitments on emissions in the convention, it gave no direct recommendations to the COP, but simply decided to 'transmit for consideration and appropriate action' the two proposed protocols from AOSIS states and from Germany to the COP (INC, 8 March 1995: 51).

The positions of states at this point fell into three main groups. Most EU countries, and now the EU itself, were in favour of a mandate to tighten up the commitments in the convention, but not in favour of agreeing cuts at the COP1 itself (*ENDS Report* 241, February 1995: 41). A group known as the 'JUSCANZ' group, made up of the delegations of Japan, the US, Canada, Australia and New Zealand, were prepared to accept that the commitments were inadequate but not to mandate that they be strengthened, particularly in the form of targets and timetables. The US and Australia were most hostile to the mention of 'reductions' in any agreed text from Berlin, and were also suggesting that, if industrialised countries' commitments were to be tightened, then developing countries should start undertaking commitments, especially the more affluent and industrialised ones. Developing countries were still at this point arguing that tightening up the commitments should not be negotiated until the state of implementation of existing ones was known. In the words of the G77 Chair, the delegate from the Philippines, 'active negotiations for... amendments of the Convention should take place only when we are sure that even the present commitments... can realistically be met' (quoted in Shlaes, 1995: 5).[29]

At Berlin, the negotiators produced what many NGO commentators felt was highly disappointing. They had the option of agreeing a formal protocol on CO_2 emissions on the lines of either the AOSIS or the German protocols, but opted simply to adopt a decision to start a process aimed at 'strengthening the commitments in Article 4.2 (a) and (b) of the Convention' (INC, 6 June 1995: 5). The decision, known as the Berlin Mandate following a US proposal (INC, 24 May 1995: 22), did formally state that the parties believed the existing Articles 4.2 (a) and (b) were inadequate, but simply deferred a decision on how to strengthen them. They agreed that the strengthened agreement should be negotiated by the Third COP in 1997 (INC, 6 June 1995: 6).

However, the final agreed text was noticeably stronger than many countries had wanted. The oil-producing states, as well as China and the Russian Federation, had all opposed proposals to make the text specify that the commitments needed strengthening.[30] While the AOSIS states were clearly unhappy that no agreement had been reached on emissions reductions at Berlin (INC, 24 May 1995: 24), a push by India and other G77 states to isolate the oil producers seems to have ensured that the negotiators came away with a text that mandated negotiators to negotiate strengthening Articles 4.2 (a) and (b), by 1997 at the latest. After an Indian-led G77 text was blocked by oil producers, India convened a group composed simply of 'like-minded states' which tabled a proposal, known as the 'Green Paper', which became the basis for the 'Berlin Mandate' (Earth Negotiations Bulletin, 1995: 28). India was thus credited, along with the EC, of brokering the deal with which countries left Berlin (*ENDS Report* 243, April 1995: 43–4). In the end, the text was prevented from being stronger largely by the Republican victory in the Congressional elections in the US, which significantly curtailed the freedom of the US negotiators. This led to many seeing the US as adopting the same role as the one they had played in Rio (*New Scientist*, 8 April 1995: 4).[31]

In addition to agreeing the Berlin Mandate, which went further than many expected, the technical aspects of the negotiations were also agreed at Berlin. Apart from a disagreement about the rules of procedure, with OPEC countries trying to insist on consensus decision-making (giving them a veto), considerable progress was made on issues such as the methodologies for compiling inventories of greenhouse gas sources and sinks, as well as institutional issues. The GEF was confirmed as the financial mechanism (despite the objections of developing countries), and the structures of the Subsidiary Bodies on Implementation and on Scientific and Technical Advice were agreed (INC, 6 June 1995).

CONCLUSIONS

Like Rio, Berlin was criticised by environmentalists for not going far enough, in particular for not agreeing a protocol there and then to reduce CO_2 emissions. Also like Rio, it was probably as good a compromise as could have been achieved at the time, given the constraints outlined briefly above. Most press coverage suggested it was a 'cautious success'.[32] Berlin went further than many commentators thought it would, because of the last-minute G77 switch led by India, and perhaps also because of a gradual change in the composition of industry pressure on governments. The next chapter analyses some of the main political features of the negotiations, hinted at here, before moving on to deeper explanatory and interpretive questions.

Chapter 4

The politics behind the negotiations

We cannot permit the extreme in the environmental movement to shut down the United States. We cannot shut down the lives of many Americans by going extreme on the environment.
(George Bush at UNCED, quoted in the *Guardian*, 1 June 1992)

Let this be the end of selfishness and hegemonism, the end of callousness, irresponsibility and deceit. Let a just economic order be instituted.
(Fidel Castro at UNCED, quoted in the *Guardian*, 13 June 1992)

INTRODUCTION

Essentially, the climate negotiations can be seen as involving two great conflicts. One is between the United States and almost everybody else (but predominantly the other industrialised countries), over the commitments to be undertaken on limiting emissions. And the other is the perennial North–South conflict. This chapter examines more systematically what lay behind the different states' positions, and looks at the general factors which help explain the groupings of countries which influenced the dynamics of the negotiations and the final form of the Climate Convention.[1]

As the previous chapter suggested, the two most politically salient parts of the negotiations so far have concerned the commitments of industrialised countries regarding limiting their carbon dioxide and other greenhouse gas emissions, and questions of financial resources and technology transfer to developing countries. However, differing political factors can be identified which help to explain the struggles over these issues. After outlining the content of the conflicts on these two issues, this chapter describes those factors and what aspects of the outcomes of the negotiations they allow us to explain.

I shall try to illustrate some general analytical points throughout the chapter. One is the importance of domestic politics: if we are to try to explain the developments in the negotiations, to do so without reference to domestic political developments and conditions in various polities would be fruitless. Another is the changing role and importance of international institutions. While these can be seen to have played a crucial role in bringing global warming on to the political agenda, their role declined significantly as the issue moved into a UN one-state-one-vote forum. As the issue progressed from being one of problem identification and definition towards formal negotiation, the states-as-dominant-actors model identified by realists delivers a more (although not wholly) adequate account of the situation. Correspondingly, the importance of international institutions in influencing outcomes declined.

POSITIONS ON THE MAJOR CONFLICTS

The Intra-North conflict

As was emphasised during the discussion of the negotiations, one of the most prominent issues debated was the question of what commitments to limit greenhouse gas emissions industrialised states would be prepared to undertake.[2] There was never any question that developing countries would be bound by such commitments; there was general recognition that their emissions would necessarily grow as they developed (although the US and Australia began to question this after Rio). The only question seriously debated was whether developing countries would commit themselves to limiting the rate of growth of their emissions, but here it was quickly pointed out that they had inadequate indigenous capital or technological resources to fund the investment which would be required for this. Thus the predominant debate was between the United States and virtually all other industrialised states, about the commitments they would undertake to limit their emissions.

As pointed out in the previous chapter, the debate moved considerably. The US moved from opposition both to quantified targets and timetables and to the specification of any individual greenhouse gases, towards the text which they finally accepted (see Chapter 3 for this text). The EC, generally along with Japan, and the other industrialised countries fairly consistently proposed texts which would impose quantified targets on industrialised states, stating that carbon dioxide and other greenhouse gases (not including those controlled under the Montreal Protocol) should be stabilised at 1990 levels by the year 2000.[3] Some also proposed texts which would then commit those states to reducing emissions after that date. After Rio, this picture is slightly more mixed, with the US's position initially moving to one of leadership after Clinton's election, but then reverting to a position hostile to significant strengthening of commitments after the congressional elections in 1994. The EU initially went into crisis over problems of implementation of its target, but later picked up momentum to push for reductions.

The outcome of Rio is clearly nearer to the preferences of the US than to the original texts of the other states. The US's alternative to 'targets and timetables' was to commit states to establishing National Strategies and plans of policies and measures which they would enact to limit emissions. This is largely what is contained in the final version of the convention. However, inclusion of texts mentioning quantified amounts of CO_2 regarded as desirable objectives arguably gives significantly more weight to the National Strategies approach, by giving benchmarks against which the strategies can be evaluated. Thus it could be suggested that the US position moved. At Berlin, other states were again able to push the US towards accepting mention of reductions in the 'Berlin Mandate', although here it is less clear that the US was in fact hostile to this, but that the US Administration was under great pressure from Congress.

The North–South conflict

The North–South conflict was an equally pervasive part of the negotiations.[4] In the structure of the convention, North–South issues surfaced in many places. In particular, it was prominent in the Principles section, in the Article on the Objective of the Convention, and in the Articles on Financial Resources and Technology Transfer.

There were many principles which developing countries wanted to see put into the convention. In contrast, several industrialised countries would have preferred there not to be a Principles Section at all. This conflict was based on the idea, accepted by both North and South, that putting clauses in the Principles section (rather than in the Preamble) would create precedents and potentially create new general principles of international law. In particular, there was resistance from the North, especially the US, to the idea of including the Sovereignty Principle. In the Declaration of the Stockholm Conference on the Human Environment in 1972, sovereignty in the use of natural resources was included as an Article. However, this was only a declaration, not a convention, and so carries less legal force. There was concern that including it as a principle in a convention might bind states on other issues in the international arena.[5] This, of course, appears to have been the objective of many developing countries, to establish their sovereign right to use of their own natural resources (Hyder, 1992). It would enable them more easily to expropriate multinational companies should they so wish, but it would also protect them from what they saw as 'ecocolonialist' attempts to control their development strategies by the North.

Another contentious principle in the North–South context was that of 'common but differentiated responsibility'. This effectively stated that, while global warming was a global problem, states had different responsibilities for dealing with it based on their historical contribution to the greenhouse problem, and on their respective capabilities of addressing it. Again, much of the controversy was not so much about the content, since no-one argued that industrialised countries should not as a practical matter take the lead in dealing with the problem, but more about whether or not to include it as a principle of their responsibility.

In the end, the North largely got its way on these issues. While a Principles section was included, the principle of sovereignty was moved to the Preamble,[6] and the 'common but differentiated responsibilities' principle was less clearly worded in terms of identifying the relative rights and responsibilities of North and South than earlier drafts had been.

North–South conflicts flared over other issues as well. Early on in the negotiations, India had proposed that the Objective of the convention should specify that, over time, emissions levels in different countries should converge at a common *per capita* level, a proposal supported by many other developing countries (INC, 26 June 1991: 12). This was based on their arguments about the implications of equity for the climate convention, but was flatly rejected by northern countries (except by France, and for a time New Zealand). However, this issue had largely died by the fifth session, in February 1992.[7]

However, most of the North–South conflict occurred over the issue which became known as 'financial resources and technology transfer'. There were two aspects to this conflict. The first was about what commitments industrialised states were going to make to transfer finance and technology to developing countries, partly to help adaptation to global warming, but predominantly to invest in energy-efficient technologies, so that developing countries' development occurred while growth in emissions could be minimised. The logic of this was that, since the North was the group of countries which both was historically responsible for global warming, and had the economic and technological capacity to address the problem, it followed that, in the strong version of the argument (often put forward by the Indian and Chinese delegations), developing countries could be put under no obligations under the convention. However, in order that global warming should not be aggravated further, finance and technology to promote less-polluting development in the South should be forthcoming from the North.

While the North accepted much of this argument in principle, what happened in the end was that, since the political will to promote such large-scale transfers was lacking in the North,[8] the convention collapsed into placing basically no obligations, even conditional on external funding, upon developing countries. In practice the only commitments the developing countries were left with were ones to establish national inventories of their greenhouse gas emissions sources and sinks (United Nations, 1992: Article 4.1 (a)). As I have argued elsewhere (Paterson, 1992b), the effect of this was that, while it appears to be a victory for developing countries in terms of making all their commitments conditional on finance and technology, those countries have little incentive from the convention to limit their emissions growth.

The second aspect of the North–South conflict over finance was the location of the mechanism through which to organise multilateral financial transfers. In this regard, the South clearly lost. The best they could do was ensure that the Global Environmental Facility (GEF) was only an 'interim' body.[9] It was understood, however, that use of the GEF could be made permanent if future negotiators so decided. The GEF was subjected to extensive criticisms throughout the negotiations, both from developing countries and from the environmental NGOs, but the ability of industrialised countries more easily to control expenditure which went through the World Bank led them to insist on the GEF being the location.

The industrialised countries generally insisted that the GEF should be the body through which financial transfers are organised for climate change.[10] Again, the US and others diverged. The US (supported by the UK) argued that the financial assistance under the convention should simply be channelled through the GEF. The EC and other industrialised countries (except the UK) suggested that the GEF should be used, but that spending should be kept under the control of the Conference of the Parties (Bodansky, 1992: 20). The developing countries had proposed creating a mechanism specifically for the purpose of administering funds allocated under the Climate Convention, arguing that the GEF is undemocratic and lacks transparency in its operations. Their point was to create a mechanism which was under the direct control of the Conference of the Parties, and thereby subject to one-state-one-vote rules, rather than being subject to the voting procedures of the World Bank which are weighted by financial contribution. India's initial proposal in early 1991 was that the decision-making structure would be like that established for the fund involved in the revised Montreal Protocol, namely that decisions (where consensus could not be achieved) would be made by a two-thirds majority of all parties, involving simple majorities of both developed and developing country parties.[11]

Criticisms of the GEF by developing countries had much to do with an underlying mistrust of the World Bank. These critiques have been well rehearsed elsewhere, but here it is simply worth mentioning that they focus on its domination by industrialised countries, the alleged secrecy surrounding its operations, the neoliberal economic ideology which pervades its mentality, lack of consultation with local peoples affected by its schemes, and its insensitivity to environmental concerns. It was seen as 'hiding the true culprits of environmental destruction – the industrialized countries – while diverting resources from development priorities' (El-Ashry, 1992: 5).[12] As Caroline Thomas has pointed out, the World Bank has moved in some of these directions during the later 1980s, but insufficiently so for many developing countries and environmental NGOs (Thomas, 1992: 79–91).[13]

THE POLITICS BEHIND THE CONFLICTS

The different positions of the US and the other countries were not purely arbitrary. Taking those positions as given, without explaining how they arise, is inadequate. All this would allow us to say would be that, since each country had different declared interests, either the negotiations arrive at some lowest common denominator outcome, or mechanisms such as side-payments are used to induce some states to accept outcomes they would not otherwise agree to. However, this tells us only a small part of the story of why a particular outcome was arrived at. We need, therefore, to examine the differing political situations within each country or group of countries.

The differences lying behind the divergent positions can be organised under three main headings. The first of these is the differing levels and types of dependence on energy resources. This has had a number of effects. Countries which are highly dependent on imported energy have been more likely to advocate strong action on global warming and a strong convention, since that position simultaneously improves their balance of payments and reduces their dependence on OPEC. By contrast, countries which are highly dependent on oil for their export earnings have been hostile to international abatement policies. Another group of countries is comprised of those which have large indigenous energy resources but are not necessarily dependent on them for exports (such as the US or China), who have also generally been hostile to action. In the latter case it is not simply that energy dependence has affected decisions in the here and now. Differing historical levels of energy dependence have encouraged cultures and practices which now influence policy. Fossil energy abundance has helped the power of energy lobbies develop, has hindered the development of energy efficiency, and affects perceptions of the economic costs of reducing emissions.

The second factor is the influence of the international political economy, and states' positions within it. This can be seen notably in the North–South conflict, which centres around questions of wealth and economic dependence. In particular, positions adopted by developing countries with regard to the need for additional funding and technology transfer can largely be explained by the weakness of states in developing countries, exacerbated by the debt crisis still pervasive in most developing countries.

The third factor which has influenced states' positions in the negotiations has been their perception of the implications of allowing global warming to go unabated. This can broadly be described in terms of countries' projected vulnerabilities to the impacts of potential climate change. At the one extreme there are the small island states, some of whom stand to all but disappear as countries in some scenarios of global warming in the twenty-first century, and who have been the most vociferous advocates of cuts in CO_2 emissions. At the other extreme, again, is the US Administration which, under the Bush Presidency, had estimated the costs of climate impacts to the US to be fairly mild. This factor clearly interacts strongly with the question of wealth. Countries may be equally badly hit by sea-level rise, for example, in the purely physical sense (e.g. Bangladesh and the Netherlands), but have greatly differing resources to cope with those impacts.

Energy dependence

Arguably the most important factor in explaining the difference between the positions of the US and other industrialised countries, and to a lesser extent between countries generally, is the underlying difference in energy resources and the structure and culture of the energy industries.[14] These differences are widely written about. Three groups of countries are readily identifiable.

The first of these includes those countries which are heavily dependent on fossil fuels for export income and have little other source of wealth. The most obvious of these are the OPEC countries, which are extremely dependent on oil exports. Saudi Arabia, for example, earns 87 per cent of its foreign exchange from oil (IEA, 1992b: 148). This group of countries was clearly the most hostile to a convention which included mention of limiting CO_2 emissions, and to revisions which strengthened those commitments. They were very vocal in the negotiations, Saudi Arabia probably speaking more than any other country, as was mentioned in the previous chapter. And many of their interventions can only reasonably be interpreted as deliberate attempts to slow the process down. For example, there was an ongoing tale by which, whenever the phrase 'environment- ally sound technology' was used, as it commonly was in parts of the text referring to development of alternatives to fossil fuels, Saudi Arabia and Kuwait would insist on intervening to make sure the words 'safe and' were inserted before 'sound'. This was partly to try to exclude nuclear power from the discussion (narrowing the policy options of states pursuing abatement measures), but more importantly it was designed to slow down the negotiations. They also engaged in other strategies, opposing not only quantified targets on greenhouse gases, but objecting to specific mention of CO_2 as a greenhouse gas (on the grounds of scientific uncertainty), emphasising that the focus should be on sinks for greenhouse gases rather than sources,[15] suggesting that much more research was needed before action was warranted, and arguing that oil-dependent countries should be among those countries selected for special consideration (alongside small island states, states subject to drought, etc).[16]

The second group of countries comprises those who, by contrast, are relatively dependent on imported energy. In particular, most of the European countries, as well as Japan, are significant energy importers. Japan is the most extreme example, supplying only 2 per cent of its own fossil energy supply (Tanabe and Grubb, 1991: 288). But other figures are also illustrative. Excluding the UK and Norway, which account for about 85 per cent of Western European oil production, Western European countries produced only 29.2 million tonnes (mt) of the 555.4mt they consumed in 1992 – in other words, only 5.3 per cent. Thus, most European countries are similarly as dependent on imported oil as Japan, and in 1988 oil provided 41 per cent of energy consumption in Western Europe.[17] Thus they have strong incentives from a balance-of-payments point of view to reduce emissions, and have not built up strong energy- dependent cultures.[18] Only the UK, Norway and Australia are energy exporters, and only Australia has been one for a significant amount of time. And it is worth noting that, at least regarding the UK and Australia, these states could be reasonably characterised as less strongly committed to their targets than some others such as Germany or the Netherlands.[19]

Partly for this reason, and partly for the historical conception (at least in the UK) of an Anglo–American 'special relationship', the UK played the role of broker between the US and other industrialised countries on the question of emissions targets, with both Michael Heseltine and Michael Howard visiting Washington when each was the UK's Secretary of State for the Environment, to try to change the US position or negotiate a compromise text.

A third group is composed of those countries with large resources which have fostered a particular energy culture. They have either industrialised on the back of cheap and abundant energy, or anticipate doing so in the near future. The US and China are the most obvious of these, although it has also influenced other large developing countries such as India, Brazil and Mexico.

The US is politically the most important of these. It is the second largest oil producer, the second largest natural gas producer and the largest coal producer in the world (Andresen, 1991: 21). It has developed with the benefit of cheap and abundant energy supplies, and correspondingly low prices. As a result, a 'gas-guzzler' culture has emerged which makes it very difficult culturally for the US to contemplate restrictions on energy use. One analyst has suggested that 'the history of US energy demand and the existing resources, infrastructure and institutions make the US economy as dependent upon fossil fuels as a heroin addict is on the needle' (Rayner, 1991: 277).

The historical consequences of these differences in the relationship which different countries have to energy resources are threefold. These have had a synergistic effect on the propensity of countries to develop strong climate policies. First, they have contributed strongly to the development of energy efficiency within particular countries. Countries with large energy resources have significantly more energy inefficient economies than those who have to import much of their energy.[20] Countries which have to import significant amounts of energy have had strong incentives to minimise their energy use to reduce balance-of-payments problems. For example, the ratio of energy consumption to GDP in the US is 0.28, while in Japan it is only 0.18[21] – in other words, Japan consumes only about two-thirds the amount of energy per unit of production as the US does, a significant difference for countries with about the same *per capita* GDP. This trend generalises to most of the industrialised world.

Furthermore, countries with high levels of energy efficiency appear more likely to adopt strong climate policies than those with poor levels (see also Rowlands, 1994: 142). There was debate before and during the negotiations about whether countries which were already efficient should commit themselves for further action. Japan, for example, at one point suggested that it should be exempt from commitments since it was already so efficient. However, early fears of this possible obstacle to negotiations seemed to evaporate, as countries with high efficiency seemed to be developing stronger climate policies. The same balance-of-payments logic continued to operate, combined with a technological confidence born of success in achieving improvements in the past, and perceptions of possible export advantages in developing more efficient technology early.

Another consequence of these differences in energy dependence is that political lobbies organised around those resources have become more powerful in countries more dependent on energy production. In the US, lobby groups, especially from the coal and oil industries, were given special privileges within Administration decision-making. As Alan Miller has pointed out, even during the last period during which there was a President in office who was sympathetic to the EPA (President Carter), the Department of Energy and lobby interests were still able to block EPA initiatives (quoted in *Tiempo* No 6, September 1992: 14). At the negotiations, representatives of the 'Climate Council' and the 'Global Climate Coalition', two coalitions of industry groups (primarily representing the coal and oil industries) essentially concerned to prevent anti-greenhouse policies in the US, were constantly to be seen alongside the formal US delegation, when they were not urging the Saudis to delay the negotiating process as a whole (see, for example, *ECO*, 8 May 1992: 3).[22]

The third result of differing types of dependence on energy helps explain an economic logic underlying why the US had a different position to most other industrialised states. Along with the greater predominance of neoliberalism in American economic thinking, the underlying dependence on fossil energy fed into differing perceptions of the costs of action. The US perceived the costs of reducing emissions to be significantly higher than did the Europeans or Japanese. Particularly influential studies were undertaken in the US which suggested that the costs imposed on the US economy of reducing emissions by even small amounts could be very high indeed. The series of studies undertaken by Alan Manne and Richard Richels (e.g. see Manne and Richels, 1990) were particularly influential. They argued that reducing CO_2 emissions by 20 per cent would cost the US economy between \$800 billion and \$3.6 trillion, costs which were cited by the 1990 Economic Report of the President.[23]

Again by contrast, many European states and Japan, and researchers working in those countries, have in general shown a greater optimism about the likely economic impacts of reducing emissions. This is not so much that they have estimated lower overall costs for reducing emissions, although they appear to have done this to an extent. Rather, a greater confidence can be clearly sensed.[24] In addition to a generally more optimistic assessment about the economic costs of reducing emissions, many of the European countries have sensed particular economic advantages in developing a leadership in abatement technologies. As the IEA stated, 'if a reinforced policy of environmental protection leads European companies to an adaptation of their marketing and R&D efforts ahead of others, these companies will in the future be better placed on world markets' (IEA, 1991).[25]

This clearly provides much of the background for the differing strengths of each country's climate policies. But, combined with the particular strength of neoliberal ideology in the Bush Administration – exemplified in this regard by the Council on Competitiveness headed by Vice-President Dan Quayle, which looked, among other things, into the damaging effects of US environmental policy on US businesses – it also helps explain why the US had such a particular objection to quantified targets on emissions, which it repeatedly held to be inefficient.[26]

The international political economy

The North–South conflict, based on questions of wealth and economic dependence, accounts for large amounts of the struggles in the negotiations. Underlying the North–South battles over specific issues were a variety of fears in both North and South. An argument which was prevalent in the US was that the effect of emissions limitations upon the North would be annulled if emissions growth in the South, particularly in large countries such as India and China, was allowed to go unabated. Emissions from developing countries are widely projected to grow rapidly as industrialisation continues, while emissions in Northern countries are roughly stable, or growing only slowly. Emissions from developing countries are currently about 26 per cent of global fossil CO_2 emissions (IPCC, 1990b: xxxiii).[27] However, Lashof and Tirpak give projected figures for this proportion of over 50 per cent by 2025, and the IPCC give a figure of 44 per cent for that date, on business-as-usual assumptions (Lashof and Tirpak, 1989: 87–8; IPCC, 1990b: xxxiii). CO_2 emissions in OECD countries were basically stable between 1970 and 1990 (IEA, 1992b: 33), although they are generally projected to grow in the future (an assumption which derives largely from the collapse in oil prices in 1986).

At its most extreme, some in the North regarded the way the South operated in the climate negotiations, as in the UNCED process generally, as an attempt to revive the agenda of the New International Economic Order (NIEO) of the 1970s. It was regarded as simply another means through which arguments could be generated to persuade Northern countries to engage in large-scale North–South transfers.

Despite its extreme tone, this charge had an element of truth in it. Certainly, many developing countries explicitly stated that the climate negotiations and UNCED generally were, for them, primarily economic negotiations. One stated bluntly: 'We from the south do not view this as an environment conference. We view it as an economic conference' (Holloway, 1992: 9). In a more closely argued manner, Hyder states that:

> The developing countries want to focus on structural questions: on greater access to world markets, attracting more capital and investment, resolving the debt problem, achieving access to science and technology, and acquiring additional finances for technology development.
>
> (Hyder, 1992: 326)[28]

On the other hand, when restricted purely to the INC forum, the G77 position was that 'the INC is not the correct forum for addressing the new international economic order' (James Naadje [Ghanaian delegate to the INC, then Chair of the G77], quoted in Bodansky, 1991: 4).

Most of the fears of the South can be most plausibly interpreted as stemming from the general desire to counter any potential 'ecocolonialism' on the part of the North. The basic premise of the arguments of most Southern countries was that their *per capita* CO_2 emissions were below the level at which the IPCC had said it would be necessary to stabilise atmospheric CO_2 concentrations; i.e. they were under 40 per cent of the average global *per capita* emissions level. Therefore they could not be held responsible for global warming. Their worry was that Northern countries were trying to get them to agree to commitments to resolve a problem which they had not caused in the first place. They were most aptly expressed in a widely used cartoon, depicting a Westerner getting out of a large car, talking to someone from a developing country in the process of cutting down a tree. The caption reads 'Yo! Amigo, we need this tree to save us from the greenhouse effect'. These fears were also fuelled by the controversy between the World Resources Institute in Washington and the Centre for Science and Environment in India (discussed below). The fears were that behind the attempts to put obligations upon developing countries was a more general attempt to hamper their economic growth.

A good example of the way in which their fears were reinforced by the actions of Northern states was the insistence of the US on using the term 'technology cooperation' rather than 'technology transfer'. This was widely (and correctly, since the US made it fairly clear that this is what it intended) interpreted to mean that, instead of technology transfer, which implies a one-way obligation to transfer technology from North to South, technology cooperation implied an equivalent two-way obligation. Kazuo Matsushita, officer in charge of technology issues on the UNCED Secretariat, was frank on the issue: 'We like to talk about "technology cooperation" and not "technology transfer" ... "Technology Transfer" implies a one-way transaction and that is not the case' (quoted in *Network 92*, August 1991: 1). It was interpreted to mean that the US wanted to be able to use in the North technologies developed in the South. Given the power of Northern multinationals, many developing countries felt this would end up being a one-way transfer of technology from South to North, perpetuating Southern dependence.

This dependence has a number of features, discussed in more detail in Chapter 8. First, Southern countries are dependent on external sources of capital, to finance and provide the technology for development. The immediate context of the debt crisis is an extreme form of this capital dependency. This has produced an inability to invest in alternatives to large-scale fossil fuel use, since large portions of export earnings are taken up in debt servicing. Second, they are dependent on the main world markets in the North. It is difficult to envisage possibilities for raising capital autonomously given their declining terms of trade due to unequal exchange; any state capital needs to be spent on funding export-led growth to repay debts. Third, they are dependent on Northern dominated institutions. The conflicts over the World Bank as the institution organising North–South transfers concerning global warming are illustrative of the resentments produced by this dependence. Much of the conflict over this has been about wishing to institute a more democratic form of decision-making. Fourth, the state in developing countries is itself weak with regard to the internal effectiveness of its operations, to an extent that assumptions about sovereignty in those countries are implausible (Jackson, 1990; Saurin, 1995). These weaknesses of states are a product of dependency, in particular of the colonial legacy.

Perceptions of the costs of impacts

The question of vulnerability to impacts contributes to an explanation of two things. It helps us to explain differences within the South. A continuum on this question can be drawn in terms of vulnerability to those impacts, from the small island states, through the Least Developed

Countries (LDCs), the large developing countries and the Newly Industrialised Countries (NICs), to the OPEC countries. It also helps, perhaps, to explain some of the differences between the EC and the US.

The countries of the Alliance of Small Island States (AOSIS), and to a lesser extent, the Least Developed Countries (largely of sub-Saharan Africa, many of whom are highly vulnerable to desertification), are the countries for whom this question is most salient. They were highly vocal during the negotiations, being critical even of proposals for stabilisation targets for CO_2, and calling for actual cuts in CO_2 emissions. At its founding, AOSIS called for a climate change convention which, alongside emphasising general Southern concerns about finance and technology, highlights that the small island states were the only group of states consistently calling for 'immediate and significant cuts by developed countries in the emissions of carbon dioxide and other greenhouse gases' (quoted in Faulks, 1991).[29] They remained highly critical of the level of commitment by the industrialised countries to limiting emissions, arguing both that they were inadequate on environmental grounds and that they fell short of the negotiating remit established by the UN General Assembly and the Second World Climate Conference (AOSIS, 1992). They also argued for an accelerated stabilisation target, at 1990 levels by 1995, as late as the February 1992 session (*ECO*, 19 February 1992).

Their vulnerability, in particular to sea-level rise, is acute. Some countries possibly stand to disappear as a result of global warming. The Maldives, for example, is a chain of 1,190 islands, none of which are higher than two metres above sea level (Thomas, 1992: 124).[30] Thus, very small sea level rises will inundate groundwater supplies of freshwater, destroying crops through salination, and making the islands uninhabitable (even before they become actually submerged). This likelihood may be exacerbated by increased storms and the flooding they cause (Thomas, 1992: 125). Many other countries are similarly vulnerable. Ince cites the Maldives, the Line Islands, the Marshall Islands, Tokelau, Tuvalu, Kiribati and Tonga as the most vulnerable (Ince, 1990; Thomas, 1992: 124). In addition, many of them are among the poorest of developing countries, with little financial resources to invest in technology to combat these effects.[31]

Among other developing countries, the question is much more ambiguous. For the large countries, they sense a vulnerability to the potential impacts of global warming, but they also sense a certain weapon in the large size of their own emissions (largely a product of the size of their populations). For them, and more importantly for the Newly Industrialising Countries of East and South-east Asia, the priority is development and access to technology. For OPEC countries, any concern for vulnerability to impacts is overridden by their oil dependence.

The question of vulnerability to impacts also contributes, although by only a small amount, to an explanation of the different positions of the industrialised countries. The perception was widespread in Bush Administration circles that costs to the US of adapting to projected climate change were in fact not particularly great (Paterson and Grubb, 1992: 302). But there was also a wider perception in the EC that the costs of adapting to climate change could be high. In particular, Europe would arguably be more vulnerable to sea-level rise than the US and, given the assumption that large numbers of environmental refugees may be created as sea-level rises, might be more vulnerable to increasing migration from worst hit areas, both because of past links through imperialism with those countries, and because of the already higher population density in Europe than in the US. Thus, global warming readily gained a political urgency in Europe which it lacked in the US.[32]

CONCLUSION

The categories outlined above help us to explain much behind the different groups which emerged during the negotiations. In the North, we can identify two broad groups, with the US ranged against virtually everybody else. The position of the US was based primarily on a historical abundance of cheap fossil energy which made its perception of the costs of action very high, and on a wealth which made its perception of the costs of the impacts of global warming (to itself) low. By contrast, other countries, to varying degrees, were more dependent on imported energy, which, along with a greater sense of vulnerability for climate impacts, allowed for more scope to envisage policies to reduce emissions.

In the South, five groups can be identified in the negotiations, which can largely be explained by these categories. The AOSIS states, driven by an intense concern with their vulnerability to climate impacts, pushed for stringent abatement measures, as did the LDCs. Both these groups also pushed for compensation for victims of global warming, and for general Southern positions on financial resources and technology transfer. In the middle were the most influential developing countries, a group based largely on the size of its members (largely, China, India, Brazil, Mexico), who were most strongly driven by questions of development and the alleviation of poverty. The NICs were not particularly vocal in the negotiations, but when they spoke it was generally to push for technology to enable them to develop faster (Ramakrishna, 1990: 429–30). Finally, the OPEC countries acted to block agreement in general, but also more specifically to try to water down commitments by the industrialised countries to limit CO_2 emissions.

The negotiations were significantly affected throughout by particular political events outside the formal negotiating arena. The general constraints imposed by political factors in various countries have already been outlined. Here it is necessary to outline some events which affected the course of the negotiations.

The 1992 US election intervened as a factor in the negotiations during that year. All the potential Democratic candidates favoured a quantified target on CO_2 emissions on the European model. Clinton also said he would give '"serious consideration" to cuts of 20–30 per cent by 2005' (*ECO*, 18 February 1991). This injected a dynamic into the US's position, and it might well be possible to attribute some of the change in that position to this. As suggested in the previous chapter, although the US held out on its major point that it would not accept a quantified target, its position as a whole moved considerably. It is reasonable to suppose that the US Administration felt some need to move in the face of what looked like becoming a Democratic challenge with significantly more electoral credibility on global warming, and on environmental issues generally, than it had itself. Despite the fact that Bush made an attempt to say that he was protecting American jobs by refusing to give in to the pressure, a certain amount of movement would enable him to say that he was doing what was possible under the conditions, should such a claim become politically necessary.

However, once in office, President Clinton was unable to deliver on his pledges. He brought the EPA Director into the Cabinet for the first time in the US, and proposed an energy tax, both to raise money in order to cut the budget deficit, and to reduce emissions. However, this proposal was watered down after intense lobbying of Congress by US industry. Other attempts to improve the US's climate policy, for example by some in the debate over the Energy Policy Act 1992, were similarly blocked (Eikeland, 1993). Finally, the Republican victory in the 1994 Congressional elections meant that any initiative Clinton had previously been able to take on global warming was removed, producing a US position which was similar to that which had been adopted by Bush.

In the EC, developments were somewhat affected by the internal debate about the implementation of its stabilisation target. During 1991–92, a strategy emerged to implement the target, but this was immediately troubled by two factors. The first, and most important, was the general debate within the EC over the Maastricht Treaty on European Union. In particular, the subsidiarity concept was highlighted in the treaty, especially by the UK government who used it (unsuccessfully) to stave off opposition to the treaty from its own MPs, and by the Danish referendum which rejected the treaty. The effect of this debate on subsidiarity was to alter the developments within much of the EC Commission's work. Three of the four programmes, THERMIE, ALTENER and SAVE, which had been devised to implement the target, were drastically cut back, it now being argued that these were more appropriate as national measures.[33]

The other factor concerned the difficulties the Commission has had in putting into practice the fourth arm of the strategy, the carbon/energy tax. The details of this tax were announced on 25 September 1991. It would be levied on the basis of 50 per cent on the carbon content of energy, and 50 per cent simply on the energy, and would be set at US$3 per barrel of oil equivalent, rising to US$10 per barrel by 2000. However, by the time the details were announced, it had already become hampered, not least by highly intensive lobbying by European industry (according to the *Economist*, [19 May 1992: 91] the heaviest lobbying of the EC it has ever engaged in). This lobbying was organised through the Union of Industrial and Employers' Confederations of Europe (UNICE), which sought to pressurise both the Commission and the Council into stopping plans for the carbon tax, fearing it would hit their competitiveness (Skjaerseth, 1994: 29).[34] Subsequently the tax was made dependent on similar measures being introduced in other industrialised countries (as UNICE had wanted), and significant exemptions were granted for the most energy-intensive industries (Grubb and Hope, 1992: 1111). Estimates suggested that the combined effect of the measures would now no longer be adequate to stabilise the EC's emissions (Grubb and Hope, 1992: 1111). In particular, by making it dependent on like action elsewhere, the EC lost any credibility it had as a world leader on global warming.

The combined effect of the problems faced in the EC was that the pressure the Europeans were putting on the US was less credible than it could have been. Throughout the negotiations, the EC had pressured the US to change its position, even in forums outside the INC or the UNCED Preparatory Committee, such as the G7 Summit in London in July 1991 (Johnson, 1991). The EC Environment Council issued a strong statement on 12 December 1991, declaring the EC's position on UNCED, including its commitment both to its CO_2 target and to increased assistance for developing countries (*Network 92*, January 1992: 11). However, this was undermined as increasingly it seemed that the measures the EC was planning to implement to meet its target were faltering. The US persistently claimed that the targets of most other industrialised countries were merely political tools, not backed up by the measures to implement them, and the more the EC's measures faltered, the easier it became for the US to resist pressure within the negotiations.

On North–South issues, the negotiations were also affected by issues arising outside the formal negotiating arena. They were seriously affected by the ability (or otherwise) of the developing countries to act as a bloc. In June 1991, they appeared to be doing this, through the Beijing Ministerial Declaration on Environment and Development (INC, 24 June 1991). The Chinese government hosted a ministerial-level meeting on 19 June in Beijing, attended by large numbers of ministers from various countries, in order to present a united front to the industrialised countries. The declaration was taken very seriously within the negotiations in Nairobi, as an expression of the views of most developing countries. Unfortunately for them, the developing countries were largely unable to maintain any semblance of unity within the negotiations (for the reasons outlined above), thereby significantly lessening any leverage they may have had.

The North–South debate was also significantly fuelled by the World Resources Institute's publication *World Resources 1990–91* (World Resources Institute, 1991). This publication drew a furious reaction from analysts at the Centre for Science and Environment in India, who wrote a lengthy critique, entitled *Global Warming in an Unequal World: A case of environmental colonialism* (Agarwal and Narain, 1991). Agarwal and Narain claimed that the WRI's report was 'based less on science than on politically motivated and mathematical jugglery. Its main intention seems to be to blame developing countries for global warming and perpetuate the current global inequality in the use of the earth's environment and its resources' (1990: 1). They argued that the way that the WRI calculated a country's 'net emissions' (emissions minus the amount assumed to be re-absorbed by a countries' sinks, e.g. its forests) of greenhouse gases, was highly spurious and politically driven. The publication of these two books, right at the start of the negotiations, provided ample evidence for many in the South of what they felt were the North's real intentions in the negotiations, and to an extent causing distrust of Northern NGOs.[35]

This chapter has given explanations for the divisions which existed on the two major questions in the climate negotiations – the commitments to be undertaken by industrialised countries to limit CO_2 or greenhouse gas emissions, and the commitments to be undertaken regarding North–South transfers of technology and finance. I have suggested that the primary explanations for these divisions can be found in the types of energy dependence of different countries' economies, their location within the world political economy, and their perceptions of the costs of the impacts of global warming itself. We now turn to a consideration of more general theoretical claims about international relations and the explanations they would offer of the politics of global warming.

Chapter 5

Anarchy, the state and power

Now the building of more coal-fired power stations or chopping down rain forests, even if on the other side of the world, is a destructive blow at our nations, an act of aggression as much as sending warships to shell New Orleans, or Miami or Harwich. They (politicians) might say that we would have to instruct certain countries to limit their carbon emissions and that if they refuse we should defend ourselves by bombing their power stations, and, yes, sending in troops to protect rain forests.

(Moss, 1991: 41)

Taking the work of Kenneth Waltz, in particular in his *Theory of International Politics* (1979), as representative of this school of thought, this chapter tries to outline how neorealist theory would analyse the politics of global warming. The focus will be on two interrelated forms of neorealist explanation within International Relations; those which focus on power (between states) as the cause of outcomes, and those which focus on anarchy as a generator of outcomes. I will try to suggest why neither gives an adequate account of the politics of global warming, and why both in some senses might be positively dangerous.

The chapter will begin with an exegesis of neorealist theory. It will ignore some aspects which I regard not to be of central relevance for the present purposes. For example, I will not deal with the parts of Waltz's theory which examine balance-of-power theory, and only touch a little on his treatment of the implications of bipolarity and multipolarity. Following this, I will look at differing neorealist accounts of international cooperation: those based on power, and those based on anarchy, and the logic of collective action. Finally, I will offer an evaluation of the strengths and weaknesses of neorealism with respect to global warming.

NEOREALIST THEORY

The basic premises of Waltz's theory are as follows. First, his is a systemic theory. That is to say, it takes as its basic level of analysis the international system, and seeks to explain outcomes in terms of the structure of that system. Hence the alternative appellation, coined by Keohane (1989d), of 'structural realism'. This is not to say that unit-level factors, such as ideology, economics, or the personality of leaders, are unimportant, but that theories which focus on these factors are, for Waltz, not strictly speaking *international* political theories. He argues this on the basis that, to be an international political theory, a theory must conceive of its subject matter (international politics) as a bounded domain, something which theories that focus on state decision-making processes do not, in his opinion, do. For him, they are theories of foreign policy. However, not only does he assume that unit-level factors are not, strictly speaking, in the international domain, but also that structural factors are more important in explaining outcomes in international politics.

Throughout his discussion, Waltz illustrates his theory by contrast to domestic political systems, and by analogy with microeconomic theory. The structure of the international political system, according to Waltz, has the following three basic features. First are its ordering principles. These are that: 'Formally, each is the equal of all the others. None is entitled to command; none is required to obey. International systems are decentralized and anarchic' (Waltz, 1979: 88).

The international system is thus one of self-help. As Waltz accepts, this merely requires an assumption 'that states seek to ensure their survival' (Waltz, 1979: 91). The system can operate with any other combination of state motivations, from 'the ambition to conquer the world to the desire merely to be left alone' (Waltz, 1979: 91). This is considerably weaker than the assumption made by some other realists, that states are self-interest (defined as power) maximisers. Following this assumption, Waltz simply asserts that the 'structure selects', i.e. some state strategies are rewarded by the system's operation, and others are not, a fact which acts as a conditioning factor (in Waltz's eyes a strong and often determining one) on state decision-making.

Waltz's second feature of the structure of the international political system is the character of the units. These are taken to be states. Their character is not used to refer to the internal composition of states, but involves the more straightforward assertion that states are functionally similar; they are 'like units'. 'International politics consists of like units duplicating one another's activities' (Waltz, 1979: 97). This fact is a product of the condition of anarchy: 'Anarchy entails relations of coordination among a system's units, and that implies their sameness' (Waltz, 1979: 93). Waltz defends the assertion that states are like units in the following manner. While accepting that 'States vary widely in size, wealth, power, and form', he argues that the important feature is that they 'are alike in the tasks that they face, though not in their abilities to perform them' (Waltz, 1979: 96). Calling them like units is 'to say that each state is like all other states in being an autonomous political unit. It is another way of saying states are sovereign' (Waltz, 1979: 95). And sovereignty need not imply the ability to do as each state wishes, merely that 'it decides for itself how it will cope with its internal and external problems' (Waltz, 1979: 96).

In this section, Waltz also asserts the state-centrism of neorealist theory. While accepting that transnational phenomena, such as corporations, social movements and international institutions, are not irrelevant, this for Waltz is primarily a question of facts and processes, rather than of structure. 'When the crunch comes', he says, 'states remake the rules by which other actors operate' (Waltz, 1979: 94).

The third feature of the international political structure is the distribution of capabilities. This distribution shows us the structure of a particular system. Thus, 'the structure of a system changes with changes in the distribution of capabilities across the system's units' (Waltz, 1979: 97). This means that the structure of an international system is defined by the number of states which can be described as great powers. Thus we can get bipolar or multipolar systems, each of which have different characteristics. The second thing which the distribution of capabilities tells us is that 'changes in structure change expectations about how the units will behave and about the outcomes their interactions will produce' (Waltz, 1979: 97).

NEOREALISM, COOPERATION AND GLOBAL WARMING

Illustrates weakness in

For neorealists, therefore, outcomes in international politics will be conditioned by the fact of anarchy in the international arena, the fact that consequently outcomes will be produced by power struggles, and the fact that the most powerful states will in general be able to get their own way. Because of the basic assumption that the primary feature of international relations is the anarchic nature of the system, the problematic question for transnational issues such as global warming is about securing international cooperation between states. Neorealist theory is, however, rather pessimistic about the possibilities for extensive international cooperation. It puts forward a general hypothesis that any

finding soltn to G W.

cooperation will be short-lived, and will in general reflect the preferences of dominant states within the system.

Such international cooperation which neorealists accept has occurred is explained by them in two different ways. The first is through hegemonic stability theory, which argues that there needs to be a single dominant state in order that cooperation can occur. The focus here then is on power as a producer of outcomes. The second focuses more simply on anarchy, and draws on game-theoretic analyses about cooperation under anarchy, in other words about the production of collective goods.

Hegemonic stability theory

Cooperation, within the neorealist literature, has most commonly been explained through hegemonic stability theory, which argues that stable cooperation can only occur when there is one state which is hegemonic within the system. Hegemons are distinguished from states which merely dominate, by having their power legitimated by those subject to their control. Hegemonic stability theory argues that cooperation will only occur on a widespread scale when there is one state which is 'powerful enough to maintain the essential rules governing interstate relations, and willing to do so' (Keohane and Nye, 1977: 44).

Hegemonic stability theory, as originally outlined by Charles Kindleberger, emerged to explain the evolution of economic regimes (Kindleberger, 1973; Gilpin, 1987: 72). In particular, it was developed to explain the emergence and maintenance specifically of a liberal world economy in the nineteenth and twentieth centuries (Gilpin, 1987: 73). It was argued that there are 'three prerequisites – hegemony, liberal ideology [in the hegemonic power], and common interests [between the other major states] – which must exist for the emergence and expansion of the liberal market system' (Gilpin, 1987: 73). Hegemonic stability theory focused on the necessity of US hegemony for construction of the international economic regimes established in the 1940s and the instability of these regimes following the (perceived) decline in US hegemony. This is not to suggest that international cooperation cannot continue as a hegemon's power declines, since congruent interests of major powers may make it possible for existing regimes to continue. It does, however, suggest that such continued cooperation will become more strained (Gilpin, 1987: 91).

Hegemonic stability theory was also then used to analyse the historical development of the world political economy, following up the argument that hegemony was necessary for the development of a liberal world order. For Gilpin, the use of hegemonic stability theory is a corrective to world systems theories which, for him, are too economistic. He casts the theory in explicitly neorealist terms:

> The theory of hegemonic stability begins with the recognition of the intensely competitive nature of international relations. The modern nation-state is first and foremost a war-making machine that is the product of the exigencies of group survival in the condition of international anarchy.
>
> (Gilpin, 1987: 85).

The reasoning behind hegemonic stability theory is derived from theories about public goods. Under conditions of relative equality in large-number systems, no single actor will pay the costs of producing a public good. This is both because each actor cannot individually do enough to provide the goods, and because each does not have enough of a stake in the provision of the goods. In a hegemonic situation, by contrast, a hegemonic state, by virtue of accounting for large portions of a particular activity related to the production of a public good (e.g. market share, or emissions of a particular pollutant), will have a disproportionate interest in providing the public good, and a disproportionate ability to provide the good (Waltz, 1979: 196–9). Specifically, it would involve the hegemon having to gain benefit of a proportion of the public good large enough to cover the costs of providing it (Snidal, 1985: 581).

For some, the existence of a single hegemonic state is required to generate cooperation. Waltz's proposition is merely that 'the smaller the group ... the likelier it becomes that some members – the larger ones – will act for the group's interest, as they define it, and not just for their own. The greater the relative size of a unit the more it identifies its own interest with the interest of the system' (Waltz, 1979: 198). He is, however, rather ambiguous in this regard, since his concluding chapter clearly argues that extensive international cooperation is *only* possible under current conditions under the leadership of the United States (Waltz, 1979: 210).

Some writers have applied the theory more widely than its original focus on the maintenance of a liberal economic order, suggesting that it might explain more general patterns of international cooperation. They suggest that, in other areas also, the existence of a hegemon is a necessary (although not a sufficient) condition for regimes to be established. Thus, in Keohane's outline of the basic tenets of the theory, 'hegemonic structures of power, dominated by a single country, are most conducive to the development of strong international regimes whose rules are relatively precise and well obeyed' (Keohane, 1980: 75). The reasoning is similar to the more restrictive application used by Gilpin. 'Hegemonic powers have the capabilities to maintain international regimes that they favor. They may use coercion to enforce the rules; or they may rely largely on positive sanctions' (Keohane, 1980: 78).

Hegemonic stability theory has been widely criticised as an explanation for regime changes in international politics. In particular, Susan Strange cites many attempts to apply it, which have found that it provides an unconvincing explanation of regime change in many areas.[1] Two major objections to its analyses are often put forward. First, some object that it is simply incorrect on theoretical grounds to argue that a hegemon is a necessary condition for cooperation to occur. Snidal (1985) even contends that, under particular conditions, cooperation may be enhanced as a hegemon's power declines. This objection has been behind some of the game-theoretic analyses of cooperation within a largely realist framework (see below).

The other principal objection is to the assumption of US hegemonic decline. Hegemonic stability theory emerged to explain the decline of liberal economic regimes in the post-war world in terms of the decline of US hegemony. 'Hegemonic stability theory seeks sources of erosion [of regimes] in changes in the relative capabilities of states' (Keohane, 1980: 78). However, many analysts refute the assertion of such a US decline. Perhaps the most vocal is Susan Strange, who argues that misleading statistics, and a misleading concept of power, are used to establish US decline. She argues that, for an analysis of power in international relations, structural power is more important than relational power, and that, in this measure, the US remains hegemonic, perhaps even stronger than before (Strange, 1987: 553). In the security, production, finance and knowledge structures, she gives (compelling) evidence that US power remains undiminished. By focusing on relational power, she argues that American academics have used statistics, such as those for trade, which generate misleading conclusions. They lead to a conclusion that US power has declined as its trade balance and proportion of world trade has declined. On the basis of arguments about structural power, however, she suggests that persistent deficits are in fact a sign of strength (a point often made about profits of firms in oligopolistic situations). Her explanation for the breakdown of regimes in the 1970s and 1980s is thus one which focuses on the negative effects of US policy. Paradoxically, despite cataloguing objections to the analytical relevance of hegemonic stability theory, Strange appears committed to its central point. Concluding her article, she writes that 'collective action is still possible but *only* when the United States takes the lead – when, in short, it still chooses to act as leader' (Strange, 1987: 574).

Another question remains about hegemonic stability theory, that of whether the power of the hegemon is fungible. In other words, is a hegemon in the international system able to translate this power across issues, or does cooperation in an issue depend mainly only on the power structure within an issue-area? Keohane (1980: 84–95) highlights this problem and plausibly suggests that a strong version, which seeks to explain cooperative patterns in terms of the overall structure of international politics, would not be particularly useful. This is argued both because power resources are simply asserted not to be fungible, and because hegemonic stability theory would not then be able to account for the differential rate of decline of different regimes (Keohane, 1980: 85). Keohane argues that 'a differentiated, issue-specific version of the hegemonic stability thesis has greater value than the overall structure version' (1980: 86). Thus, in the oil issue area, he uses the changes in US dependency on imports, and relative changes between the US, Western Europe and Japan, as indicators of dominance in that issue-area, and monetary reserves as a percentage of world reserves as an indicator in the monetary issue-area. This question is of obvious relevance regarding global warming, since it begs the question of what the relevant indicators of power resources in this area are, and it will be returned to.

The argument presented here is that hegemonic stability theory is largely useless because of the way the realist notion of hegemony is defined.[2] Application of the theory would require us to be able to make a reasonable assertion about the existence or otherwise of a hegemon, which I hope to show is not possible.

It would be reasonable to suggest that the only candidate for the role of hegemon in this context would be the US. It is also certainly the case that the vast majority of those involved in the climate negotiations regarded US participation as essential (Paterson and Grubb, 1992). Here, considerations about the US's proportion of emissions were vital. The argument ran that, since the US constituted about 25 per cent of world total CO_2 emissions, it would be crucially important to involve them in the Framework Convention. And it is not difficult to establish that it was US opposition to any stronger wording which was crucial in leading to the convention taking its final wording, particularly regarding Article 4.2 on commitments. Repeatedly throughout the negotiations, the US remained hostile to quantified targets for industrialised countries' emissions, while almost all other OECD countries made proposals for stronger wording than the US was prepared to allow (see Chapters 3 and 4). It was a clear sign of US strength that the other states did not simply ignore the US and sign a treaty without it. Any discussion of hegemonic stability theory in this context, however, centres around the interpretation of these facts. In contrast to the suggestion that US *hegemony* meant that no agreement which went beyond what the US was prepared to accept was possible, it is perhaps more simply that the condition of *anarchy*, combined with the US's proportion of world emissions, meant that an agreement without the US was not considered viable.

We need, therefore, to start with an assessment of whether it is reasonable to regard the US as a hegemon in the case of global warming. As indicated above, I am largely convinced by Susan Strange's arguments about US power remaining hegemonic within the overall system. However, I am unconvinced that this translates easily into power within the global warming negotiations. Therefore we need to fall back on Keohane's use of hegemonic stability theory disaggregating into different issue-areas. But then, in an 'issue structure model', it appears very difficult to establish what are the relevant criteria for judging what a hegemon's power resources would consist of in relation to global warming. For the oil, or monetary, issue-areas, Keohane was able relatively easily to establish relevant measures (1980: 86–7). But for global warming, this appears to be difficult to do. Percentage of world emissions is the obvious candidate, since this corresponds directly to a state's ability to affect the outcome of a regime defined in terms of limiting emissions. But it is difficult to envisage how this can be used as a power resource. In other areas the measures used to establish capabilities can be seen to be directly useful to a state in interstate relations. For example, in oil, relative dependence on imports translates more or less into relative ability to withstand market disruptions. Percentage of emissions does not translate into either power as resources or power as control over outcomes in any easy way. And to the extent that it does, it is in a purely negative sense. States which account for a greater part of a problem, such as CO_2 emissions, are more essential if the cooperation is to be effective than are states with negligible emissions. The US is more important in this issue than is Senegal. In this sense, despite the caveats outlined above, proportion of emissions could be a source of power.

Within the issue-area of global warming, to construct a measure of power resources would be inherently problematic.[3] Beyond the negative effect of percentage of emissions, the primary considerations would seem to me to be factors which were mentioned in Chapter 4, particularly relative susceptibility to climatic changes and relative ability to reduce emissions. Both of these would be very difficult to reduce to a single measure of power resources, since each is itself a composite measure, and each is plagued by huge uncertainties compounded by the interest which each state has in massaging figures, especially on its ability to reduce emissions.[4] Also, it is not clear which way power goes in that situation. Countries which can reduce emissions easily should have significantly more freedom of manoeuvre in negotiations, but, on the other hand, countries with high (perceived) costs of reducing emissions have an interest in weak international controls, and thus possibly argue more strongly for their preferred solution, because of the perceived damage caused by not getting that solution.[5]

An additional complicating factor would be that, even if the assumption of US hegemony held, there is no good reason to believe that the assumption also holds that a hegemon identifies its interest with that of the system as a whole. Even if the US could be considered hegemonic, it does not follow that it has a disproportionate interest in a strong global warming regime, since that depends on its assessments of the costs of the impacts of global warming to *itself*.

Of course, an alternative explanation of the importance of the US might simply be drawn from the implications of the realist assumption of anarchy. Since an anarchic realm is a realm of coordination, in Waltz's terms (1979: 88), it follows that consensual processes are required to generate international cooperation. This leads to what is often referred to as the lowest common denominator effect: cooperation occurs at the lowest level which each state will accept (Sand, 1990: 5). However, this risks ignoring the fact that, for any particular cooperative project, some states are more necessary than others, as noted above. This therefore implies, however, that the neorealist emphasis on the structure of anarchy is useful, since it allows us to explain the US's ability to thwart greater global abatement efforts.

The basic problem with an analysis based on power is that it assumes that it is possible to establish where power lies. Underlying this is neorealism's assumption that the basic power resources are military and economic. Power is then fungible across to other issue-areas. Through this mechanism, neorealist theory can become tautologous, by simply stating that the locus of power is in states which get their preferred outcome in any given conflict. Looking at global warming, the assumption that it is easy to assess where power lies becomes highly problematic.

This can be seen in two contexts. First, within the industrialised countries, it is not clear which bloc of states is the most powerful. One of the foremost struggles within the global warming negotiations was certainly an intra-North struggle over the content of the commitments the Northern countries would undertake. While the section above on hegemonic stability theory gave some reasons for believing the US to be dominant in the global warming issue-area, this remains contested. In particular, it was suggested that much of the US's power in the area came from the widespread perception of the necessity of US participation, and hence from the very perception of US dominance. Thus US dominance is rather ambiguous and susceptible to challenge. Certainly, at the same time as US participation was regarded as crucial – and this is why important concessions were made, for example on the wording of Article 4.2 on Specific Commitments on Emissions Stabilisation – the activities of other OECD states cannot be interpreted as implying acquiescence in that dominance. Use of the term hegemony consequently becomes problematic, since it implies the legitimation of the hegemon's power by other states.

The point here is merely to highlight problems in predicting outcomes from the distribution of capabilities in complex issue areas such as global warming, because of the problem of identifying the distribution of capabilities. This was examined above in relation to the problems of identifying a potential hegemon.

It can also be highlighted by looking at the global warming negotiations in a North–South context. North–South issues were also highly contentious in the negotiations. I have suggested elsewhere that the interdependence involved in global warming, in particular the fact that the South will increasingly account for greater and greater proportions of total world emissions in the future, gives at least some states within the South power resources within the negotiations.[6] While it is by no means clear that this mechanism is at work, it does highlight the problems that exist in identifying precisely where power resources lie, a prerequisite in predicting outcomes on the basis of the distribution of capabilities.

A deeper objection might be raised here, that neorealists have a limited conception of power. Stewart Clegg (1989) gives an account of theories of power which reveals a substantially wider array of views than Waltz (along with many other IR writers) seems aware of. Waltz simply talks about power in terms of capabilities (1979: 98), which seems to correspond to a notion of 'facilitative power' (the ability to get things done) which Clegg associates with Talcott Parsons, Michel Foucault and Anthony Giddens (1989: 2, 15). Waltz implicitly relates the notion of capabilities to abilities to control outcomes, or 'one-dimensional', agency-centred, conceptions of power (A getting B to do what they would not otherwise have done) (Clegg, 1989). But he never shows how capabilities and influence are related, and there is a tension between the two conceptions of power. Keohane gives a slightly modified version of realists' conceptions of power, suggesting that they use it to refer to 'resources that can be used to induce other actors to do what they would not otherwise do' (Keohane, 1989d: 54). This clearly links facilitative and agency conceptions, but it remains the case that, if neorealists wish to continue to base explanations on power, they could well benefit from a more adequate treatment of that subject such as is given by Clegg (1989).

Cooperation under anarchy[7]

Others within the neorealist school suggest that cooperation is possible without a hegemon. This has been termed the 'cooperation under anarchy' school. Much of their work has emerged in response to what were seen as weaknesses of hegemonic stability theory (Snidal, 1985). The analyses of this group straddle neorealism and neoliberal institutionalism (see below).[8] Drawing largely on insights drawn from game theory, they see endemic cooperation as possible under conditions of anarchy. However, they do not in general suggest that such cooperation alters the fundamentally anarchic character of the international political system.

The reasoning of the 'cooperation under anarchy' school is game-theoretic in character (Oye, 1986). They look at game-theoretic work undertaken (e.g. Axelrod, 1984 or Taylor, 1976) which focuses primarily on the implications of iterating game situations; for example, of Prisoner's Dilemma (PD), or of Chicken or Stag Hunt. They reasonably assume that, in international political situations, states expect to continue to interact with each other. For PD and Stag Hunt, cooperation becomes significantly more likely to occur when iterated, while Chicken becomes less cooperative, since a party which builds a reputation for defecting is more likely in a Chicken game to deter another party from defecting, mutual defection being catastrophic (Oye, 1986a: 12). Under PD and Stag Hunt, however, the opportunities for building up trust, building incentives to cooperate (for example, through strategies of reciprocity such as 'tit-for-tat') are greatly enhanced, so long as there is no *prespecified* end to the game which the players know in advance.

This school specifies three main conditions which affect the likelihood of cooperation under conditions of anarchy. These are that there are mutual interests to be realised, that the 'shadow of the future' is long, and that the number of players is reasonably small (Axelrod and Keohane, 1986).

That there need to be mutual interests to be realised is an obvious condition for cooperation to be possible. If mutual interests are automatically realised, then cooperation is unnecessary; the game is

'Harmony'. If there are no mutual interests (in game-theoretic terms, if DD is preferred to CC), then cooperation is not possible since none of the parties desires it; the game becomes 'Deadlock'. It is only if there are mutual interests between states, but that these are not automatically realised through the autonomous actions of each state, that cooperation becomes a potential issue.

The 'shadow of the future' being long refers to how much actors value payoffs realised in the future. The longer the shadow of the future, the more likely states are to cooperate. This is because, in an iterated situation, if state A defects today, state B may retaliate tomorrow. Therefore if A values the outcome tomorrow, defecting today then becomes less rational (Axelrod and Keohane, 1986: 232–4).

The size of the group is also often considered to be important. As groups get bigger, transforming situations from a two-person to an n-person game, cooperation becomes more difficult (Axelrod and Keohane, 1986: 234–8).[9] This is primarily because strategies of reciprocity, such as tit-for-tat, which significantly enhance possibilities for cooperation in two-person games, become more difficult to apply in large-number systems. It becomes more difficult to identify defectors, simply because the situation is more complex. It can also be more difficult to focus retaliation specifically towards a defector in a multilateral situation. For example, trade restrictions designed to sanction a defector may well also hurt third parties. Third, in multilateral situations, there may be fewer incentives for members of the group to punish defectors. In trade, for example, states who do not apply sanctions against a defecting state would have advantages over those who did.

Looking at the game-theoretic literature on cooperation, we notice a significant difference to Waltz with respect to the importance of strategies. For Waltz, structural constraints are strong,[10] while the game-theoretic literature emphasises much more strongly the importance of strategies adopted by states to achieve cooperation. The structural constraints – which they accept exist in the structures of the game being played – once known, however, also reveal the possibilities for state action. This becomes more important, since one of the strategies open to states is to try to change the structure of the game in the first place.

An important assumption underlying game-theoretic explanations is the rationality assumption.[11] This is the assumption, derived from rational choice theory, that states act in instrumentally rational ways; that is, they seek to maximise their ability to meet given goals (security, welfare, etc.) in as efficient and effective a manner as possible.[12] While technically involving an assumption that actors have theoretically perfect information about the options open to them (which, for game theory, involves knowing what other states would do in given circumstances), this is usually relaxed using the concept of 'bounded rationality' (Elster, 1986a; see also Keohane, 1984). It is worth mentioning since it underlies the logic of game theory, and is something which I will return to in the discussion of its applicability to global warming. If use of game theory depends on the rationality assumption, we must first ascertain that states do in fact behave in this manner.

In some respects the 'cooperation under anarchy' school more closely resembles the neoliberal institutionalist theories outlined in the next chapter. It is certainly the case that some of the writers (e.g. Keohane) explicitly propound institutionalist theories. Furthermore, many of them emphasise the importance of institutions as able to influence the structure of the games which states play. Snidal (1986: 56) certainly believes that game theory is a way out of the neorealist/institutionalist impasse, by specifying conditions under which institutions will or will not be likely to form. Also, the solutions which others suggest (e.g. Axelrod and Keohane, 1986) for alleviating some of the obstacles to cooperation outlined above, in particular concerning the shadow of the future and the number of players involved, are explicitly institutional. They suggest that, by constructing regimes and institutions, states may lessen some of these problems, for example by improving monitoring which makes defectors easier to identify, or by stabilising expectations which makes the shadow of the future longer. The parts of their arguments which elaborate the role of institutions will be dealt with in the next chapter.

Game-theoretic insights associated with the 'cooperation under anarchy' school would lead to a different account of international cooperation on global warming. The existence of a hegemon ceases to be a necessary condition for the generation of cooperation, so we are not left with the problem of identifying a possible hegemon and arguing over whether hegemony actually exists.

However, at least for a question such as global warming, the rationality assumption (even limited to bounded rationality) is highly problematic. Use of game theory (and arguably of realism more generally) depends on a notion that states act rationally in the sense outlined by rational choice theory. Therefore, if the rationality assumption does not hold as an explanation of state motivation and behaviour, use of game theory as an explanation of outcomes becomes tenuous.

This does not mean, of course, that game theory cannot be used as a model of the situation which states face. I shall continue by outlining the assumptions on which such models might be based. However, constructing such models is unlikely to provide good explanations for outcomes if the behaviour of the actors involved does not conform to its presuppositions.

A game-theoretic account would begin by assessing the potential for cooperation based on two of the features outlined above: the number of actors, the length of the shadow of the future, and the possibility of mutual gains; and the structure of the game. Game theorists stress that the smaller the number of actors involved, the greater the likelihood of cooperation, and that asymmetries of power within the group do help (Snidal, 1985). This assumption would lead to pessimistic projections at the superficial level, since in the issue of global warming, the majority of the states in the world are involved. In the negotiating sessions for the Framework Convention, there were between 102 (for Chantilly/Washington) and 148 (for New York) states participating. Thus, while the assumption that, for practical purposes, most of these states were irrelevant or can be reduced to blocs is a reasonable one, it remains problematic to identify the most important states or blocs involved.

Chapter 4 outlined how the countries in the negotiations could be broken down into a number of groups – the US, the EC and others, large developing countries, NICs, AOSIS, LDCs, OPEC – however, this still leaves us with a relatively large number system.[13] Furthermore, the assumption that these groups are internally coherent is itself problematic.[14]

Thus, on the criterion of the number of actors, game theory might lead us to be rather pessimistic about the likelihood of cooperation.[15] On its other criteria for successful cooperation, game theory produces more ambiguous results. Regarding the possibility of mutual gains, it is clear that this is possible. It is clear that it is generally regarded by most actors that $CC>DD$.[16] However, global warming clearly involves a situation where both relative gains are very important, not least since the uncertainties involved in assessing the potential impacts of global warming make overall assessments of absolute gains for any particular state almost impossible, and each state's assessment of what a gain actually is will differ greatly. What the economic game-theoretic work which has been undertaken does tell us (see Note 7) is that the gains from economically optimal agreements are very unevenly distributed (Kverndokk, 1992: 20–1). Kverndokk estimates, for example, that China would be particularly badly hit. Therefore, in the absence of strong side-payments to induce those countries to participate, it is unlikely that countries such as China will cooperate in enacting policies to limit CO_2 emissions. This could constitute at least part of the explanation for the perceived weakness of the convention on North–South issues. While the convention did specify that 'new and additional financial resources' would be made available by industrialised countries to developing countries, it was clearly understood that this would be of a limited scale; thus, developing country commitments were correspondingly limited to preparation of inventories of sources and sinks of greenhouse gases (United Nations, 1992: Article 4.2.3). Insufficient side-payments were provided to induce the cooperation of those parties which would lose out most strongly under the terms of the convention.[17]

At first sight, the shadow of the future is undeniably long with regard to global warming. Notwithstanding scientific uncertainties, states can and do expect to be engaged in ongoing negotiations on the issue for the foreseeable future. This is not simply an assessment based on the assumption that global warming will not go away as a problem and therefore states will have to negotiate. Before Rio, states clearly understood that negotiations would be ongoing, even in advance of the convention's entry into force. As the initial negotiations came to an end, the negotiators quickly organised interim arrangements to operate until the convention came into force, and the negotiations continued after UNCED. Moreover, the convention, along with some of its interim arrangements, specified timetables when some of the articles in particular, such as Article 4 on Commitments, were to be reconsidered in the light of new evidence, up until 1998. States have clearly anticipated interacting for the foreseeable future, and it is plausible, therefore, that this would have some effect on their strategies in the present. This, according to the game-theorists mentioned above, increases the likelihood of cooperation, unless the game structure were Chicken. However, the shadow of the future does not only involve an expectation of future interaction, but also requires an attitude that values positive outcomes in the future relative to gains made in the present. And it is by no means clear that that attitude exists, state decision-making still being dominated by short-term electoral and fiscal considerations.

An assessment of the likelihood of cooperation on global warming derived from game theory would also have to involve assessing the question of the type of game which is involved. Since PD and Stag Hunt become more cooperative when iterated, while Chicken becomes less cooperative (see above), the precise structure of the pay-offs matters. Some analyses of the game structure underlying the politics of global warming have been undertaken. In some works, the assumption of a PD structure is made (Dorfman, 1991). On the other hand, Ward (1993) argues that the structure is more plausibly interpreted as one of Chicken.

Chicken is largely characterised by the players' mutual aversion to DD, but the preference for DC over CC. Thus, states would wish to employ 'commitment tactics', committing themselves to defection in order to induce cooperation in others. Thus, it could be possible – as Ward does (1993: 204) – to interpret the actions of the US, the former Soviet Union, and China, as being versions of commitment tactics. He cites the US's claims that insufficient evidence exists to provide a basis for policy change and that its costs of reducing emissions would be too great, and China's use of ethical arguments about developing countries' lack of responsibility for global warming, as evidence of these tactics.

Of course, alternative interpretations of these actions are possible. Within the game-theoretic framework, but providing us with an analytical problem, is the fact that the game structure might look different depending on who you are. Thus, it might also be a reasonable interpretation of the US's actions that it simply regards DD as a preferable outcome to CD, or even to CC. In the first case, this would imply that the US was acting as if the game were PD (and it was avoiding the CD outcome by itself defecting);[18] in the second, that it regards there not to be gains to be had through emissions reduction. In other words, for the US, the costs of action exceed the benefits of greenhouse gas abatement. This is certainly a reasonable interpretation of the Bush Administration's so-called 'no regrets' strategy (see Gray and Rivkin, 1991, for an outline). However, other countries, (for example those in the EC) clearly regard DD as potentially disastrous, implying a Chicken structure. This is arguably an inevitable occurrence in regime creation, in that, before a regime is created which lays down norms and rules to guide behaviour, the definitions of cooperation and defection are themselves contested.

The problem, of course, within a Chicken structure attributed to global warming is that, while DD may be widely perceived as disastrous, it is (a) a long (unspecified) time away, and (b) the public good of avoiding DD can, in theory, be provided by less than all states, and certainly by different states unequally. The implication of this for strategic interaction is that it encourages commitment tactics in the short term, since there is significant latitude for changing strategy in the longer term. A state is not fixed to the same strategy for the next forty years. Ward's point (1993: 231), that established regimes need not only to encourage conditional cooperation through stabilising expectations, but to discourage commitment tactics, is therefore especially important.

As noted above, game theory lays considerably more emphasis on strategy and agency than does neorealist theory as exemplified by Waltz.

Thus, once the structure of the game has been identified and outlined, it could be possible to account for the cooperation, or lack of it, by focusing on the strategies adopted by states in the negotiations. Some of these were outlined above. Another line of analysis would be to interpret the actions of EC states as conditional cooperation designed to encourage like cooperation.[19] Certainly, the manner in which the unilateral targets were announced by industrialised states during 1990–91 seems to support this interpretation. This is plausible, especially as the targets were often announced directly in the face of arguments which emphasised how unilateral action was *of itself* unimportant. The announcement of the EC target in October 1990 was explicitly designed to influence the outcome of the Second World Climate Conference and to precipitate international negotiations (Haigh, 1993). The fact that many of these commitments were qualified with riders stating their dependence on 'similar action by major greenhouse producing countries' (in the words of the Australian target) also suggests that they were designed to induce like action.[20] Hare comments that the Australian target's qualification 'highlights the very real concern of many nations that large polluters, like the USA, should not be allowed a free ride on the actions of smaller countries' (in *ECO*, 29 October 1990). However, since there are, of course, no clear rules guiding behaviour, retaliation against defection is difficult, since identifying defection is complicated in a 'pre-regime' situation.

However, this interpretation relies ultimately on the rationality assumption involved in game theory. I hope to show more fully in the next chapter why this interpretation of state action on global warming is problematic. Here, it is enough to note that I regard it as more plausible to interpret actions such as the EC's (and many individual states') announcement of a target as a part of the EC's sense of its role. The EC wished to play the role of a world environmental leader. To do this, it needed to make symbolic actions such as the announcement of a CO_2 target. However, it had no clear goal to pursue, against which the rationality of its action could be judged, or interpreted as a strategy.

Game theory tells us more about the structure of states' incentives for cooperating in particular ways (presuming rationality and reasonably clear state preferences) than it actually explains the bargaining which occurred during the climate negotiations. Those negotiations can be more easily characterised as a series of attempts to work out what the lowest common denominator in fact was, and by states which wanted as strong a convention as possible in order to push more reluctant states as far as possible. There were thus numerous attempts to reformulate the language of Article 4.2 (a) and (b), in order that it would become more acceptable to the United States. The introduction and lengthy discussion (both inside and outside of formal negotiating sessions) of the 'pledge and review' concept, by the UK and Japan (Grubb and Steen, 1991), the constant rewording and renegotiating of the text on specific commitments on CO_2, and the final drafting of a text acceptable to the US at the 'resumed' fifth session during April–May 1991, are all most plausibly interpreted in this manner. Interpreting the US's intransigent strategy as a commitment tactic seems misleading, since it makes assumptions about US preferences which are fundamentally ambiguous. Using game theory as a tool for analysis only really helps us understand the underlying incentives to cooperate, rather than the cooperation which has occurred to date.

DEEPER PROBLEMS

The deep assumption made by neorealists is that states can be treated as units with given interests generated by their position within the international structure. This is misleading when looking at environmental issues such as global warming. First, as outlined in the section above on hegemonic stability theory, since the 'distribution of capabilities' with respect to global warming must be regarded as fundamentally ambiguous, analysing outcomes at the international level purely by reference to this structural factor is bound to be inadequate. Thus the internal political processes of (at least some) states are crucial to an understanding of the politics of global warming at the international level. The inadequacy is in part because, while, for traditional security concerns, it may be more reasonable to take state interests as given, for global warming, and other environmental issues, states' interests are fundamentally more ambiguous. While Waltz's guiding assumption that a state seeks to survive is a reasonable one, it is virtually useless in analysing global warming, except in the case of the small island states, who are at risk of disappearing as states as a consequence of global warming. These states, of course, have been politically very vocal in the global warming negotiations, but not particularly influential. State interests depend much more on internal characteristics, such as the factors identified in Chapter 4: for example, the structure of the energy industries, the perceived impact of global warming, and so on. State interests are fundamentally ambiguous in relation to global warming in this sense. Does a state have an interest in preventing the potential projected impacts of global warming? Or does it have a greater interest in preserving the existing structures of industry and the economy? And to what extent are these interests actually in conflict with each other?

In relation to global warming and neorealism, what is theoretically very important is that the answers to these questions will vary from state to state based on characteristics specific to them, and thus state interests cannot be deduced from the nature and structure of the international system. This is Waltz's rationale for treating them as given.[21] He does not state that internal political processes are irrelevant, merely that the structure of the international system is more important in influencing state behaviour. However, this is inadequate for understanding the politics of global warming. Interstate interactions on an issue such as global warming cannot be characterised in the same way as those on security relations. Thus, even if the structure of the system could be adequately described, it could not be expected to be a good predictor of state behaviour.[22] Consequently, a focus on domestic politics, which Waltz in particular among neorealists regards as largely irrelevant, is in fact necessary to an analysis.

The other misleading aspect of neorealism's state centrism in this case is its assumption that states are the only relevant actors for analytical purposes. The historical chapters in this book provided ample evidence as to the importance of both international organisations and non-governmental organisations. The point to be emphasised here is that the international organisations involved – predominantly WMO, UNEP and the IPCC – cannot in any meaningful sense be regarded as epiphenomenal. Waltz states that, while international organisations and institutions do exist, their role and functions can be discounted; i.e. they can simply be viewed as functionaries of the interstate system. 'Whatever elements of authority emerge internationally are barely once removed from the capability that provides the foundation for the appearance of those elements. Authority quickly reduces to a particular expression of capability' (Waltz, 1979: 88). They cannot, for him, be viewed as having any independent influence. This statement is inadequate with respect to global warming. While having been initially set up by states, the roles of these organisations clearly reveal some autonomous influence over outcomes. Were Waltz correct we would, for example, expect the intense lobbying by the US delegation, along with OPEC delegates and industrial lobbyists, in the IPCC to have had much greater effect. Lunde's account of the final IPCC Plenary in Sundsvall, Sweden, is particularly instructive (1991: 100–10). He shows how those actors' views were rejected, and thus an outcome was achieved which was opposed to the interests of major players in the international system, and which made objections to international action significantly more difficult to sustain. This point will be followed up and enlarged upon in the next chapter.

With NGOs, it is more difficult to establish their role, since they were not formal players in the process. It is, therefore, more difficult to establish particular cases of their influence. However, it is hard to conceive that their very high profile, their persistent lobbying (in large numbers), and their links to the media both internationally and in their own countries, were without effect.

One case of influence can be cited as an illustration. The convention eventually ended up with a clause (Article 4.2 [b]) which enabled industrialised countries to stabilise their emissions 'individually or jointly'. The purpose of this phrase was to increase the economic efficiency of implementation by permitting investment in abatement abroad to offset growth in emissions domestically. It was a half-way house between strict national targets and fully tradeable permits. The origin of 'joint implementation', as it became known, was a workshop organised by the Center for International Climate and Energy Research, an NGO based in Oslo, in July 1991 (Hanisch, 1991).

A related problem is neorealism's assumption that international politics is fundamentally anarchic and that this anarchic nature is not amenable to change. It was suggested above that the anarchy assumption gives a better account of how the US was able to determine how far global abatement efforts would go than do assertions about the US's hegemonic power.

However, the assumption of anarchy is problematic in a number of ways. While the characterisation of the system as essentially a self-help system seems initially appealing in relation to the dramatic conflicts which occurred in the negotiations on global warming, it remains misleading. Fundamentally, Waltz's insistence on the clear separation of structure and process becomes problematic. It relies on an assumption that structure (more or less) determines outcomes, and thus particular processes are not important; like international institutions, they are epiphenomenal. However, this assumption is unable to provide us with explanations as to how particular issues get on to the agenda. Neorealism thereby suffers as an explanatory theory through its static treatment of international politics. Waltz himself is open about this feature of neorealist theory. The underlying reason why neorealists neglect this aspect of international politics is because they regard the basic underlying characteristics of the system to be robust and unsusceptible to change. The problem here is that, when we focus on any particular issue, it is inevitably dynamic in character; it rises on to the agenda, is (or is not) dealt with by the politicians, and the international response to it evolves. Sometimes the problem goes away. However, all these dynamics need explaining if we are to gain a fuller understanding of international politics.

The point is that neorealism has no tools to understand these dynamics (Ashley, 1986: 265). For global warming, a process has emerged largely without reference to a pre-existing international structure (defined in Waltz's terms). Within its framework, the assumption of anarchy leads us to rely purely on the distribution of capabilities as determinants of what gets on the international agenda. Powerful states are able to get issues of interest to them on to the agenda. Reflecting on the material presented in Chapter 2 in particular, this is clearly an inadequate account of the process of agenda setting in the case of global warming. But beyond this, it fails to account for how the process of agenda setting affects in important ways the context within which states negotiate. The assumption of anarchy suggests that such negotiations occur in some sort of vacuum, with given state interests and the distribution of capabilities generating the outcome. However, the process of how an issue gets on the agenda will affect the negotiating structure. It implies that, as Milner argues, the strategic interdependence faced by states, based on their continuing interactions, and their assessment of their interests, will be just as important a *structural* feature of the negotiations (Milner, 1991: 81–5). And the processes by which the agenda, for example on global warming, was set (*not* by sovereign states operating in an anarchic environment) will affect their perceptions of where they fit within this structure. Fundamentally then, according to Waltz's criteria for judging an assumption, the problem is simply that, when analysing the international politics of global warming, the assumption of anarchy, defined simply as absence of a central governmental authority, is not a *useful* one. Since, for Waltz, the distribution of capabilities determines outcomes in an anarchic situation, it follows that, as that distribution cannot in any precise fashion be described, the assumption of anarchy loses value as an assumption. And, as I have tried to show, it also gives us no tools for analysing agenda setting.

CONCLUSIONS

Explanations of the politics of global warming based on neorealist theory are largely unconvincing. While intuitively the notion of anarchy gives some insight into how collective action problems work, the explanations fall down because they rely ultimately on the assumption that states are individual utility (or power) maximisers. As will be developed further in the next chapter, detailed analysis of state practices on global warming does not bear this assumption out; rather, states' interests are constituted intersubjectively, and states spend most of their energy on working towards some sense of what their interests are, rather than in trying to realise some pre-given interest. And regarding explanations based on power, the notions of power which realists derive from their study of military relations between states is inappropriate, since there is no clear way in which a power structure works in relation to the issue of global warming.

However, not only are realist analyses unconvincing, they are arguably self-fulfilling – and (from a normative point of view) dangerously so (Wendt, 1992: 411; Scholte, 1993: 21). Since realists view the international system as necessarily unchanging, they produce analyses which emphasise continuity and whose policy implications are that states should not expect cooperation from other states, and should be wary of cooperative ventures, for example by worrying about relative gains. But the important point is that realism has been politically hegemonic, at least since the Second World War, which has meant that the dominant way in which policy-makers have thought of international politics has been as conflictual. This has a number of effects, including entrenching existing power relations.

An example of how realist assumptions of the noncooperative nature of international politics could be argued to have influenced the position of the US on global warming and benefited the already powerful, could be seen in the following. The US frequently made the argument during the negotiations and in other forums that it would be irrelevant for it to take substantial action on global warming if developing countries would not also undertake commitments to reduce the rate of growth of their emissions. Developing countries claimed they were willing to undertake these commitments provided they would be financed by the North. The US argument (as well as being based in the political infeasibility of facilitating North–South transfers at that point) was clearly based in assumptions about potential 'free-riding' on the provision of a collective good, such as (relative) climate stability. The US was unprepared to cooperate unless it had cast-iron guarantees that other countries would also, and assumed (being historically informed by realists) that such a level of cooperation would not be forthcoming. The theory becomes self-fulfilling. But the discussion on the game-theoretic aspects of neorealism above showed that such a situation is non-determinate; mutual cooperation cannot be presumed, but it certainly cannot theoretically be precluded. Thus, since the US is likely to be hit less severely by the potential impacts of global warming (if only because it has the financial resources to cope with adaptation), than, for example, Bangladesh or the small island states, realism (if only unintentionally) benefits the already privileged, by giving them theoretically reasonable grounds not to cooperate.

Another way this could be illustrated is that some analysts have used realist analogies drawn from the area of security relations to try to explain international environmental politics. Some of the conceptual borrowing is remarkably blatant, and reveals its own inadequacies clearly. The quote from Norman Moss (1991) given at the beginning of this chapter is the most clear example. However, these security analogies are misplaced. The underlying structure of these problems is qualitatively different from that of security problems, and analogous reasoning is therefore not viable (Porter and Brown, 1991: 19). As Thomas states, 'The traditional approach (to security) based on military preparedness to meet an external threat to a sovereign state is inadequate' (1992: 151). Borrowing concepts about military security will not enable us to understand the politics of environmental problems. While an expanded concept of security[23] is sometimes useful to account in particular for the direct impacts of environmental and resource problems, through the generation of competition over scarce resources, or of political instability, it tells us little about the politics of ameliorating those problems (Deudney, 1990). (It also, as Thomas points out, involves an explicit rejection of realist accounts based on the sovereign state and the preponderance of military matters.) Whether or not they generate military conflict, environmental threats are not direct threats from another nation state, and are not resolvable by military means. But analysing them as if they did follow such a logic will produce damaging consequences if acted upon.

Despite these caveats, neorealist theory does tell us something about the politics of global warming. It helps us to focus on the conflictual aspects of the negotiations, and elucidates some of the reasons why cooperation has been difficult to achieve. It leads us to think of it in terms of a collective action problem, through its conceptualisation of anarchy. Its primary weaknesses are its neglect of international institutions and domestic politics, and its effective structural determinism which leaves us unable to account for the process and for agenda setting.

Chapter 6

Cooperation and institutions

The purpose of this chapter is to outline and analyse neoliberal institutionalist theories of IR in the light of the experience of global warming.[1] While these accounts vary in some respects, they hold certain common positions which differ in significant respects from neorealist positions, and serve as a basis for discussion.

Within the debate on global warming (and global environmental change generally), this line of thought is very important, since it provides the basis of many prescriptions for the forms which international responses should take. Institutionalist assumptions lie behind the proposals, included in the Climate Change Convention, and more widely in the UNCED process, to create new international bodies within the UN system (for example, the bodies created in the convention, or the Commission on Sustainable Development proposed in Agenda 21 at UNCED, and created by UNGA). Chapter 1 reviewed some of the statements made by proponents of this position. The viability of many of these proposals depends on the assumption that institutions matter, and the ability to demonstrate the conditions under which they matter.

The general line of argument in this chapter will be that there are two types of institutionalist thought, which require different types of analysis. The first is one which reduces the concept of an institution to formal organisations, an approach which often happens in practice even while this reduction is denied in institutionalist theory. Here, it is not difficult to show that, at particular points, the role of international organisations such as WMO and UNEP has been immense. It is also possible to specify reasonably closely the conditions under which their influence declined.

The second type of institutionalism uses a broader concept of institutions, and again, here, there are two underlying approaches which, to an extent, compete as explanations for the existence, prevalence and importance of institutions. One is a rational choice/game-theoretic explanation, typified by Axelrod and Keohane, where institutions are means by which rational actors realise joint gains. The other is a line of thought, associated more with Oran Young, or with the 'reflective school' identified by Keohane (1989b), in which the growth of institutions is a product of the actors in International Relations being more role players than status or utility maximisers (Young, 1989b: 209–13). These are not mutually exclusive (as Young himself suggests), since norms could reinforce (long term) self-interested behaviour, and indeed repeated (self-interested) behaviour by an actor could generate norms and the sense of a role within that actor. However, they remain in a certain tension. If the first explanation prevails, then we would expect institutions to emerge only when the conditions for fruitful cooperation, outlined by game theorists and given in the previous chapter, prevail (i.e. a long shadow of the future, small number of actors, potential joint gains). In the latter case we would expect institutions to be more extensive and prevalent.

In general, I hope to show that neoliberal institutionalism provides a more adequate account of the international cooperation on global warming than does neorealism. However, I will also argue that the norm/role-based account is more convincing than the rational-choice one, but that this leads us into fields of critical enquiry into which some institutionalists, such as Keohane, do not want to go.

NEOLIBERAL INSTITUTIONALISM

Neoliberal institutionalism centres on the work of Robert Keohane, although others involved would include writers such as Oran Young. Perhaps a good way to start is to look at its intellectual origins. It is a product of the development of thought about international law going back at least to Grotius, and the line of international thought which went, through Kant, to the Idealists at the time of the creation of the League of Nations. The perceived failure of much of this thinking to produce a decline in international violence in the inter-war period led to the resurgence of realist thought in Carr and, after the Second World War, in Morgenthau and others. Thus, despite the emergence of the UN after the Second World War, institutionalist thought declined.

What led to its re-emergence in new forms was the growth of international interdependence and regional integration (particularly the EC) in the 1950s and 1960s. One strand of this thought was the functionalism of David Mitrany and Ernst Haas. However, the evolution of functionalism and its substantial modification combined with the developments within realism, particularly through game-theoretical constructs (see the previous chapter), to produce a new set of ideas about international institutions and their role and power.

Initially, however, the new institutionalist thinking was not rationalised in this manner. One could take as an early form the 'International Organization model' outlined in Keohane and Nye's *Power and Interdependence* (Keohane and Nye, 1977). Keohane and Nye defined 'International Organization' as another type of structure in the world system:

> One can think of governments as linked not merely by formal relations between foreign offices but also by intergovernmental and transgovernmental ties at many levels – from heads of state on down. These ties between governments may be reinforced by norms prescribing behavior in particular situations, and in some cases by formal institutions. We use the term *international organization* to refer to these multilevel linkages, norms, and institutions.
>
> (Keohane and Nye, 1977: 54)

Keohane and Nye emphasised that this type of structure becomes an independent factor in explaining outcomes in international politics. They argued that the networks of organisation will be 'difficult either to eradicate or drastically to rearrange' (Keohane and Nye, 1977: 55).

Their other major emphasis was on the concept of 'organizationally dependent capabilities'. These capabilities, such as 'voting power, ability to form coalitions, and control of elite networks' (1977: 55), increasingly influence outcomes. They cite the one-state-one-vote system in UNGA, and the influence of UNCTAD on the international trade regime, as evidence of these capabilities.

Although the terminology is slightly different, the usage and intention of Keohane and Nye is very similar to later work. However, they remain slightly less confident about the ability of institutions to survive sustained hostility from major powers. While accepting that institutions are difficult to destroy or change radically once set up, especially under conditions of what they term complex interdependence, they do state that powerful states can destroy them if they object particularly strongly, once the treatment of an issue gets 'above a certain level of conflict' (1977: 58). This contrasts, for example, with Young who, writing much later, places significantly greater emphasis on the durability of international institutions. 'Existing regimes or institutional arrangements often prove highly resistant even to assaults spearheaded by one or more of the great powers', he suggests (Young, 1989b: 64).

Institutionalist thought received a great impetus in the early 1980s through the growth in the literature on international regimes. Of particular note was the special issue of *International Organization* in 1982 on the subject, later published as a book (Krasner, 1983a). Stephen Krasner himself significantly developed the line of thought by elaborating some of the ways in which international institutional arrangements affect outcomes by influencing state behaviour. He suggested that these ways include the following: affecting states' calculations of how to maximise their self-interest; altering states' (perceptions about their) interests; being themselves a source of authority to which states can appeal; and altering states' capabilities (Krasner, 1983c: 358).

Indeed, institutionalism and regime analysis could, in some lights, be seen as almost synonymous. Both emphasise the impact of arrangements within which formally sovereign states are enmeshed, and which are held to influence their behaviour. The definition of regimes given by Krasner – which is by now almost universally cited – is remarkably closely related to Young's or Keohane's definition of an institution. Krasner defines regimes as:

> sets of implicit or explicit principles, norms, rules, and decision-making procedures around which actors' expectations converge in a given area of international relations.
>
> (Krasner, 1983b: 2).

Young defines institutions as 'social practices consisting of easily recognized roles coupled with clusters of rules or conventions governing relations between occupants of these roles' (Young, 1989b: 32). Keohane gives an alternative: 'persistent sets of rules (formal and informal) that prescribe behavioral roles, constrain activity, and shape expectations' (Keohane, 1989a: 3). Young intends the usage of institutions to be much broader than that of regimes. He regards regimes as a subset of institutions, dividing international institutions into international orders and international regimes. Orders are broader sets of aggregate arrangements. Thus there is an international economic order, within which there are regimes for trade, monetary relations, etc. (Young, 1989b: 13).

Furthermore, the most prominent critique of regime analysis came in markedly realist terms. Strange's (1983) objection to regime analysis was essentially that regimes, or institutional arrangements, are ultimately epiphenomenal in determining outcomes. She states explicitly that her argument is 'realist in the sense of continuing to look to the state and to national governments as the final determinants of outcomes' (Strange, 1983: 338).

Within Keohane's later work, institutionalist ideas were developed largely through some of the internal inconsistencies felt to be present within neorealism. In particular, he followed through game-theoretic logic, borrowing in particular from the work of Axelrod (1984), to argue that, even under what might initially be realist conditions (a state of international anarchy), it is theoretically easy to envisage how long-lasting cooperation could emerge, and that this cooperation could produce institutions which became important in their own right as influencers of outcomes. This is where the break with realism lies. Realism could accept that cooperation could occur between self-interested actors, but not that this cooperation could change the basic framework within which those actors interacted. Institutionalist thought suggests that, in many cases, the institutions come to be determiners of outcomes alongside the preferences of states (Keohane, 1984).

Arguably the most succinct and formalised account of institutionalist thought comes in Keohane's essay 'Neoliberal Institutionalism: a Perspective on World Politics' (1989a). There, Keohane gives the following account of the new institutionalist thought. Institutionalists accept the basic premise of realists that international relations is fundamentally a condition of anarchy in the sense that states lack a common government. However, in contrast to realists, institutionalists argue that world politics is also fundamentally institutionalised.

He makes explicit a significantly different assumption, which leads liberal institutionalists to emphasise institutions. Realists assume that states are relative gains maximisers; they have to be because they are always in danger of invasion, in the medium-term even from current allies. Therefore, for realists, 'the fundamental goal of states in any relationship is to prevent others from achieving advances in their relative capabilities' (Grieco, 1988: 498, quoted in Keohane, 1989a: 10). Therefore a centrally different assumption made by liberal institutionalist such as Keohane is that states are absolute gains maximisers. This is acknowledged in the game-theoretic literature to make cooperation more likely.[2] Keohane accepts that the principal concern with relative gains accurately describes some relationships (he cites those of the US–the Soviet Union, Iran–Iraq, and India–Pakistan), but argues that, in most instances, states' margins of survival are not small. Thus, theoretically, it is unlikely that states will worry about relative gains when they do not expect to be threatened by force, and empirically, he asserts that the relative gains assumption does not hold for many relationships, such as US policy towards (Western) Europe or Japan, or within the European Community (Keohane, 1989a: 10).

To assert that world politics is fundamentally institutionalised means that 'much behavior is recognized by participants as reflecting established rules, norms, and conventions, and its meaning is interpreted in light of these understandings' (Keohane, 1989a: 1). Thus, without suggesting that states are highly constrained by international institutions, he argues that:

> state actions depend to a considerable degree on prevailing institutional arrangements, which affect
>
> • the flow of information and opportunities to negotiate;
> • the ability of governments to monitor others' compliance and to implement their own commitments – hence their ability to make credible commitments in the first place; and
> • prevailing expectations about the solidity of international agreements.
>
> (1989a: 2)

He also later gives two other reasons why institutional arrangements are important. First, they affect the incentives facing states. In some situations, they make it possible to do things which otherwise would be impossible (he cites the UN Secretary-General's mediation between Iran and Iraq). In others, they affect the costs associated with various courses of action, such as in arms control treaties. Second, they may also affect 'the understandings that leaders of states have of the roles they should play and their assumptions about others' motivations and perceived self-interests' (1989a: 6). This effect is deeper than many others; it turns the role of institutions from being purely regulative into being constitutive of state interests.

Keohane suggests that two key conditions must hold, for the institutionalist perspective he develops to be relevant. First, 'the actors must have some mutual interests'; second, 'variations in the degree of institutionalization exert substantial effects on state behavior' (1989a: 2–3). He suggests that there is ample evidence to show that these conditions hold in general in contemporary world politics.

He then gives an account of three different types of international institution, splitting them up into 'formal intergovernmental or cross-national nongovernmental organizations', 'international regimes', and 'conventions' (1989a: 3–4). He suggests that looking at variations between these types of international institution can help identify where institutionalisation of an issue-area is most important. However, it is not simply that the more institutionalised (i.e. the more organisations are involved) an issue is, the greater the importance of the institutions (1989a: 6–7). There remain definitional ambiguities related to institutionalist thought. There is a tension between the theoretical definitions, such as those outlined by Oran Young (1989b), which emphasise that institutions are not the same as organisations, and the practical usage which frequently operates as if institutions are roughly synonymous with organisations. Young's definition, cited earlier, is obviously significantly wider in its implications than simply involving the analysis of organisations, 'material entities possessing physical locations (or seats), offices, personnel, equipment and budgets' (1989b: 32). However, much usage simply conflates the two, presumably because it is simpler to examine the latter than the former. Certainly, in the less theoretically oriented literature – for example, that mentioned above which deals with UNCED – institutions are treated as completely synonymous with organisations (e.g. regarding the Commission on Sustainable Development).

Two distinct lines of thought come from each of these uses of the term 'institutions'. The latter produces a simple methodology where it is simply necessary to examine on a case-by-case basis the direct and indirect effects of international organisations on influencing outcomes in particular cases. Thus it would be possible to examine the roles of UNEP and WMO in the politics of global warming, something which Chapter 2 was designed to enable us to do.

However, the earlier definition of the term leads us down a more theoretical enquiry into the nature of IR itself. If institutions in the sense which Oran Young uses are prevalent, then we get a picture of international relations which is considerably more rule-governed, and not dissimilar to the image given by Hedley Bull,[3] than a realist world of self-interested status or utility maximisers.[4] We are then led to analyse the outcomes in terms of the evolution of norms, and the effect of those norms.[5]

This case is more difficult to evaluate, since it amounts to an ontological claim rather than to a simple hypothesis which can be examined. It provides a set of alternative assumptions to those used by realists about the nature of international relations and the underlying motivations behind actors' behaviour. However, by looking at the more limited case, we may get some insight into the deeper picture. If it can be demonstrated that institutions as organisations influence outcomes, state behaviour and state motivations, then it becomes easier to claim that state behaviour itself is based less straightforwardly on autonomous assessments of self-interest. In effect, the door is opened for a claim that norms play a much greater role in state behaviour than realists would accept.[6]

There are, then, two questions provoked by institutionalist thought which are of particular interest with respect to global warming. The first is:

why do institutions become prevalent? Clearly, answering this question relies on some assumptions about state behaviour. As Young points out, we can use three main sorts of these assumptions. Hardened realists assume states are status maximisers, in which case institutional arrangements will play a negligible role in international affairs, except in the sense – pointed out by Cox (1986: 219) – that institutions serve to further the interests of the already powerful. An assumption which gives a greater role for institutions can be that states are self-interested utility maximisers, an assumption Young associates with Keohane, Krasner and Stein, and which leads to the game-theoretic analyses outlined in the previous chapter. Alternatively, states can be treated as 'occupants of more or less well-defined roles whose actions are heavily constrained by the requirements of the roles they occupy' (Young, 1989b: 211). Young suggests that this view is best understood in Rawlsian terms. This viewpoint is, however, also identifiable in the 'reflective' school outlined by Keohane in his 'International Institutions: Two Approaches',[7] associated by him with Hayward Alker, Richard Ashley, Frederic Kratochwil and John Ruggie (Keohane, 1989b: 161). Young suggests that 'there is no need to make a definitive choice among the behavioral models' (1989b: 213), but his institutionalism surely leads him to be unconvinced of the value of the first assumption. However, it seems plausible that either utility maximising or role playing behaviour could lead to a prevalent role for institutions in the generation of outcomes. Indeed, if the utility maximisation is expressed as a form of rule utilitarianism, there is a significant overlap between the two types of behaviour.[8]

The second question which institutionalism provokes is: what are the mechanisms by which international institutions influence outcomes and state behaviour? The lists provided by Krasner (1983c) and Keohane (1989), cited above, remain a useful point of departure. Another list is given by Haas, Keohane and Levy in their volume specifically on international institutions and environmental problems (1993). They suggest that institutions function by 'increasing governmental concern, enhancing the contractual environment, and increasing national political and administrative capacity' (Levy, Keohane and Haas, 1993: 424).

Collectively, these lists suggest two main forms of institutional effect. First, institutional arrangements affect states' incentives – the ways in which states try to maximise pre-defined utility functions. This could be by making certain courses of action possible, by providing negotiating forums or mediators, through altering the information available to a state, by making it possible to make agreements because state X feels more confident that state Y will comply as a result of the institutional arrangement, or by being a source of authority to which states can appeal. Second, they affect the constitution of those utility functions. The dissemination of information is a major factor in this, as is the socialisation involved in the way in which institutions are held to lead to a state having a sense of its role within a system.

Two other mechanisms mentioned by other writers are worth highlighting here. Oran Young adds another important aspect. He emphasises how state decision-making is normally bureaucratised, channelled into standard operating procedures (SOPs). Subsequently, one of the sources of influence which international institutions have is being written into those SOPs (Young, 1989b: 79). Compliance with many international agreements may then simply become routinised.

Keohane and Nye (1974) give another source of influence. International organisations help the generation of transgovernmental coalitions, or groups of officials within government departments or agencies, who come to 'jointly use resources to influence governmental decisions' (1974: 220). The existence of international organisations legitimates regular contact between these officials, since states (or, more precisely, higher-level officials) have already committed themselves to the principles of joint cooperation through the creation of the organisation.

GLOBAL WARMING AND INTERNATIONAL INSTITUTIONS

Clearly, international institutions (both in the sense of organisations and in the wider definition) have been highly involved in the politics of global warming. But the question is whether or not they have been important in producing outcomes, independent of the preferences of states.

Institutions as organisations

To evaluate the claim that the various international organisations which have been involved in the development of the politics of global warming have been important in influencing outcomes is a relatively straightforward task. The principal organisations involved have been WMO and UNEP (and their joint organisation, the IPCC), ICSU (an INGO), then, later, the broader UN system through the INC (with a secretariat housed in UNCTAD), and finally the convention bodies – the interim and then permanent secretariat, the Conference of the Parties, and the Subsidiary Bodies. In addition, some other organisations were peripherally involved. For example, the International Energy Agency (IEA) produced a regular update of countries' policies and targets, including a book produced after UNCED (IEA, 1991; 1992a; 1992b). Arguably, this contributed to the development of those policies, and to the emergence of a general international norm that such policies were desirable.

I would argue that the international organisations involved have been highly important in generating outcomes in relation to global warming, and that their influence cannot be reduced to mere epiphenomena of state preferences. However, the role and importance of these organisations has varied over time. Two main temporal splits can be located – at the start of formal negotiations in February 1991, and then following the convention's signature in June 1992. Prior to 1991, international organisations were highly important in several political processes: development of the cognitive base which underpinned later policies; construction of state preferences; and, to a lesser extent (in terms of importance), political pressure on states. After the start of negotiations in early 1991, the ability of these organisations to influence state behaviour declined significantly. States' involvement in the issue moved into a context with which they were more familiar – formal interstate negotiations. At this point, the more traditional state concerns became prevalent. The concern with distributive questions, state (perceived) self-interest, focused on by realists, became more important in determining outcomes. However, it is important to note that Keohane and other institutionalists also emphasise that negotiating agreements remains difficult, for much the same reasons. Then, after Rio, the organisations created by the convention again started to become more important. In particular, the secretariat was given much more autonomy, doing much of the work that the subsidiary bodies would later begin to carry out.

The importance of the organisations mentioned can be illustrated in several developments. The primary roles of international organisations were as generators of cognitive development and as agenda setters. To an extent, the first of these will also be dealt with in the next chapter, where the focus is on the communities of scientists who generate the knowledge. In institutionalist analysis, the focus is on the importance of the organisations themselves.[9] Chapter 2 illustrated the importance of international organisations, in particular IMO/WMO, along with ICSU, in collating and disseminating meteorological and climatological data, and in stimulating research in particular areas. The development of research into global warming as a climatological issue can be seen to have been stimulated at crucial points, particularly during the IGY, and in the series of conferences which began in the early 1970s. A fairly strong consensus on global warming had been generated by Villach in 1985.

Until the establishment of the IPCC in 1987–8, the process was largely out of the control of state decision-makers, and in the hands of the scientists themselves. The initiation of the IPCC appears to have been, at least partly, a politically led process. But even this was dependent on the knowledge previously generated by the scientists through bodies like WMO, and transmitted by them to state decision-makers. Thus the development of knowledge fostered by international organisations was crucial in altering state perceptions of self-interest, at least to the point that global warming became a political issue which required a response.

This is not the same, of course, as saying that international organisations then determined the form of response that states developed. Such a claim would be deeply problematic. Clearly, the ability of organisations like WMO to affect the cognitive base on which states act is not matched by any ability (by WMO or any other organisation) to affect states' decision-making on what came to be determined in many states by economic criteria. The altered perception of self-interest was only partial, and still had to compete with pre-existing, historically conditioned, political preferences within states.

This goes a long way to explain why the more overt political pressure-group type of activity, particularly associated with UNEP, has failed to produce results in changing state behaviour. Much recent institutionalist writing has emphasised how the role and importance of international organisations is not through political processes of a pressuring nature, but more through their ability to provide public goods, alter perceptions, stabilise expectations about others' actions, and so on. Thus an institutionalist would not particularly expect exhortations like those of Mostafa Tolba (then Executive Director of UNEP) to have much effect.

However, being at the forefront of the scientific debate on global warming did enable international organisations to act as agenda-setters, setting out the parameters, not only of the scope of global warming as a scientific and environmental problem, but also of its political characteristics, and the scope of potential political solutions. The presentation of information by specialists to lay persons is never purely technical; it will always carry political implications and the political perspectives of those involved. And political negotiations do not exist in an information vacuum. The presentation of information to decision-makers will necessarily influence the decisions they make. It is at this point that Keohane and Nye's concept of 'organizationally dependent capabilities' (1977) becomes useful. Because many of those high up in many of the international organisations involved were from developing countries, the political prescriptions put out by those organisations were largely from a perspective which explicitly dealt with problems of North–South inequality, delegitimising any potential Northern attempts to construct the problem differently. Subsequently, while many Northern states have, for example, refused to engage in significant North–South transfers, they were prevented from being able to frame the problem as one where all states had equal obligations, which some states clearly would have liked to have done, and which would have produced significantly different negotiating conditions.

The international organisations were crucial in this process, in their role as agenda-setters. They were in a position to influence strongly the way in which information was presented. In particular, they highlighted the disparities in *per capita* emissions across countries. They took sides explicitly in debates over 'eco-colonialism' throughout that period (see Chapter 4). Examination of the IPCC's Policymakers summaries, or the Scientific and Technical Declaration of the Second World Climate Conference (SWCC), amply illustrates the political nature of those statements (Houghton *et al.*, 1990; IPCC, 1990; McTegart *et al.*, 1990; SWCC, 1990). For example, the SWCC Declaration stated that, 'In order to stabilize atmospheric concentrations of greenhouse gases *while allowing for growth in emissions from developing countries*, industrialized countries must implement reductions even greater than those required, on average, for the globe as a whole' (SWCC, 1990: 501, emphasis added), and that 'industrialized countries and developing countries have a common but differentiated responsibility for dealing with the problems of climate change. The problem is largely the consequence of past patterns of economic growth in the industrial countries' (SWCC, 1990: 502).

In the period before 1988, the role of WMO was very great in influencing both cognitive development and agenda setting. This can be seen in several of the developments outlined in Chapter 2, but a brief presentation of some examples here is worthwhile.

WMO was closely involved in the International Geophysical Year of 1957–8 (IGY). This involved many experiments which advanced the state of climatic knowledge, and in particular led to the continuous measurements of CO_2 at Mauna Loa, Hawaii, which directly caused a resurgence of climate research, as it quickly demonstrated that all the anthropogenic CO_2 was not absorbed by the oceans. Later, WMO was directly involved in collecting data on CO_2, temperature changes, etc., in the light of the greenhouse theory.

WMO actively fostered a scientific consensus on climate change throughout the 1970s and 1980s. Of note were the Stockholm Conference of 1974 (on climate modelling), the Norwich meeting in 1975 which ended speculation about possible global cooling because of other industrial pollutants, the World Climate Conference of 1979, the establishment of the World Climate Programme in 1979, which itself led to the Villach Conference which proved to be the turning point in the politicisation of climate change as an issue, and the establishment of the IPCC, which finally consolidated the consensus originally reached at Villach. The fact that the IPCC was heavily politicised does not discount the fact that it still generated what was treated as an authoritative account of scientific consensus on the climate change issue, while framing the problem politically in a particular way. Supporting Young's statement cited earlier, no state withdrew from the IPCC's deliberations (even though the US in particular objected to some of its findings), but on the other hand, states (e.g. the US) were able to ignore its recommendations. But then, it was not a formal negotiating body establishing an international treaty.

A move away from international organisational influence can be detected from 1988 onwards, when particular national governments took up the initiative in fostering a political consensus on global warming, largely through a series of international conferences, and through the establishment of unilateral targets on greenhouse gas emissions. The various conferences, from Toronto to the establishment of the INC, were sponsored by individual governments or groups of governments, and, while members of international organisations attended, they did so only in an advisory capacity. However, it is worth noting that the biggest and most prestigious of those conferences, the Second World Climate Conference, in November 1990, was initiated by WMO and ICSU.

When we get to the INC, two comments are worth making. On the one hand, before Rio, there was little direct political role for the officials in the INC Secretariat. While they clearly had strong normative beliefs with regard to global warming (see Chapter 3, Note 6), they were confined to a technical role by the member states (secretariats in other negotiations have been given a much greater political role). Only the Executive Secretary, Michael Zammit Cutajar, held significant political influence with delegations. Thus, formally, there was little institutional effect in the INC.

On the other hand, there is a strange irony. The institutional arrangements of the INC, structured as they were in the universal, sovereign-state equality system of the UN, formalised realist assumptions about international cooperation and made strong agreement more difficult. The resulting agreement was much more likely to be a lowest common denominator agreement, given the institutional arrangements.[10]

However, once the convention was agreed, its rules and norms tempered these effects. The text of the convention delimited the terms of possible debate, made certain positions untenable, and became a resource for certain other positions. In addition, the bodies servicing the convention were in particular given significantly more freedom to make proposals, allowed leeway in how they interpreted requests or instructions from the INC meetings, and so on (see Chapter 3).

Thus, by simply looking at the importance of international organisations, a strong case can be made that those organisations were influential, in particular in affecting states' conceptions of their self-interest. While the conception put forward, that global warming should be seen as a social bad and should be slowed by aggressive state policies, particularly by industrialised countries, was by no means wholly internalised, and conflicted strongly with competing conceptions of state interest (economic growth, competitiveness, etc.), it was still successfully advanced during the period after Villach in 1985, primarily within international organisations. This is in accordance with the institutionalist expectations outlined earlier.

Institutions, in the sense of formal organisations, were also important in altering states' incentives. The UN system provided a ready-made negotiating forum which states already understood and were able to use. Arguably, this explains the rapidity with which negotiations were convened and completed, a speed commented on by many writers (Bodansky, 1993: 2), even while environmentalists complained that they were excessively slow (see Chapter 3). The information disseminated by the IPCC also provided a cognitive basis for many states' negotiating positions and strategies. For example, the announcement in the IPCC 1992 Update that CFCs were less important than had previously been thought, strengthened the hand of the Europeans and others at the expense of the US, which still wished to retain its 'Comprehensive Approach' (see Chapter 3 for details).

The broader usage – institutions as roles and rules

Of course, restricting the notion of institutions to that of formal organisations and their rules and procedures leaves out a significant portion of what many institutionalists want to claim. That is, that the notion of international institutions can be used to describe much broader patterns of interaction, where states occupy roles whose rules then come strongly to influence state behaviour, even when a particular state may not feel that complying with those rules is in its short-term interest. Developing this broader usage, one of the interesting features of climate politics was the norm-generating process which occurred between 1988 and 1991, through the spate of unilateral declarations of targets to limit emissions by industrialised countries. An international institution (in Oran Young's sense), centred on the 'easily recognized roles' of the industrialised states involved, and having their targets as the primary rules, was emerging.

This, I would argue, is difficult to explain in realist terms. A realist would have to argue either one of two positions. The first is that states were simply behaving in bad faith; that the targets were established purely for ideological reasons, and were either ones the states had no intention of meeting, or were in reality very easy to meet. There is a certain amount of plausibility in this, especially in the latter sense, since the history of energy forecasting clearly shows a tendency to over-project energy demand (and hence CO_2 emissions) for political purposes (Baumgartner and Midttun, 1987).

The second line of argument a realist could use is that states were 'testing the waters'; engaging in conditional cooperation, cooperating in order to elicit cooperation (Ward, 1989). However, this remains a problematic interpretation in the face of persistent US 'defection' throughout 1991–2 since, on such a basis, other industrialised states ought to have reneged on their commitments. This realist interpretation leads us into an institutionalist conclusion, namely that what institutions could have done (and to an extent, however imperfectly, did do) was create 'stable expectations' about what precisely constituted cooperation and defection.[11]

However, this criticism seems to me also to undermine game-theoretic institutionalist accounts. Writers adopting this position could interpret the 1988–91 'unilateral targets' process in the same sense, as in Keohane's discussion of reciprocity (Keohane, 1989c). But these analyses assume a predefined notion of what constitutes cooperation and defection, notions which clearly did not exist for CO_2 targets in that period. It is a misleading interpretation to say that the states who set targets were cooperating *in order* to elicit cooperation, since states who refused (e.g. the US) cannot properly be called defectors. States still had to negotiate a definition of what constituted cooperation and defection on this issue, and what the public good they would collectively be trying to provide would be.

It seems more plausible to interpret this 'unilateral targets' process in the following way: instead of engaging in strategies to meet pre-defined ends (CO_2 abatement), states were in a process of redefining those ends (defining CO_2 abatement as a collective good). The establishment of targets is then seen less as a strategy for eliciting like behaviour from other actors, than as a signal to other actors as to what initial steps are involved in acting on the new norm, in other words to intersubjectively come to some understandings about what norms concerning global warming *mean*.

During the period leading up to the Berlin COP, another prevalent feature of these negotiations could be interpreted in a similar way. During this period, (almost all) industrialised countries were stating that existing commitments were inadequate and needed strengthening. It was, however, becoming clear that many of them, if not most, would fail to meet their existing commitments. Again, a realist could interpret this as acting in bad faith to defend the national interest. But it seems more plausible that states have been grappling intersubjectively with the question of what norms they might need to develop in order to respond to global warming. A contradiction between public pronouncements by governments (declaring that existing commitments need strengthening) and current state practices would not, therefore, be a problem which needs explaining. As Kratochwil and Ruggie point out, this contradiction between expressed norms and observed behaviour is only a problem for those, like realists and (rationalist) liberal institutionalists such as Keohane, who try to infer, on positivist grounds, intersubjective meanings from behaviour. At the root of the problem is that rationalist analyses of regimes (either liberal or realist) have an intersubjective ontology (regimes are about meaning and norms between states) but an objectivist epistemology (so that meaning has to be observed through behaviour) (Kratochwil and Ruggie, 1986: 764).

This interpretation could be supported by some statements by participants in the negotiations themselves. For example, the focus of the interpretation by EC negotiators of the text in the convention on limiting emissions was that there was a 'common understanding' that countries will stabilise emissions, regarded as important in itself (Pearce, 1994b). Benedick – in the climate negotiations an observer, but senior US negotiator in the ozone negotiations – indicated that there was a strong sense that the process was one where states gained some identity as 'good international players' through participation in the climate negotiations; 'no one can turn their back on a process like this and expect to survive in the world of international diplomacy' (quoted in the *Guardian*, 12 April 1995: 5). Perhaps the best illustration is from Bo Kjellen, head of the Swedish delegation:

> The shared understanding of the complexity of the undertaking created a sense of common purpose among the negotiators. All realized that they had to learn from each other, that there are many different skills and types of expertise needed in this extremely

complicated and uncharted field, and that no one country or individual possessed the key to success. It was truly a joint undertaking.

(Kjellen, 1994: 150)

It can therefore be seen that, at least up to 1991, institutions were very important in influencing outcomes regarding global warming. However, looking at the later period, after formal negotiations had started, the development of these norms and their acceptance by states seems to have frozen. The role of institutions seems to be more limited in this period, with state behaviour being more easily interpreted within a framework of realist assumptions. Ironically, this could be precisely because, at this point, the interactions on the issue became formalised within the UN *organisational framework*, which imposed its interstate, universal, consensual method of decision making. Previously, the generation of norms could occur among participating states because states not amenable to the norms could simply be ignored.

QUESTIONS OF POLITICAL ECONOMY

The above discussion suggests that a neoliberal institutionalist account of the politics of global warming is more adequate than a neorealist one. However, a major weakness is its conceptualisation of the relationship between politics and economics. Liberals tend to assume that politics and economics are largely autonomous spheres of human activity, and that this separation both is and should be preserved in order that trade and human welfare can be maximised. They would tend to suggest that states operate autonomously from economic organisations such as large corporations, and they act as an aggregated 'national interest', much in the same way that realists assume. Keohane tries to disentangle the two, and explicitly denies that his position assumes the 'superiority of markets to state regulation of an economy' (1989a: 10). However, these two aspects of liberalism, the political and the economic, cannot be so neatly disen-tangled. Certainly, it is reasonable to infer from his *After Hegemony* (1984) that Keohane does, in fact, adopt a liberal position on political economy.

However, examining the politics of global warming undermines such a conception of political economy. Large corporations, particularly those in the energy sphere, hold great influence over many states' positions. The positions of the OPEC countries are clearly the extreme case;[12] but the same applies to many other countries. The US was clearly influenced by the oil and coal lobbies, not least because the then President Bush himself had an oil background, but more importantly because of the prevalence of those lobbies within the US political system, and the political importance of the resources they control and produce. It would be possible to argue that the power of the energy lobby within the US system was what lay behind the expressions of scepticism about the climate problem, along with the personal influence of the US Chief of Staff, John Sununu. In the EC, European industry mounted its largest-ever campaign against any EC proposal against the carbon tax (*The Economist*, 9 May 1992: 91–2), and was clearly successful in getting the original proposals substantially modified.[13] I have given a fuller account elsewhere of the role of these groups in formulating US and EC climate policy and its position within international negotiations (Paterson, 1993). Here, it is simply important to emphasise that it is difficult to reconcile the role of the energy lobby in the US with the liberal presumptions of most existing institutionalist theory. Chapter 8 will develop this critique into an analysis of climate politics, based on a more adequate account of this political economy.

CONCLUSIONS

I have tried to show that neoliberal institutionalism provides a more adequate account of the international politics of global warming than does neorealism. Institutions, both in the weak sense of merely referring to international organisations, and in the strong sense of rules conferring roles on actors (states), have been extremely important in generating the outcome, defined simply as the Framework Convention. What is more, neoliberal institutionalists counter potential neorealist criticisms by accepting the basic anarchic and state-centric nature of IR, and that cooperation will not be easy to achieve. This allows them still to account for the problems experienced, during the negotiations, in reaching anything other than a lowest common denominator agreement, a factor which would be emphasised by neorealists.

I have also tried to suggest that the rational-choice account of why institutions become important and prevalent in international society, given by Keohane and others, provides a less convincing explanation than that which interprets the states as playing roles and trying, intersubject-ively, to develop norms and a sense of what their interests are in relation to global warming. This seems to me to be plausible, primarily because rational-choice accounts usually focus on how states achieve predefined ends, whereas the other approaches allow more space for accounting for how ends themselves are redefined.

The ideas explored by what Keohane (1989b) calls the 'reflectivist school' may therefore have much to offer here. This term subsumes writers from a host of different positions, many of whom would feel uneasy with being seen as liberal institutionalists. Here, I will just briefly outline how the ideas put forward by Alexander Wendt (1987; 1992), among others, are useful.

Like Keohane, Wendt starts with a realist ontology of the world as composed of states existing in a condition of anarchy. Wendt, however, argues – in a similar fashion to the argument given above – that state interests cannot be taken as given by the structure of international politics. He starts from a position, drawn from symbolic interactionist social theory, that 'people act toward objects, including other actors, on the basis of the meanings that the objects have for them' (1992: 396–7). The importance of this is that the interests of particular states in particular situations cannot be deduced from structural factors. Wendt claims that this means that anarchy has no necessary properties – in particular, that the contemporary states-system as a self-help system is one which is socially constructed. Other sorts of systems, for example where states identify their interests with those of other states, could logically emerge from the condition of anarchy.

Thus the central point in relation to international institutions is that, within this framework, those institutions can be seen as part of the structure of international politics, whereas in both realism and liberal institutionalism they are seen as effects of state action, not part of the basic structure (see also Dessler, 1989). Since the interests of states depend on the meaning which particular objects, events and other states, etc., have for them, and the identity that meaning gives them, it follows that institutions, through which these meanings are intersubjectively produced, are constitutive of state interests. This relates to the point made by Kratochwil and Ruggie, given above, that the logic of an intersubjective ontology requires an epistemology which takes this production of meaning seriously.

International institutions, in this view, therefore, are the 'preconditions for meaningful state action'; they 'constitute state actors as subjects of international life in the sense that they make meaningful interaction by the latter possible' (Wendt and Duvall, 1989: 53). This claim begins to look like an even deeper structuralism than that of neorealism. However, Wendt then introduces a structurationist position derived from Giddens, whereby states and international structures are mutually constitutive of each other. While state practices, therefore, are made meaningful by international institutions, they also reproduce (and sometimes help to transform) those institutions and structures (Wendt, 1987).

This perspective would allow us to see the negotiation process over global warming in terms of the production and reproduction of state identities. At a deep level, basic international institutions such as sovereignty were reaffirmed, and in some ways altered (for example the whole debate about the 'sovereign use of natural resources' had evolved since its original conception at the Stockholm Conference in 1972 – see Pallemaerts, 1993). Also, at a general level, the identity of particular states as 'leaders' in international affairs was fought over. But, concerning the specific issue of global warming, this helps us to see it in terms of states producing and reproducing their identities as environmentally conscious states (e.g. Germany, the Netherlands, Sweden), or spokespersons for the developing countries (e.g. India, China). It also helps us to see how these meanings depend for their existence on being intersubjectively reaffirmed (and contested). The emerging norm, that industrialised states should stabilise their CO_2 emissions, can be seen as a (partial) transformation of their identity in relation to global warming. It is a consequence of global warming having attained a meaning for them as a threat to be countered.

Chapter 7

Science, politics and global warming

We have been given the Earth to look after, and we have also been given the science and technology to do it.

(John Houghton, quoted in Shackley, 1994: 2)

INTRODUCTION

The politics of science is a pervasive theme in international environmental politics, and global warming is no exception. Thus it is no surprise that some writers have developed theories as to how this politics works. Within IR, the prevailing approach is the 'epistemic communities' approach, developed by Peter Haas and others. This chapter tries to evaluate the utility of this approach. In a manner similar to that used in previous chapters, it concludes with a look at alternative approaches to the relationship between science and politics regarding global warming, developed mainly within the sociology of science by people like Brian Wynne (1994) and Simon Shackley (1994) and, most recently, to very good effect within IR by Karen Litfin in her book on ozone depletion (1994). These approaches are also more consistent with the general constructivist approaches in IR outlined at the end of Chapter 6.

EPISTEMIC COMMUNITIES

Largely in response to the increasing number of international environmental agreements which have been signed since the beginning of the 1970s, several analysts have highlighted the role of transnational scientific and technical groups in international politics. Given that these analyses were developed to explain environmental politics, we might expect them to have something to say about the emergence of a regime on global warming. There are some notable features which distinguish this approach from those of neorealists and neoliberal institutionalists, discussed in earlier chapters.

As a contrast to neorealist theory, which stresses the difficulties in securing international cooperation, this literature addresses some factors which might explain why international cooperation has sometimes been easier to achieve than realists would expect. It is also useful in identifying why neorealists and neoliberal institutionalists over-emphasise the unity and dominance of states as actors, as it encourages us to look at the groups of *people* who initiate cooperation, rather than which state(s) start the process. This helps us break down the domestic–international divide, by showing how the actors who, in some circumstances, forge international cooperation have strong transnational links and operate both within the state, in formal terms, and outside it, in universities, environmental non-governmental organisations (NGOs), and so on.

Second, in contrast to neoliberal institutionalist models, cooperation is generated by specifically identified agents, rather than simply abstracted states. Neoliberal institutionalists suggest that the interdependence between states in a particular issue-area often (but not always) makes state strategies to secure cooperation viable, but they still assume an international structure largely defined by anarchy. In contrast, epistemic community models suggest a greater freedom of manoeuvre for some agents in forging cooperation.

The most recent, and currently prevalent, way of theorising in this way is the 'epistemic communities' model developed, in particular, by Peter Haas. The definition of such a community has gradually evolved. A special issue of *International Organization* on the approach defined what is currently the consensual definition. An epistemic community is defined there as:

> a network of individuals or groups with an authoritative claim to policy-relevant knowledge within their domain of expertise...They adhere to the following: (1) shared consummatory values[1] and principled beliefs; (2) shared causal beliefs or professional judgement; (3) common notions of validity based on intersubjective internally defined criteria for validating knowledge; and (4) a common policy project.
>
> (Adler, 1992: 101n1)

There are several points of relevance when using this approach to look at global warming.[2] First, this definition leaves open the nature of the professional's knowledge; a definition which would fit would be to define knowledge, in Ernst Haas's terms, as 'the sum of technical information and of theories about that information which commands sufficient consensus at a given time among interested actors to serve as a guide to public policy designed to achieve some social goal' (Haas, 1980: 367–8). The knowledge is recognised as a social construct but its relationship to an outer 'reality' is left open.[3] However, it is intended to be possible, within this framework, to hold completely realist or relativist epistemological positions.[4]

Second, the claim to authority through which these groups may become politically empowered is through their ability to generate acceptance of their knowledge as valid. Here, the point often made is that the knowledge which they generate and control becomes politically important and influential when the consensus among the epistemic community is sufficient to be convincing to the external political community. Although it often requires the consensus to coincide with lay perceptions of the problem, this is not always the case. Much of the environmental legislation and international agreement enacted in the 1980s *preceded* the surge in public interest in environmental issues in industrialised countries from about 1987 onwards (Haas, 1990a: 353).

It is not adequate, however, to explain their ability to generate acceptance of their knowledge through reference to the ideological hegemony of science. Different branches of the natural sciences generate different conclusions about specific causal mechanisms, and the struggle of an epistemic community is often within the natural sciences.

Third, these communities are themselves politically motivated and goal-seeking. The knowledge they generate tends to lead them to share common beliefs about a particular problem. Their transnational contacts and participation in negotiations often cement this shared view. Thus, as actors in the socio-political sphere, they tend to act towards the resolution of problems which they themselves have been instrumental in defining in the first place. The other side of this is that they develop a self-interest in maintaining themselves in international bodies and in their professional position. As Peter Sand has observed, 'Since transnational contacts enhance the professional status of participants, they create strong incentives for continuing and expanding international agreements' (Sand, 1990: 29).

Fourth, it is important to remember that the implications of this approach are different from those of an approach which focuses on *consensus* as a spur to political action. Many authors highlight how consensual knowledge may stimulate international cooperation and action on an issue (Haas, 1980; Rothstein, 1984; Underdal, 1989; Lunde, 1991).[5] It is not necessary here, however, to have full consensus between all relevant 'experts'. Thus the obvious fact that some climatologists dissent strongly from the IPCC consensus does not *necessarily* mean that international cooperation is unlikely. The point is that certain subgroups of the wider scientific community – i.e. the epistemic community – may be able, under certain circumstances, to make sure that it is they to whom policymakers turn under conditions of uncertainty. The evolution of this approach has been to move away from describing how *knowledge* acted in the international sphere, to accounting for *who* was generating this knowledge and acting on it politically. In Peter Haas's words, 'The ideas would be sterile without carriers' (Haas, 1992: 27). Thus the actors which drove agreements such as the Mediterranean Action Plan (MedPlan) were not unitary nation states, but actors whose goals were largely transnational and were defined according to the scientific disciplines to which they belonged.

Writers who stress this approach do not suggest that this model necessarily should replace older theories. For example, Haas, in his analysis of the MedPlan, also ascribes some relevance to neorealism and historical materialism (Haas, 1990: chs 6 and 7). Many constraints are placed on the activity and influence of epistemic communities. In particular, 'epistemic agreement [is] possible only in those areas removed from the political whirl' (Haas, 1992: 5). This is indeed a significant limitation on the applicability of the theory, and one to which we will return in relation to global warming. On the other hand, Adler's case of the emergence of ideas about nuclear arms control would seem to be a counterfactual to this suggestion (Adler, 1992). What these writers do emphasise is the following:

> we acknowledge that systemic conditions and domestic pressures impose constraints on state behaviour, but we argue that there is still a wide degree of latitude for state action. How states identify their interests and recognize the latitude of actions deemed appropriate in specific issue-areas are functions of the manner in which the problems are understood by the policy-makers or are represented by those to whom they turn for advice under conditions of uncertainty.
>
> (Haas, 1992: 2)

There is (at least) one problematic part and one ambiguity involved in the theory which affect how we apply it to global warming, and which therefore require discussion. The problematic part is this. Haas (1990; 1990a) has argued that a feature of these groups is that they are politically empowered, by which it is meant that they have often become entrenched in national bureaucracies, especially since the establishment of Environment Ministries in many countries in the early 1970s. He shows how, in relation to the MedPlan, many of the ecologists who had transnational contacts with other ecologists or marine biologists, and who were highly involved in the negotiation of the Climate Convention and protocols associated with the MedPlan, were also well established within their national bureaucracies (Haas, 1989). Furthermore, variance in relation to a particular state's commitment to and compliance with these agreements could be explained, in this case, in terms of how well established these groups are domestically.

> The strongest supporters of the MedPlan were the countries in which the epistemic community was most active ... Algeria, Egypt, France, Greece and Israel – the states where the epistemic community became most strongly entrenched – adopted more coherent forms of pollution control ... Elsewhere – where the epistemic community was weaker – states signed and ratified the Land-Based Sources Protocol, but have not taken steps to integrate such objectives into the rest of national policy-making.
>
> (Haas, 1990: 218–19)

Much of this is simply because environmental agreements require a significant monitoring element, the implementation of which is necessarily delegated to scientists and technicians. However, this involves politically empowering them to provide the knowledge about what needs monitoring, how to do it, when an agreement is being breached or should be strengthened, and so on.

However, in most recent versions of the theory, the entrenchment of epistemic communities in national bureaucracies is dropped as a condition for being termed an epistemic community. Of course, as a condition for them to be politically influential, their entrenchment remains important, but it does not seem a reasonable characteristic to expect in order simply to refer to them as epistemic communities. The point here is that, if we simply say that when entrenched in bureaucracies they are influential, we fall into two problems. On the one hand such a statement is question-begging in the extreme – we need to investigate how and why these groups become politically privileged in such a way. On the other hand it is not such a huge claim to say that bits of state bureaucracies influence outcomes – the point is to see how influential these groups are relative to other parts of the state (concerning global warming, relative to energy, economics, and transport ministries in particular).

Several answers have been given to the question of how epistemic communities become politically empowered. The most simple structural precondition is that, when confronted with highly complex technical issues characterised by great uncertainty, policy-makers turn to experts for advice. These will frequently be members of epistemic communities. Haas suggests that crises offer openings for epistemic communities, as decision-makers turn to new sources of advice (Haas, 1992: 34). However, this is a part of the theory which is underdeveloped.

The ambiguity in the theory is that, in early versions of this line of analysis, these groups were assumed to be transnational in character. Many of the negotiations leading to environmental agreements which have occurred since 1970 have been organised with UNEP as the leading actor. The scientists involved in the negotiations have often been associated with UNEP, and their links to each other are manifest. They also become heavily embedded in the international organisations set up by those agreements to monitor compliance and review research (Sand, 1990: 29).

However, in the more recent versions of the theory, the insistence on the transnational character of epistemic communities has been dropped (*International Organization*, 1992: *passim*). This has widened out the potential scope of the analysis by allowing epistemic communities to be purely national. The literature on which those advocating the model can draw is now much broader, and they seem to have shown a wide variety of situations in which it is applicable (*International Organization*, 1992: *passim*).

It also, however, produces two hypothetical processes of international cooperation which could occur. The first is where a purely national epistemic community manages to gain acceptance of its ideas domestically, and then the implementation of this policy nationally extends out to other states. Adler (1992) gives an example of this in relation to arms control, when the arms control community in the late 1950s and early 1960s was able to get arms control accepted as a US policy, and then set about convincing the Soviet Union's defence experts and policy-makers. Here, the theory could be combined with general theories about strategic relations and realist notions of hegemony.

However, where the epistemic community is transnational in character, a different process of cooperation would evolve, since the ideas on a particular issue would develop in several states simultaneously, if not at an even rate in all states. In this case, the role of international organisations would be greatly enhanced, and arguably the potential for much more deep-seated cooperation would be present, since it would not be susceptible to changes in the ability of the community in one state alone to maintain its privileged access to decision-makers.

EPISTEMIC COMMUNITIES

Predictions of the epistemic community approach

To the extent that an epistemic community (or communities) exists over global warming, and to the extent that it has been able to gain a hegemonic position in policy-making fields in the major states involved, we should expect it to have been able to influence the outcome strongly. Put another way, the outcome of the negotiations on global warming ought to be explicable in terms of how well the epistemic communities had been able to secure for themselves niches in the relevant policy-making circles, either through traditional bureaucratic systems or through non-formal but recurrent access to decision-makers.[6] We should, therefore, expect that the content of the signed international agreement would reflect the policy project and principled beliefs of the epistemic community.

Is there an epistemic community?

The first step we need to make is simply to ask whether there is an epistemic community or communities. While the intuitive answer to this question would be 'yes', a little, more thorough, investigation is required. We need to see if a group of people whose authority derives from their 'recognized expertise and competence . . . and an authoritative claim to policy-relevant knowledge' (Haas, 1992: 3) exists, and if these people share the four characteristics outlined above.

I would argue that such a community does exist in relation to global warming, and can be identified around the group involved in the IPCC, especially in Working Groups I and II. It has many members who have been highly involved in WMO, in UNEP, in ICSU prior to the IPCC, and who were involved in the First World Climate Conference. It has some who go back as far as the IGY in 1957. This group was and is recognised to have 'expertise and competence' in relation to producing policy-relevant knowledge for global warming. And it does have the characteristics outlined above.

First, its members do share 'consummatory values and principled beliefs'. Despite the fact that we would expect people to differ over how to take decisions under uncertainty even if they agreed on the nature and extent of the uncertainty, the IPCC was able to produce consensual statements with regard to how it believed societies should respond. The overview of the IPCC's First Assessment Report contained many such normative beliefs. The following selection should demonstrate this:

The IPCC recommends a programme for the development and implementation of global, comprehensive and phased action for the resolution of the global warming problem under a flexible and progressive approach.

Every effort should be made to find replacements (to CFCs) that have little or no greenhouse warming potential . . .

Industrialized and developing countries have a common but varied responsibility in dealing with the problem of climate change and its adverse effects. The former should take the lead in two ways: i) . . . Industrialized countries should adopt domestic measures to limit climate change by adapting their own economies in line with future agreements to limit emissions. ii) To co-operate with developing countries in international action without standing in the way of the latter's development by contributing additional financial resources, by appropriate transfer of technology. . . .

(IPCC, 1990: 9–10)

These principles were elaborated on in the Scientific and Technical Declaration of the Second World Climate Conference, 'which involved 747 participants from 120 countries' (SWCC, 1990: para. 1). The declaration included statements such as:

nations should now take steps towards reducing sources and increasing sinks of greenhouse gases through national and regional actions, and negotiation of a global convention on climate change and related legal instruments.

In order to stabilize atmospheric concentrations of greenhouse gases while allowing for growth in emissions from developing countries, industrialized countries must implement reductions even greater than those required, on average, for the globe as a whole.
(SWCC, 1990: Summary Statement, para.2; and Part II, para.4.1).[7]

These extracts seem to demonstrate a normative consensus between IPCC participants, a consensus which could be described as being that action should be taken to mitigate possible global warming despite the remaining uncertainties, and that such mitigation should take into account international inequalities (Lunde, 1991: 153–5).[8]

Second, the group's members share 'causal beliefs' about the process involved in global warming. Peter Haas argued in 1990 that such a community in relation to global warming was only 'incipient', on the basis that its consensus on causal beliefs is not strong enough. 'Although atmospheric scientists speak of their certainty that some climate change is unavoidable from the introduction of greenhouse gases, they are much less sure about the timing, extent or distribution of the effects' (Haas, 1990a: 359). This seems to be too strict.[9] The elements of scientific consensus outlined in the IPCC report would seem to be sufficient to qualify for consensus on causal beliefs. It is also clear, as Leiv Lunde has shown, that the substantive edge of this consensus sharpened during the 1980s (Lunde, 1991: 135–9).

The relevant statement in the IPCC Report which, in my view, demonstrates consensus on causal mechanisms is:

> We are certain of the following: . . . Emissions resulting from human activities are substantially increasing the atmospheric concentrations of the greenhouse gases: carbon dioxide, methane, chlorofluorocarbons (CFCs) and nitrous oxide. These increases will enhance the greenhouse effect, *resulting on average in an additional warming of the Earth's surface.*
>
> (Houghton *et al.*, 1990: xi, emphasis added)

Other elements of this consensus are that 'carbon dioxide has been responsible for over half the enhanced greenhouse effect in the past'; projected increases in emissions 'will result in a likely increase in global mean temperature of about 1 °C above the present value by 2025 and 3 °C before the end of the next century'; and the topic of projected sea-levels rises (Houghton *et al.*, 1990: xi). Given the uncertainties surrounding climate science, and the rapid development of scientific knowledge during the 1970s and 1980s, a statement that they were 'certain' that current trends would warm the earth is a significant indicator of agreement on causal beliefs. Prior to this, no such certainty had been expressed by scientists *as a community*, rather than as individuals.

Third, the group shares 'common notions of validity based on internally defined criteria for validating knowledge'; i.e. they share an acceptance of various mechanisms for testing their beliefs about global warming, such as a number of types of models, including General Circulation Models (GCMs), the evidence of changing global average temperatures since the Industrial Revolution, or the value of their various scenarios.

This criterion is perhaps the most strained in relation to the global warming epistemic community. There have been some fierce debates over methodologies for modelling, measuring and calculating climate change. In particular, there has been great controversy over the hegemonic status of GCMs within climate modelling, which has clearly been as much about access to research funding and particular disciplinary battles as over 'purely' epistemic issues (Shackley *et al.*, n.d.). Lunde cites two major controversies within the epistemic community. One is between the geophysicists who tend to generalise about the system as a whole, and 'ecoparticularists' (geologists, biologists, ecologists) who focus on small areas to measure change (Lunde, 1991: 22). The second is over using 'palaeoanalogues', i.e. measuring prehistoric temperatures and CO_2 levels through ice core samples, and using these to predict climatic changes from increased CO_2 levels – a technique favoured by scientists of the one-time Soviet Union – as opposed to climate modelling, favoured by Western scientists. However, these disputes have been contained and resolved within the IPCC framework and, for example, both palaeoanalogues and modelling results were included in the first IPCC report (Lunde, 1991: 28).

Finally, the members share a common policy project. An integral part of the IPCC process was the work of Working Group III on policy responses. While it was evident that WGIII was heavily politicised, it also reflected certain shared beliefs of the epistemic community: that the information and knowledge they had generated in relation to global warming was worth acting on; that uncertainty was not an excuse for inaction; that North–South inequalities needed to be addressed in responding to global warming; and that emissions of CO_2 should be strongly limited. The policy project they espoused is a reflection of their shared 'values and principled beliefs', as elaborated above.

In relation to the ambiguity in the theory outlined above, the community involved in global warming is genuinely transnational. While there is a predominance of scientists from the industrialised countries in general, and from the US in particular, most of the process by which scientists generated and developed their knowledge has been transnational. Thus, in relation to the discussion of the model above, we would expect the second process of cooperation to emerge; i.e. a process in which several states are involved in the formal initiation of cooperation on the issue, and where the international organisations in which the epistemic community is active are highly involved. Variance between the outcome and the prescriptions of the epistemic community would then be explained by the interventions of states where the epistemic community was not active or had not managed to secure its project as state policy.

The adequacy of epistemic community explanations

If we look at global warming, we find two main themes. First, an epistemic community was very important, if not crucial, in relation to how global warming emerged on the political agenda. Its identification of the problem, its active fostering of a consensus on the nature of the problem, and its agency in pushing for a political response, were all important in explaining why global warming became a political issue high on the international agenda. However, once global warming became a negotiating issue, the influence of the epistemic community declined and became more diffuse. That is to say, while they still evidently had a role in defining and redefining the problem[10] which had some influence on the negotiations, these were minimal relative to other factors.

Agenda setting

This section will seek to establish that the epistemic community outlined above was extremely important in establishing global warming as a political issue about which states needed to negotiate some sort of agreement. The first part will retrace the emergence of global warming as a scientific and then a political issue through the agency of international organisations such as WMO and UNEP. Since the epistemic community was transnational and organised within those organisations, this illustrates the involvement of the epistemic community.[11] The focus here is on both the evolution of the scientific consensus on global warming, and how these organisations precipitated political negotiations from this consensus. Second, it looks at the involvement of particular members of the community, many of whom have been involved in climate science and in international scientific cooperation since at least the IGY of 1957–8, and traces their active involvement in the fostering of a scientific consensus between scientists from the relevant disciplines. Third, it suggests that the epistemic community was able to get global warming on to the agenda without significant entrenchment in national bureaucracies in many countries, a paradox for the epistemic community theory as it has evolved so far.

The history of the science and the international development of climate as a political issue, described in Chapter 2, can plausibly be interpreted in terms of the effects of the development of an epistemic community on the subject. A number of points are worth making in this regard. Chapter 2 gives more detail on many of the events and developments mentioned here.

Throughout the early development of the International Meteorological Organization (IMO), participants remained primarily meteorological scientists, even while IMO was an intergovernmental body. The motivation for international scientific cooperation seems to have been partly economic, but also partly the realisation by scientists of the inevitably transnational nature of their science. The IGY stimulated the international activities which helped foster the emergence of an epistemic community among meteorologists. This can be traced through the WMO's research programmes – the World Weather Watch and the Global Atmospheric Research Programme (GARP).

This community became increasingly aware, during the 1970s, that a significant global warming could be the result of the increase in the atmospheric concentrations of various trace gases, in particular of CO_2, an increase which was largely due to human industrial activity. Part of this was simply an increased understanding of how human societies were sensitive to climatic variations; during the early 1970s, the focus of GARP's activities moved towards understanding *climate* and its underlying characteristics, rather than simply weather patterns (Cain, 1983: 81). But there was also an increased recognition of the possibility that human activities could significantly affect climate, and therefore of the necessity of increasing research on this possibility. David Davies, then Secretary-General of the WMO, was happy to declare as early as 1972 that:

> Although a fully satisfactory model to forecast the climatic consequences of greater levels of carbon dioxide is not available, the best current predictions indicate that by the year 2000 the effect of added carbon dioxide will be about one-half degree Celsius warming of the average global temperature which, in some sections of the world, could have significant effects on weather patterns and agricultural and industrial productivity.
>
> (Davies, 1972: 333)

It is thus plausible to trace the evolution of the scientific consensus on global warming back to the beliefs of members of the epistemic community (see more on individuals below).[12] Two conferences in the early 1970s, the Study of Man's Impact on Climate (SMIC) conference of 1971, and the conference on the 'physical basis of climate and climate modelling' in 1974 (see Chapter 2 for details), reveal the early development of awareness of the potential of climate change, and the institutionalisation of the scientific response. SMIC produced a 300-page document, which provided the background for the discussion of climate change at the UN Conference on the Human Environment in Stockholm in 1972. The latter, according to Lunde, was 'one of the first general climate change assessments of truly global character, with about 70 leading climatologists from all over the world participating' (Lunde, 1991: 13–14). This conference was chaired by Bert Bolin, who almost twenty years later chaired the IPCC, indicating a continuity over two decades of the people involved.

By 1979, at the World Climate Conference, WMO's climatological community was stating that it thought it 'plausible that an increased amount of carbon dioxide in the atmosphere can contribute to a gradual warming of the lower atmosphere, especially at high latitudes' (WMO, 1979b: 714). This is less positive than Davies's statement above, reflecting the need to produce consensus documents. However, as Lunde points out, it reveals that the consensus on the possibility of global warming had sharpened considerably during the 1970s (Lunde, 1991: 73–5), as a result of research efforts coordinated under GARP. The conference also urged nations 'to foresee and to prevent potential man-made change in climate that might be adverse to the well-being of humanity' (WMO, 1979b: 713).

During the 1980s, the scientists involved in WMO, and increasingly also in UNEP, became progressively more active in fostering what became a scientific consensus[13] within the meteorological and climatological communities: that global warming was highly likely to occur and could have severe societal impacts. They were highly involved in organising the three crucial events mentioned in Chapter 2: the 'Villach Conference' of 1985; the 'Villach–Bellagio Workshops' of 1987; and the 'Toronto Conference' of 1988. More importantly, they were also instrumental in setting up the World Climate Programme (WCP) and the IPCC. These three events and two organisations established between them the scientific consensus which was widely perceived to have emerged at the end of the 1980s. Research within the WCP developed during the 1980s, and was used, in particular at the Villach Conference, to consolidate a consensus within the epistemic community on the basics of global warming. This consensus provided the impetus for the interstate negotiations on how to respond to global warming which took place in the INC. Without the activities of these scientific communities, the existence of the negotiations cannot ultimately be explained.

In the IPCC we can see the epistemic community at its most organised. It was the biggest politically organised consensus process yet undertaken to assess the state of scientific knowledge on climate change. It had many participants who had been involved in earlier assessments such as the Villach Conference, most prominently Bert Bolin, who by now chaired the IPCC. Its architects strengthened the consensus within the epistemic community, by making it dominated by geophysicists and meteorologists and largely leaving out ecologists (Lunde, 1991: 85), and by what can be interpreted as at least a partially deliberate exclusion of particular scientists who held views which were deeply hostile to those of the majority of climate scientists (see Chapter 2).

The IPCC produced the most strongly worded statement of the scientific consensus to date and, as outlined above, provided evidence of its normative belief that something had to be done about global warming. While such a belief had existed at least since the World Climate Conference in 1979, the commitment had sharpened strongly by 1990.

We can also see that particular individuals actively fostered the scientific consensus on global warming and worked for a political response. These scientists can, in some sense, be seen as representative of the wider epistemic community. Bert Bolin is the prime example. He was researching on climate issues as early as 1959, following up Revelle's early research which demonstrated that not all anthropogenic CO_2 was being absorbed by the oceans (Lunde, 1991: 63). He was involved in 'close to all international climate assessments from 1971 to 1990' (Lunde, 1991: 70). In many of these, including the 1974 Stockholm Conference on climate modelling and the IPCC itself, he was actually the Chair. Other prominent scientists who pushed for the development of climate science and for a political response include Roger Revelle, of whom it has been written that 'there are many who would never have believed in global warming if Roger Revelle had not written about it in 1957' (Beardsley, 1990: 16–17), and John Houghton, Head of the UK's Meteorological Office and Chair of IPCC's Working Group I.

What is interesting in theoretical terms is that the epistemic community in this case appears to have managed to set the agenda on global warming without any significant entrenchment in national bureaucracies. While delegates to the IPCC were largely government nominated, many in fact came from outside direct government circles. Most of the members worked in universities rather than government departments or agencies (although many leading members were from Meteorological Offices), and their influence was primarily through their involvement in international organisations, and through direct access to publics, particularly in the industrialised countries.

The negotiations

However, these actors had much less influence over the course of the actual negotiations, certainly by comparison to the MedPlan or the Montreal Protocol. Part of this is because they had got it on to the agenda without being significantly entrenched in national bureaucracies, or because such entrenchment was erratic. It is also partly a result of the political problem structure internal to global warming.

When turning to the negotiations in the INC, we notice several things. Comparing delegates to the IPCC with those to the INC, it is clear that, while many delegates to the INC were still scientists, these were predominantly from developing countries.[14] In industrialised countries, delegations had come to be dominated by foreign ministries. This is to be expected, of course, but it involved the emergence of actors who saw their primary responsibility as defending their states' perceived interest. And since the epistemic community was not politically entrenched, it was not the primary definer of state interests on global warming. There was a break in continuity in who was expressing opinions from a country on the issue. The epistemic community thus had less hold on the outcome of the negotiations.

We can also illustrate this through a comparison between the statements in the SWCC Scientific and Technical Declaration, and the final text in the convention. While some parts obviously show continuity, the substantive commitments made in the convention reveal a great disparity between the normative statements made by the epistemic community and the text of the convention.

For example, the wording of the objective of the convention bears a great resemblance to earlier statements by the epistemic community. The objective of the convention is as follows:

> The ultimate objective of the Convention and any other related legal instruments that the Conference of the Parties may adopt is to achieve, in accordance with the relevant provisions of the Convention, stabilization of greenhouse gas concentrations in the atmosphere at a level that would prevent dangerous anthropogenic interference with the climate system. Such a level should be achieved within a time-frame sufficient to allow ecosystems to adapt naturally to climate change, to ensure that food production is not threatened and to enable economic development to proceed in a sustainable manner.
>
> (United Nations, 1992: Article 2).

This compares well with the statement in the SWCC Scientific and Technical Declaration, which stated that 'The long-term goal should be to halt the build-up of greenhouse gases at a level that minimizes risks to society and natural ecosystems' (SWCC, 1990: para.2). However, if we look at what the convention commits individual states to doing, there remains a great divergence from earlier recommendations of the epistemic community. On limiting emissions, the Toronto Conference had called for a reduction in the CO_2 emissions of industrialised countries by 20 per cent from 1988 levels, by 2005. The SWCC Scientific and Technical Declaration said that the participants believed such reductions were possible, and indicated that they felt such an action to be desirable (SWCC, 1990: para.8). The politicisation of the IPCC as a pre-negotiating process, and in particular Working Group III, meant that it was unable to make similar recommendations. However, the statement that greater than 60 per cent cuts in CO_2 emissions would be needed to stabilise atmospheric concentrations can be interpreted as meaning that some cuts were desirable as far as the members of Working Group I were concerned. Since immediate 60 per cent cuts were not considered viable by anyone involved, there was no real reason to include such a statement, except to apply pressure for *some* cuts.

A more explicit call for cuts came from John Houghton, Chair of Working Group I and Head of the UK's Meteorological Office, in an article in *The Financial Times* at the time of the SWCC:

The first sort of action should be taken now to slow down the rate of global warming by stabilising or reducing carbon dioxide emissions (from both fossil fuel burning and deforestation). Secondly, preparation needs to be made now for the further action that is likely to be required to stabilise the concentration of carbon dioxide in the atmosphere at some level by about the middle of next century.

(Houghton, 1990)

Similarly, on reducing emissions, Bert Bolin stated that the international community was not doing enough. Speaking at the 5th Session of the INC in New York, while presenting the 1992 IPCC Supplement, he stated that existing commitments by some industrialised countries would only reduce future increases in atmospheric CO_2 concentrations by 4–6 per cent. He continued:

the scenarios show that far more reaching efforts are required than are now being contemplated in order to achieve a major reduction in the rate of carbon dioxide increase in the atmosphere.

(quoted in *ECO*, 21 February 1992).[15]

On North–South issues, sections of the convention follow in many ways the views of the epistemic community cited above. The industrialised countries are expected in the convention to take the lead in limiting emissions, and are expected to help developing countries develop whilst limiting their emissions growth. The wording of the Second World Climate Conference is stronger,[16] but, more importantly, it is reasonably clear that the wording on North–South issues was the result of more traditional political bargaining and compromise between North and South. At best, the epistemic community provided the South with an extra intellectual basis on which to argue its case, but since the disparities in emissions, on which arguments about burden-sharing are based, are so obvious, no great importance can be attributed to the epistemic community in this.

How can we account for the loss of influence by the epistemic community? It seems to me that there are two primary reasons. First, the epistemic community had only achieved a tenuous and erratic foothold in national bureaucracies. Its involvement in international organisations, its ability to link its ideas (however vaguely) to events in the 1980s (e.g. the US drought of 1988; and the 1980s being the hottest decade on record) and the public's sensitisation in industrialised countries to environmental issues in general in the 1980s, because of ozone depletion, acid rain and so on, had enabled it to get global warming on to the agenda without such a foothold. However, this did not allow it to determine the course of the negotiations. Other actors, primarily diplomats, but also actors from other sections of the state such as finance and energy ministries, were then well placed to get their own position across and secure its acceptance by governments in many countries.

What is also interesting is that there is no clear correlation between those who were involved in their national bureaucracies, and the positions their governments took once negotiations had started. For example, the US, which had played a large role in initiating the IPCC process, had a large proportion of participants who came from state bodies such as EPA, NOAA and NASA, although the final position of the US in the negotiations was widely perceived to be the most 'reactionary' of the industrialised countries. What appears to be the case is that, in some countries where it was well established, it was not sufficiently established in the *right bits* of the state. For example, in the US, the community was highly involved in the EPA, but this body was easily marginalised within the US political decision-making process because of its agency status and because (under Bush) it was not part of the White House.

The second, and possibly more important, reason lies in the political problem structure of global warming. As is widely recognised, a successful response to global warming has raised many more substantive issues for policy-makers than did Mediterranean pollution or ozone depletion. The costs imposed by responding are potentially much greater, since the pollutants involved go to the heart of industrial processes, particularly of energy production. Carbon dioxide is not amenable to any simple technofix in the way that CFCs – for which there are easily available substitutes – have been. Thus, the resolution of global warming is widely believed to extend into many other areas of states' jurisdiction, including energy, land-use, agriculture, economics, transport, and foreign policies.

The effect of this characteristic of global warming has been that, as it became a negotiating issue, other actors within national bureaucracies made sure that their own positions were heard. Subsequently the epistemic community found it increasingly difficult to ensure that its position was adopted as the state's, since it faced tough competition from other parts of the state. This, of course, is reminiscent of Peter Haas's statement, quoted earlier, that epistemic communities can only be influential 'in areas removed from the political whirl' (Haas, 1992: 5). But such a statement begs the question: where does the political whirl start?

ALTERNATIVES TO THE MODEL

While perhaps more sophisticated than more general accounts of science and politics in international environmental politics (e.g. Andresen and Ostreng, 1989), the epistemic communities approach still suffers, in that – as Karen Litfin points out – it both treats science as being outside politics, and sees international cooperation as necessarily requiring (and often also being a product of) epistemic consensus (1994: 4).[17] As Litfin says, 'epistemic community approaches downplay – almost to the point of neglect – the ways in which scientific information simply rationalizes or reinforces existing political conflicts' (1994: 11).

A plausible case can be made that epistemic communities, as defined by Haas and others, helped to put global warming on the international political agenda. However, a number of instances help to destabilise the model. The following are just a few examples, but more could be given. First, it was clearly not the case that an epistemic consensus neatly produced international cooperation on the climate issue. Instead, it produced resources for policymakers from different countries (or from within different parts of the state within those countries) to advance positions they preferred – it became another strategic argument at their disposal. Thus, oil producing countries were able to emphasise uncertainties (even those within the limits of the scientific consensus).

Second, the approach underplays the ways in which scientific knowledge can itself be managed by political elites. The most dramatic illustration of this was the doctoring of James Hansen's Congressional testimony by the Office of Management and Budget. They changed his testimony so that it made their policy stance more defensible, by 'weakening his conclusion that enough was known about the phenomenon to justify immediate action' (Rowlands, 1994: 76). This helps to reveal how the science, rather than being under the control of an epistemic community, became a resource which knowledge brokers, including top-level politicians, were able to manipulate for their own ends, within certain discursive limits.

Third, the approach underplays how scientific knowledge itself is always imbued with normative claims. Thus, the ways in which the 'precautionary principle' has been presented are an example of how 'questions of value become reframed as questions of fact' (Litfin, 1994: 4). Indeed, climate scientists have often recognised their own limits in this way: when asked by the INC to define 'dangerous anthropogenic interference with climate' (United Nations, 1992: Article 1), the IPCC declined on the substantive questions, stating that they were inherently political and ethical questions (Moss, 1995).

An alternative approach to science and politics regarding global warming is therefore needed. Fortunately, a considerable amount of work has been undertaken on this question, although not within IR. Shackley (1994) discusses climate research in relation to four major models of the science/politics interaction. The first, 'scientism', is where the epistemic communities approach in IR fits most easily, as it refers to those approaches which assume (if implicitly) a rationalist model of the relationship between science and politics, where science produces (value-free) information and knowledge, and politics acts on it. The second, 'science as politics by other means', suggests that scientific research managers more or less cynically advance particular claims (such as the threat of global warming) in order to increase research budgets. This was often the claim made by greenhouse sceptics such as Fred Singer and Richard Lindzen, about the IPCC and national mainstream research units, in particular about those wanting better computers for their climate modelling activities. It has also been advanced by Sonja Boehmer-Christiansen in a series of pieces which essentially amount to a conspiracy theory about the IPCC, and particularly about the British scientists involved in it (1993; 1994a; 1994b; 1995a; 1995b). She claims that those scientists have produced global warming as a threat in order both to emphasise their own policy relevance and to increase research funding; have sought scientific consensus on the issue to consolidate their position (a process which also involved constructing the problem whereby consensus was seen as something desirable in the first place); and then, after the issue got on to the agenda, emphasised uncertainties to ensure that their particular expertise remains relevant to policy makers (see, e.g. Boehmer-Christiansen, 1995a: 8–9).[18]

Hart and Victor's (1993) application of the 'garbage can' model to understanding the role of scientific elites in the climate research policy of the US is also perhaps consistent with this model, although much less conspiratorial. In this model, science and politics move in separate 'streams', interacting periodically through scientific elites acting as entrepreneurs to increase research funding. This interaction also acts as a filter through which political priorities often feed into research agendas. Hart and Victor show how the understanding of climate change in terms of weather modification shifted to one of a threat in the late 1960s, which changed the context for scientists working on the carbon cycle and atmospheric modelling, allowing those sciences to flourish. The overall interpretation is much less conspiratorial than that of Boehmer-Christiansen, but the view that scientists' interactions with policy-makers are primarily motivated by research funding and prestige considerations is similar.

Shackley's third position is one of scepticism. Here, the focus is as much on the nature of scientific knowledge as on the explicit science/politics interface. The scepticism is in relation to science's claims to provide objective, value-free knowledge. However, what this approach often focuses on is the rhetorical force of science, the ways in which scientific discourse has managed to become dominant within modern societies. Thus, science becomes both a useful strategic tool for politicians to legitimise particular practices, and a device through which scientists can distinguish their truth claims from those of 'non-scientists', in order to advance particular agendas (whether they be research related or more explicitly political).

The fourth position, 'new forms of science', is even more highly focused on the internal nature of scientific knowledge. Here, the claim is that existing scientific knowledge is reductionist and fundamentally concerns the domination of nature, a common complaint by many environmentalists, whereas what is needed is a 'holistic' science.

These models clearly indicate a more expansive research agenda for studying science in relation to the international politics of global warming. Within IR, the only major work done which is consistent with this expanded agenda is Litfin's work on ozone depletion (1994). She outlines what she calls a 'discursive practices' approach, drawing primarily on Foucauldian notions of discourse. This fits most easily with Shackley's third position, scepticism, although elements of his second are also present. In both, knowledge is itself seen as deeply implicated in power relations, and not an abstract search for objective truths. Yet the rhetorical force of scientific truth claims is recognised. Subsequently, knowledge is something which is strenuously fought over, rather than something which acts in the background as a precursor to political action.

Such an approach suggests that scientists involved in global warming, particularly 'GCMers', are engaged in hegemonic practices within climate related sciences (Shackley, 1994: 10–11). The success of GCMers in relation to other models or disciplines with climate-relevant knowledge has depended not purely on epistemic factors or on 'consensus' within a particular discipline, but rather on the compatibility of GCMs with broader political developments. Thus, Shackley suggests that GCMs have been successful because their global focus is concurrent with the focus within broad processes of globalisation on increasing complexity (one of GCM's main claims to credibility is the greater complexity they have relative to other models), and the high status of computers in an 'information age'. Scientific discourse then also becomes a strategic tool for policy-makers, both informing and justifying positions. Scientific consensus, however manufactured, does not necessarily produce political consensus. Partly this is because the uncertainty itself has different meanings for the scientists and for the policy-makers. For the former it refers to the uncertainties surrounding particular variables (e.g. clouds) and how to incorporate these uncertainties into the models, while for the latter the uncertainty is about the very relevance of GCMs to their decisions (Shackley, n.d.). In addition, reduced scientific uncertainty could make some countries harden their opposition to action on global warming, if, for example, they came to see that they would benefit from likely climate impacts (Waterstone, 1993; Shackley *et al.*, n.d.: 12).

A further example of the ways in which this discursive aspect of science is important would be to look at the battle (if tacit) over the meaning of the various terms denoting the phenomenon. During 1988–90, the meaning of terms became highly politicised. The debate was about the use of the terms 'climate change', 'the greenhouse effect', and 'global warming'. Each term had particular nuances which became symbolic of the struggles over global warming itself. The US Administration felt 'global warming' to be too alarming a term, and insisted on it being called 'climate change' which, to them, sounded more innocuous. However, this backfired to an extent since, at least in the UK, 'climate change' was felt to be more sinister, implying general uncertainty, while 'global warming' simply meant to many people hotter summers, which they were not particularly perturbed about. The 'greenhouse effect', as a term, fell out of usage once it became commonly realised that it is simply a naturally occurring phenomenon and therefore largely meaningless. But these apparently semantic fights had their roots in different scientific and political understandings of the nature of the problem, and produced particular effects in the meanings which global warming took on politically.

CONCLUSIONS

In this chapter I have tried to suggest a number of points about the epistemic communities model and what it might say about the politics of global warming, and to outline how it could be improved upon. First, I have suggested that its account is only really plausible with regard to the agenda-setting phase, when those in WMO were working to make global warming a political issue. But in this phase, it offers a more adequate account than do either neorealism or neoliberal institutionalism. It identifies the actors who played the most important role in getting global warming on to the political agenda, and provides a view of how that process operated. However, due to the political structure of global warming, the influence of those actors declined once formal international negotiations started. An additional problem noted was that, during this latter period, the state in whose bureaucracies the epistemic community was arguably the most entrenched, the US, was also the one with the most 'reactionary' climate policy.

The second point is that a theory focusing on epistemic communities provides a useful corrective to the state-as-unitary-actor assumption of both neorealism and neoliberal institutionalism. It provides a framework within which the activities of the state can be disaggregated, and a conceptual tool for eroding the domestic/international distinction which pervades much IR writing, as was emphasised in Chapter 5.

However, it is not clear that epistemic community theory as it stands at present lives up to this potential. First, the account of how an epistemic community can get its viewpoint across and influence state action remains both unclear and theoretically underdeveloped. A particular problem which global warming highlights is how the model conceives the relationship of the epistemic community, and its allies within the state, to other departments within state bureaucracies and to the industrial interests those departments often represent. It is clear from the writings at least of Peter Haas that a pluralist model of bureaucratic politics is presumed, which an analysis of global warming shows to be inadequate (see Chapter 4 on the importance of energy lobbies in many industrialised countries, and Chapter 8 for a theoretical elaboration).

Second, as noted above, Haas's assertion about the 'political whirl' leaves a lot of questions unanswered. Can we make any generalisations about what happens when an issue hits the political whirl? If one of the mechanisms through which epistemic communities are influential is through raising an issue on to the political agenda, does epistemic community theory simply offer an account of agenda setting in international politics? Clearly, Haas believes this not to be the case, at least not for the MedPlan and ozone depletion. If, however, epistemic communities are only effective by operating largely behind the scenes, as he suggests happened for the MedPlan, what does this mean about any potential for democracy in the resolution of environmental problems? These questions need to be addressed.

On both these questions, an approach which is more sceptical about the nature of scientists and scientific knowledge would be more fruitful. Focusing on science as a discourse, rather than simply the activities of particular scientists, enables us to be more sophisticated by not presenting an impression that the scientists involved in an issue are largely free from manipulation by politicians. It enables us to examine how contradictions within science are exploited by politicians and other actors. And focusing on discourse also enables us to get away from the problem of the 'political whirl' formulation, since scientific discourse necessarily interrelates with other discourses, and the focus on which one prevails is not so salient. Haas's implicit positivism means that he is searching for *the* cause of international cooperation.[19]

Chapter 8

A political economy of global warming

This chapter explores the explanations which might be offered to account for the international politics of global warming by arguments from within historical materialism. It suggests that, at least as a starting point, this provides a significantly more convincing interpretation of the empirical material covered in the book, than do the positions covered in the last three chapters.[1]

Three arguments drawn from the literature of historical materialism will be used. The examination of the relationship between the state and capital accumulation in the state theory of Bob Jessop gives a basic set of conceptual tools with which to start looking at what determines states' policies on global warming, while the Gramscian focus on hegemony, developed in IR by Stephen Gill and others, helps to avoid the tendency towards deterministic analyses often found in this perspective. Next, the literature on changes within capitalism, such as the move from 'Fordism' to 'flexible accumulation' as outlined, for example, by David Harvey (1990), and on the general phenomenon of globalisation, helps explain some of the constraints on state actions on climate change. Finally, international political economy (IPE) based in historical materialism gives the most plausible framework for analysing the North–South conflict within the climate negotiations. The overall argument will be that this framework provides a more adequate starting point for explaining the politics of the Climate Convention than do the theories examined in the previous three chapters.

THE STATE, CAPITAL AND HEGEMONY

Historical materialism treats capitalist societies as unstable, due to their basic contradictions. Consequently, the reproduction of those societies is something which has to be consciously sought. Harvey (1990: 180) gives three basic conditions for capitalist reproduction. First, capitalism requires economic growth to reproduce itself. This is a corollary of the need for firms continually to maximise profits. Second, the making of a profit necessarily involves paying workers for less than the value of what they produce (extracting surplus value). This produces a class antagonism, the continual resolution of which (i.e. control of the labour force) is necessary for capitalist reproduction. Third, as a result of its growth imperative, capitalism is technologically and organisationally dynamic. This dynamism has crucial effects on the way in which labour control is pursued by capital, and the ensuing class struggle.

The state is then seen as necessarily involved in the process of reproducing these background conditions. Marxist state theorists, such as Bob Jessop, outline how the state in capitalist society has the securing of capital accumulation as one of its main functions. Jessop argues that the capitalist state is 'charged with the responsibility for accumulation when market forces fail' (1990: 360).[2]

As a result of the state's centrality in the process of capital accumulation, the capitalist class is structurally powerful with respect to state decision-making. Gill and Law, for example, describe the structural power of capital (1988: ch. 7; 1993). This is reflected in the importance of the business climate for investment and profit-making, in the power of markets to use such tools as the 'investment strike', and the capacity to shape the 'limits of the possible' through the construction of hegemonic ideas concerning the conditions for economic growth. The international mobility of capital (compared to that of labour) heightens this power (Gill and Law, 1988).[3]

The second basic conceptual tool which we can use from historical materialism is the term hegemony, drawing primarily on Gramsci. Hegemony denotes the ideological struggles which occur over the projects of the dominant class designed to secure the basic conditions for accumulation. The process of securing those conditions requires that capital engages in continual ideological struggles to create a capacity to keep capitalist societies together. The notion of hegemony suggests that capitalist societies are not governed purely through domination, but normally through legitimating practices, in which hegemonic struggles play a central role. As Barrett puts it, hegemony is about '*the organisation of consent* – the process through which subordinated forms of consciousness are constructed without recourse to violence or coercion' (1991: 54).

Thus, transformations within global capitalism can be understood through the attempts by an increasingly transnational capitalist class to secure the conditions of capital accumulation, attempts known as hegemonic projects. The particular forms which hegemonic projects might take vary over time (for example, Fordism/Keynesianism in the 1940s–1960s, post-Fordism/neoliberalism from the late 1970s onwards), but the usefulness of the term hegemony is that it helps us to avoid deterministic tendencies within historical materialism by emphasising the contingent nature of capitalist reproduction.

Colin Hay (1994) has developed the implications of this argument for environmental problems in general. He suggests that environmental problems produce a legitimation crisis of a Habermasian sort for advanced capitalist democracies, as they create a contradiction between the state's need to intervene economically in order to create the conditions of capital accumulation, and their need to legitimate themselves (Habermas, 1975; Hay, 1994: 219). Thus, the study of environmental problems 'must be located within the *economic* context of global capitalist accumulation (within which different economies find different *modes of insertion*)' as well as within the more conventional political framework of the influence of social movements on states and the interstate politics of 'global environmental diplomacy' (Hay, 1994: 218). Even many non-Marxist works on environmental policy suggest that business and state interests are often conflated by policy-makers (Rowlands, 1994: 156). Perhaps ironically for the case examined here, Vogel (1986) suggests that the US is the exception to this, due to business (as well as wider cultural) hostility to government intervention.

This gives us significant leeway to examine the material conditions behind states' positions in international negotiations on global warming. Much of the politics of global warming becomes explicable, which would not be the case were we merely to assume that the state is a unitary, rational actor. Chapter 4 suggested that the reasons why different states adopted different positions in climate negotiations focused on three things – the relationship to energy resources, the position in the global economy, and the vulnerability to climate impacts. Of these, the first and second can plausibly be explained within this framework, while, for the last, the material resources available to the state significantly condition its vulnerability to climate impacts. The position in the global economy will be dealt with later. Here, it is useful to relate the argument from Chapter 4, about the role of energy politics in determining climate policies, to this point about the state and capital accumulation.

The state is clearly important in relation to global warming. As a collection of institutions it is clearly crucial to affecting greenhouse gas emissions, and a focus on its activities is vital. The energy sector (including transport) is the most important area of economic activity as far as global warming is concerned. Forty-six per cent of all greenhouse gas emissions come from that sector, according to the IPCC (IPCC, 1990b: xxix).[4] The state is extensively involved in the energy business in most capitalist countries, in various ways. In some it owns parts of the industry (most commonly coal, gas, railways, roads, and sometimes oil); even where ownership is not in state hands, the state plays a large role – in regulating and protecting markets, in funding research and development, in ensuring security of supply, and so on.

Large corporations are also highly involved in the production of greenhouse gases. The UNCTC estimated in 1992 that transnational corporations (TNCs) account for approximately 50 per cent of all ghg production (UNCTC, 1992: 14–15). Many of these corporations have produced position papers, stimulated research and lobbied hard on global warming. For example, IPIECA, the oil industry's energy conservation organisation, has had a long-standing research programme on global warming (Flannery and Clarke, 1991). These industry-wide groups have often been left to do much of the lobbying, to reduce the visibility of individual companies in relation to global warming (Bergesen and Estrada, 1994). Car manufacturers have also produced lengthy documents on the subject (SMMT, 1990; 1993). And of course coal and oil interests, primarily in the US, have funded one of the major lobbying groups on global warming, the Global Climate Coalition.

The messages which these companies have issued concerning global warming have been fairly unambiguous. The Society of Motor Manufacturers and Traders (in the UK), worried about the competitiveness effects of unilateral action, emphasised that any action should only take place in a 'framework of international cooperation' (SMMT, 1990). Chapter 4 showed this process in relation to the EC carbon tax. The major oil companies have been openly hostile to most government measures (Bergesen and Estrada, 1994).

The fractions of capital involved in energy are also heavily intertwined with the institutions of the state (Baumgartner and Midttun, 1987). Just taking the UK as an example, the energy lobby is regarded to be particularly influential in Whitehall; the British state is particularly vulnerable to concerns about profitability from that sector (Boehmer-Christiansen and Skea, 1991: 127). A similar situation exists with the relationship between the Department of Transport and the British Road Federation (Hamer, 1987). States have also clearly felt the need to promote business involvement in the negotiations. For example, the New Zealand delegation, in the February 1994 session, stated that there was a need for 'positive interaction with transnational business interests'

(WEC, 1995a: 4). Consequently, it is reasonable to suppose that the power of these lobbies provides one of the major explanations for the limited nature of state responses to date.

Historically, the interaction between these corporations and governments have often produced development paths which have increased greenhouse gas emissions (UNCTC, 1992). The most famous example is General Motors being allowed to buy up and shut down public transport systems in US cities to stimulate the use of motor cars (UNCTC, 1992: 55–6).

Much of the differences in industrialised states' policies can be explained through the differing relationship which their economies have to energy: in other words, to the place energy has in the overall process of capital accumulation, and the corresponding power this confers on those fractions of capital involved in energy production. Chapter 4 outlined how this played out empirically, with three groups of countries being readily identifiable – those dependent on fossil fuel exports for income, those highly dependent on fossil fuel imports, and those with large fossil energy resources (but who did not necessarily export them). The point here is that these differences make most sense when the state is understood as fundamentally enmeshed in the process of accumulation. For each of the countries in these groups, accumulation is dependent on fossil energy in different ways, and this has been the major influence on their climate policy.

State accumulation strategies have clearly made some difference here. For example, Germany's corporatist style of economic management means that business is more used to taking the lead from government and adapting to political demands, which has made the government's job easier and perhaps helps explain why Germany has found it easier to set stringent targets than has, for example, the UK, where neoliberalism means that businesses are more used to resisting government intervention. Both Cavender and Jaeger (1993: 12–13), and Hatch (1995), reveal this in detail concerning Germany, with Hatch in particular emphasising the point about corporatism. Industry involvement has also helped in some countries to put global warming on the political agenda. For example, under threat during the 1980s, the German nuclear industry actively promoted nuclear power from the early 1980s as an alternative to fossil fuels, and intensified this campaign after Chernobyl, to protect its interests (Cavender and Jaeger, 1993: 13).

The Gramscian usage of hegemony in this context is useful primarily because it shifts our attention towards asking historically contextual questions. The reproduction of capitalist societies takes particular forms at particular times, with different effects, for example, on the ability of states to respond to environmental problems. What we need to do, therefore, is to identify the relevance, both of the state–capital relationship and of the particular hegemonic struggles within contemporary world capitalism which could explain the politics of global warming. These transformations are discussed in detail in the next section. A number of debates within contemporary IPE are helpful in identifying underlying transformations within capitalism, within which the politics of global warming have operated. They can be thought of as a set of hegemonic struggles which have conditioned the capacity of the global political economy to respond to global warming. These debates clearly overlap, but the overlaps should be thought of as giving the position a cumulative explanatory value.

CONTEMPORARY TRANSFORMATIONS AND GLOBAL WARMING

In addition to explaining the background features behind states' negotiating positions and climate strategies, focusing on political economy allows us to locate the emergence of climate politics historically in contemporary transformations within the world political economy. Three related transformations can be identified: the shift from Fordism to post-Fordism or flexible accumulation; the processes of globalisation; and the move towards neoliberalism as the hegemonic project of transnational capitalist classes associated with these other two shifts.

Collectively, these help to show three things. First, they help to explain how global warming emerged in the mid-1980s on the back of a (short-lived) economic boom produced (among other things) by the shift to flexible accumulation. Second, they show how the policy space was limited by the emergence of neoliberalism, which constrained the types of policies which could legitimately be developed. Third, and perhaps most important, they show how some of the basic conditions outlined above, in particular the structural power of capital, have intensified the constraints on the development of policies to respond to global warming.

Fordism and flexible accumulation

The first of these shifts is the transition from 'Fordism' to 'post-Fordism' or 'flexible accumulation'. This terminology comes from what is usually known as the 'regulation school' (Aglietta, 1979). The focus of this school is on the mechanisms by which capitalist society is reproduced. They identify two areas in which this operates – the regime of accumulation, and the mode of regulation. The first of these refers to the way in which, over the long term, a parallel development is achieved between the conditions of production and the conditions under which production is put to social use, while the second refers to the mechanisms deployed to stabilise and adapt to the contradictions thrown up by the particular regime of accumulation (Lipietz, 1992: 2; see also Harvey, 1990: 121–2).

Contemporary capitalism is commonly thought of within this framework as undergoing a transition from a Fordist regime of accumulation and mode of regulation, to a 'post-Fordist' one, based on different organising principles.[5] For Gramsci, Fordism had four central features (Gramsci, 1971).[6] These were: the increased mechanisation, rationalisation and militarisation of the production process and the introduction of the assembly line; the incorporation of new production methods into a new mechanism of accumulation, involving wage increases which stimulated mass consumption and standardised commodities; the intensified regulation of all parts of social life; and a highly active engagement of the state in the organisation of the economy.

A number of trends which prevailed during the 1960s brought the Fordist regime to a situation of crisis by the early 1970s. Harvey suggests that the varied causes of this crisis can be summed up by the word 'rigidity' (1990: 142). The rigidities involved in labour markets and contracts, standardised mass production, state welfare schemes, fixed exchange rates and other heavily regulated aspects of global economic relations, all became, by the end of the 1960s, constraints on further capitalist growth rather than the stimuli to it that they had initially been.

The response to this consisted in a number of substantial changes to the way in which capitalism reproduced itself. The terms different writers use to describe these changes differ, as do their political implications, but the basic features of flexible accumulation (to use the phrase adopted by Harvey) are similar. The basic change, corresponding to Harvey's point about Fordism's problem being one of rigidity, is summed up by the term 'flexibility'. From this, elaborate schema can be given for the features of flexible accumulation, such as the three given by Harvey (1990: 174–9). In the production process, there is a shift from mass standardisation to the small batch production of diversified products ('just-in-time' production), which corresponds to the shift from price competitiveness to product innovation competition, as outlined by Kaplinsky (1991). In labour relations there is a shift, both to greater degrees of labour control due to increased casualisation, etc., but also to greater flexibility for (some) workers due to multiple tasks being done by workers rather than single tasks, and increases in team working. In the state, the shift is away from heavy regulation and state intervention, and extensive welfare systems, towards privatisation of welfare needs, deregulation, and so on. And in ideology, the shift is from mass consumption, towards individualised consumption, and from modernism to postmodernism.[7] These shifts were, in large part, facilitated by technological possibilities opened up in particular by developments in information technology, reflecting the third of Harvey's points about basic features of capitalist reproduction.

The emergence of flexible accumulation helped to produce an economic boom in the mid-1980s throughout most Western countries. This boom had the effect of creating the space within which it became possible to get environmental questions on to the political agenda. A spate of environmental problems came on to the agenda during this period, including acid rain, ozone depletion, global warming and deforestation. Tanzer (1992) highlights how this fitted in with the economic boom, and subsequently became more problematic after recession set in at the end of the decade.

According to Harvey, the transition to flexible accumulation has involved two central shifts. The first is the changes in information, which I will not focus on here. The second, however, is the rise of the power of international finance. Harvey locates this in the failure in the early 1970s of the Fordist/Keynesian mode of regulation to resolve the basic contradictions of capital; its only response by this point was to increase the money supply. Thus, in the 1970s, financial markets expanded rapidly to meet this additional demand for money. Eurodollar markets expanded 25 per cent annually in this decade (Harvey, 1990: 163).

The impact of this has been to make states considerably more dependent on financial markets to secure their own legitimacy (Harvey, 1990: 165), reinforcing the background point made above by Gill and Law about the structural power of capital (1988: 94–5). In addition, it has made international financial affairs in general more unstable (Gill and Law, 1988: 160–3; Strange, 1986; Stopford and Strange, 1991: 40–9). This is arguably very important in explaining the constraints upon state action on problems such as global warming. Partly, it helps us to explain why most states' targets for CO_2 emissions which were established during 1989–90 were relatively weak, and many were made conditional on like action by other states. The increased dominance of international finance means that states must be more cautious in adopting policies which reduce the likelihood of transnational investment coming their way (Stopford and Strange, 1991; Palan, 1993). It is also plausible that this has had a knock-on effect on the capacity of states to negotiate collective action – the free rider problem could become important, as the power of international financial institutions means that states have to worry more about their fiscal stability than about global warming, so they would have large incentives to free-ride on climate agreements.

The structural shifts in industrial organisation are, perhaps, more ambiguous in their environmental implications than this suggests. Many firms have made attempts to integrate environmental concerns into their reorganisation strategies. For example, the Business Council on Sustainable Development, an organisation involving many major multinationals and a major funder of UNCED, suggested in its book *Changing Course* (Schmidheiny, 1992) that reorganisation along the lines of 'Total Quality Management' (management-speak for many of the changes involved in the transition to flexible accumulation) will make firms reduce pollution, including that which results from energy use. 'More and more companies are realizing that the pollution they produce is a sign of inefficiency and that waste reflects raw materials not sold in the process' (1992: 99; Chatterjee and Finger, 1994: 124). In other words, many firms have been using environmental concerns such as global warming to legitimate restructuring, and in so doing having some effect on their environmental impact.

On the other hand, Chatterjee and Finger (1994) provide a powerful analysis of this industrialists' response to problems like global warming, and a strong argument concerning the limits upon how industrial restructuring can provide the basis for resolving these problems. They also outline how UNCED was used by major multinationals to consolidate their power within world politics and present themselves as the major legitimate players (alongside national governments) in the emergence of 'global environmental management'. And the German experience has not, by and large, been dominant in the strategies adopted by firms in other countries.

In some cases, the shift to flexible accumulation has meant that the structural power of capital has had a positive influence on the development of climate policies by particular governments. For example, the strong target on emissions reduction adopted by the German government had much to do with the technological confidence of German firms, borne out of their successes in developing pollution control technology as part of the response to acid rain – here the structural power of capital has provided extra impetus to the development of climate policies, rather than being a constraint on them. Splits within industry have emerged in a number of places. At the international level, the World Sustainable Energy Coalition, representing energy efficiency and renewable energy industries, emerged to lobby in favour of emissions reductions (1993). In Germany again, an alliance between the Bundesverband Junger Unternehmer (League of Young Entrepreneurs), and the Bund für Umwelt und Naturschutz Deutschland, the major environmental NGO in Germany, emerged in 1993 over the issue of ecological tax reform, including promoting a carbon tax (Beuermann and Jaeger, 1996). This suggests, perhaps, a deeper way in which the interests of capitalists might be discursively constructed.

Perhaps the most important, although only nascent, split in industry interests is seen in the emergence of a tentative alliance between Greenpeace and the international insurance industry (and, to a lesser extent, other parts of the financial sector, especially pension funds). This has been fostered by Greenpeace, in particular by Jeremy Leggett, and may prove to be short-lived. But, were it to succeed, given the argument about the power of financial capital in the conditions produced by globalisation and post-Fordism, it could have significant impacts in climate politics.

Leggett (1995) has aimed to persuade the insurance industry that its interests are best served by disinvesting from carbon intensive industries, in order to avoid potentially catastrophic losses due to increased natural disasters from climate impacts. His case was supported by evidence that, after a stable twenty years with no 'billion dollar cats' (disasters with over a billion dollars worth of insurance pay-outs), between 1987 and 1994 there were fifteen of these events, such as Hurricane Andrew in 1992. Many of the largest insurance companies in the world have also sounded warning notes about global warming. For example, Munich Reinsurance, the world's largest reinsurance company, was convinced about 'the trend towards more frequent and more severe natural disasters' (*Nature*, 17 November 1994), and called on governments to stabilise CO_2 emissions. One syndicate at Lloyd's of London had reduced its exposure in Florida due to fears about global warming, avoiding massive losses from Hurricane Andrew (Leggett, 1995). And major insurers, with UNEP backing, have begun to incorporate environmental risk into their insurance policies, with climate concerns at the forefront (*The Times*, 27 March 1995).

Of course, one implication of this is that we are now looking at features of climate politics where the state is not the focus of our attention. Historical materialism allows us to do this, while realist and liberal institutionalist approaches make this difficult. As Leggett points out, once the statements by insurers about global warming work their way into their practices, this could mean a large-scale shift in investment patterns from carbon industries to fossil free industries and energy efficiency, which perhaps would have as much effect on future greenhouse gas trends as do international treaties.

Globalisation

The second feature of contemporary IPE is often referred to as the process of globalisation. As early as 1846, Marx and Engels saw that capitalism would necessarily become global in scope, because of its expansionist logic; throughout the *German Ideology* they refer to the 'world market'; for example, they suggest that, as economic activity has continuously expanded, individuals have become more and more subject to 'a power which has become more and more enormous, and, in the last instance, turns out to be the world market' (Marx and Engels, 1970: 55).

This theme is developed in some of the Marxist state theory literature. For example, in 1977, Jessop suggested that an implication of the state's role in securing capital accumulation was that, as capital becomes progressively internationalised, so the state's role and forms of intervention change, to secure capital accumulation on a world scale (1977: 365). By 1990, he became more specific:

> The international scope and flexibility of capital makes it difficult for individual nation-states to monitor and control the course of capital accumulation. Paradoxically, the internationalisation of capital does not dissolve the need for state intervention. It merely makes it more difficult to achieve.
>
> (Jessop, 1990: 358).

Picciotto (1991) gives a more comprehensive analysis of how Marxists could view the state in the age of transnational capital. His argument focuses on the increasing jurisdictional conflicts between capitalist states over rights to regulate – a contradiction between the territoriality of the state and the global nature of capitalism – and attempts collectively to manage global capitalism. These attempts do not, however, proceed smoothly.

Other work makes similar points. A persistent theme in writing throughout IPE is that globalisation has radically changed the state's possibilities for economic intervention. Two pieces are worth mentioning to illustrate this. John Stopford and Susan Strange (1991) demonstrate how the processes of globalisation have produced a transformation where states can no longer exert control over national development projects, but where they simply become rivals competing for investment, which increases the constraints on all sorts of policy-making. 'As firms harness the power of new technology to create systems of activity linked directly across borders, so they increasingly concentrate on those territories offering the greatest potential for recovering their investments' (Stopford and Strange, 1991: 1). While they suggest that, in many ways, this increases the policy mechanisms available to governments, it simultaneously increases the stakes involved in policy decisions by increasing the governments' 'dependence on the scarce resources controlled by firms' (1991).

Ronen Palan (1993) develops the argument within an explicitly historical materialist framework. Like Stopford and Strange, he first shows how states are now primarily competing for investment with each other. The 1980s, therefore, have seen the rise of whole sets of policy tools, such as tax havens, R&D investment grants, subsidies, export incentives, deregulation of labour markets, and so on. He then suggests, however, that this intensified interstate competition for investment, produced by globalisation, is leading to the re-emergence of the crises of under-consumption identified by Marx in the nineteenth century, and commonly thought to have been alleviated by the emergence of the welfare state. The new 'competition state', as he calls it (following Cerny, 1990), is in a contradictory position of spending higher portions of its income on attracting business, but simultaneously having to reduce taxation, for the same reason. This, he suggests, provides much of the impetus behind both the dismantling of welfare states in many advanced capitalist societies, and the widening income inequalities within those societies. The problem is, however, that this process leads to a decline in effective demand, producing crises of underconsumption. Thus, economic crises such as those experienced at the end of the 1980s and into the 1990s, which provided heavy constraints on the development of international responses to global warming, could be a persistent constraint.

Neoliberalism

The third transformation has been the emergence of neoliberalism as the hegemonic project of dominant classes, in order to fulfil the basic conditions for capitalist reproduction identified by Harvey, under the new conditions outlined previously. This shift during the 1970s and 1980s is relatively well documented, and needs little elaboration.[8] Neoliberal ideology had three main roots in emerging economic thought in the 1970s – in supply-side economics, monetarism, and public choice theory. The policy prescriptions following from this focused on control of public expenditure and the money supply more generally (to control inflation and encourage enterprise), on control of trade unions (again to control inflation and reduce constraints on enterprise), and to 'roll back the state' economically, through privatisation and deregulation.

The effect of neoliberalism has been to narrow the available policy options. Discussion of environmental questions in general has been severely curtailed by its dominance. Discussion of environmental questions was first transformed into the ideologies of 'ecological modernisation' (Weale, 1992) and 'sustainable development', reflecting a renewed obsession with economic growth. Also, neoliberalism has led to environmental economics being almost exclusively concerned with 'market-based solutions'. These dominate policy debates on global warming and other environmental questions, with the advantages of 'market mechanisms' over 'command and control' regulation often regurgitated, rather in the form of a mantra. Regarding global warming, international debate of this sort has concerned the relative merits of methods of regulating greenhouse gases, such as carbon taxes (either international, or national but coordinated internationally), fixed targets for countries, tradeable permits, and, from early 1992 onwards, joint implementation. While fixed targets is the option which has been adopted, and which looks set to remain (largely for reasons of simplicity), tradeable permits and joint implementation have most widely been regarded by analysts and many (Western) governments as being optimal. The criteria for this relate purely to economic efficiency, where markets are always assumed, in the absence of government interference, to operate efficiently. Yet it is the hegemony of neoliberalism which leads this assumption to be so widely held, and the criterion of economic efficiency the one which trumps other values. The prevalence of neoliberalism can also be seen in the relative unpopularity of the idea of carbon taxes, especially international ones, as these involve large new international bodies to administer the large sums involved. Neoliberalism's Lockean focus on the small state objects to such bureaucracy (see, for example, the quote from Nicholas Ridley, the then UK Environment Minister, in Chapter 2).

A good illustration of how this has limited the potential to develop policies regarding climate change can be seen in relation to the Bush Administration. Neoliberal ideology had particular strength there, exemplified in this regard by the Council on Competitiveness headed by Vice-President Dan Quayle, which looked into, among other things, the damaging effects of US environmental policy on US businesses. This also helps explain why the US had such a particular objection to quantified targets on emissions, which it repeatedly held to be economically inefficient.

These three transformations give some indication of how we could look at the emergence of international policy responses to global warming. Collectively, these arguments help show how the constraints have influenced the capacities of states to respond to climate change. A persistent discourse during discussions of global warming policy was over the economic costs of action. Bush's famous quote at UNCED, 'We cannot permit the extreme in the environmental movement to shut down the United States. We cannot shut down the lives of many Americans by going extreme on the environment' (*Guardian*, 1 June 1992), illustrates the theme well. But analysis of government documents, politicians' statements, the pages of *ECO*, or the pages of policy analysts' papers about climate change, also reflect the dominance of the costs issue in the policy debate. The figures given in Chapter 4 concerning the perceived costs of action are also illustrative of this. Also revealing is the way in which many of the unilateral targets undertaken by states were made conditional on like action by other states – these include those of Japan, Australia, and the UK (IEA, 1992b: 25) – as, of course, was the EC's carbon tax proposal. That of New Zealand was made conditional upon the 'measures to achieve the target not affecting New Zealand's competitive advantage, being cost-effective . . . ' (IEA, 1992b: 25). And companies often lobbied directly on the basis of this concern; in relation to UNCED in general, for example, the International Chamber of Commerce lobbied on the basis of the recession, and of concerns about 'reduced national competitiveness' (Lees, 1992, quoted in Eden, 1994: 164). While not explicitly argued in terms of pressure put forward by globalisation, it is plausible to interpret the political salience of economic costs in terms of these increased constraints.

Given the structural power of capital, state decision-makers are unlikely to undertake potentially costly actions while under pressure from falling government revenue, increased welfare spending and falling profitability for many companies. In many countries policy-makers have made noises which show this priority of growth/accumulation. It has provided the backdrop against which it has been fairly simple for energy and heavy industry to have preferred forms of policies adopted, over the objections of environmentalists. The examples of the struggle over the EC carbon tax, of fights within the Japanese government over their CO_2 target, or the pressures on the US administration, all testify to this.

At a more general level, the policy debates on global warming have been almost completely dominated by economic concerns, reflecting the general dependence of the state on capital accumulation, and the particular forms this has taken in the transition to flexible accumulation, and as part of the processes of globalisation. The ubiquity of this focus of the policy debates is such that it becomes difficult to emphasise the historically specific nature of the concerns expressed – and it has been such that even those proposing far-reaching action to reduce greenhouse gas emissions feel compelled to argue in the language of economic efficiency. Just to take one example of the policy debates, Fish and South (1994) review policy options within industrialised countries. Of the eight features of factors affecting government decisions on reduction strategies, five are completely economic in nature, while the rest are highly affected by economic considerations. The five are: overall macroeconomic costs to the economy (measured in GNP losses); trade/competitiveness impacts; losses for particular sectors; energy supplies; and political/economic capacity to reduce emissions (Fish and South, 1994: 15). Two of these – overall GNP losses, and competitiveness effects – have been the dominant ones in policy discussions. It was the latter which persuaded the EC to insert significant conditionality into its carbon/energy tax proposal, and which has been a major limitation on the individual targets of many industrialised countries, such as Australia and the UK.

NORTH–SOUTH POLITICS

Historical materialism also emphasises that the process of capital accumulation necessarily reproduces and intensifies inequalities. This process, as capitalism has become progressively more global in scope, has meant that those inequalities have increasingly been played out across state borders. While, during the eighteenth and nineteenth centuries, inequalities within countries were much greater than those between countries, increasingly from the late nineteenth century onwards that picture has been reversed (Brown, 1992: 155–6).

Historical materialism has developed a number of ways of analysing this process, ranging from dependency theory,[9] through the world-systems analysis of Immanuel Wallerstein, to the New International Division of Labour debate (Froebel, 1980). While there are differences between them, they share an understanding that capitalism depends on exploiting and intensifying global inequalities. This position is also shared by the Gramscian writers on IPE (Augelli and Murphy, 1988). The major Marxist exception would be Warren (1980), who argues that the orthodox Marxist position is that capitalism does in fact progressively 'develop' the world as it expands.

Conflict between North and South over a number of related issues has been central to the international politics of global warming. As Chapter 4 discussed in detail, the main issues fought over in the climate negotiations between North and South have been: whether developing countries have obligations to undertake actions without those actions being conditional on provision of finance and technology by the North; what obligations the North should undertake to organise 'financial resources and technology transfer' (the negotiations jargon) to the South; which institutions should be used to manage multilateral transfers, along with the decision-making mechanisms within those institutions; and, whether those developing countries particularly hard hit by global warming should be compensated by the North for the damage caused by Northern emissions.

These issues all reflect the structural inequality in the world political economy. This provides the background under which it is possible to argue in negotiations (and which is widely accepted by Northern negotiators) that developing countries are not in a position autonomously to have significant effects on their future emissions paths. And this can be explained relatively straightforwardly in terms of the developing countries' dependent position within the world economy.

The underlying problems faced by developing countries with regard to the climate treaty are the perennial ones they face in international relations in general. Two features are of particular importance for the discussion here. One is the perennial weaknesses of the state in many developing countries, with respect both to external forces and to domestic social groups, which severely limit its political, financial, and administrative capacity to implement policies effectively, or to make significant investment decisions. The second is the more particular nature of the debt crisis in many developing countries, which continues into the 1990s. Again, this severely limits what developing countries have the capacity to do. In the negotiations, these factors underlay the claims that they felt unable to alter their emissions path without external assistance.

Most states in developing countries are weak to the extent that Robert Jackson has referred to their status in terms of 'quasi-sovereignty' (Jackson, 1990). Indeed, Cammack, Pool and Tordoff go so far as to say that 'it is a mistake to attribute too great a capacity to bring about particular ends to any actor in the Third World' (Cammack, Pool and Tordoff, 1988: 47), illustrating how misguided are the assumptions of many of those from the North when negotiating agreements, that agreements signed by states can be assumed to be implemented. This weakness has two aspects: the first is external weakness, with respect to dependency on commodities – often on only one or two particular commodities – for foreign exchange, domination by the International Monetary Fund (IMF) and, in many cases, by Western-based transnational corporations (TNCs), and dependency on the world market and, through that, on decisions in core capitalist economies – for example, on interest rate decisions in the United States, which vastly exacerbated external debt problems in the early 1980s (Thomas, 1987: 4–5).

The second aspect of state weakness is internal weakness, with respect to civil society. States in many developing countries still often contain the legacy of colonialism. For example, many countries in sub-Saharan Africa contain diverse ethnic groupings reflecting the arbitrary nature of boundaries drawn up by colonialist powers. This has fuelled much conflict within countries. Another side to this is pervasive economic and fiscal weakness, interacting of course with external weakness, which undermines the ability of many governments to govern effectively, and thus to implement political decisions.[10] The Structural Adjustment Programmes of the IMF, designed (within the IMF's monetarist framework) to cope with problems of external debt, fuelled internal instability and even riots in many countries; for example, in Zambia in 1986, in Venezuela in 1989, in Morocco and Sudan during 1981–2, and in Jamaica in the 1970s (Thomas, 1987: 60; Jackson, 1990: 126–7). This state incapacity makes it more difficult for those countries, either to participate effectively in international negotiations, or to implement treaties once they are signed (Rowlands, 1994: 213).

The debt crisis pervasive in many developing countries in the 1980s and through into the 1990s provided the background feature which underlay their position and concerns in the climate negotiations. A few simple but striking figures suffice to illustrate how this constrains the feasibility of significant investment by developing country states in climate programmes without external assistance.

By 1992, developing countries collectively had debts of approximately $128 trillion (Hyder, 1992: 334), and between 1982 and 1990 were paying on average about $12.5 billion dollars a month in debt service payments to Northern banks and governments (George, 1992: xiv). The net flow of capital from South to North during the same eight year period has been estimated at a total of $418 billion, an equivalent, as Susan George points out, of six Marshall Plans (George, 1992: xv).[11] In many countries, debt service repayments alone accounted for significant proportions of export earnings, in some cases over 100 per cent. For example, the debt service ratio, as this proportion is known, was 53 per cent for Mexico, 44 per cent for Brazil, 67 per cent for Zambia, and went to an extreme in Mozambique of 204 per cent (George, 1992: 15; Onimode, 1992: 26).[12] In other words, these countries lose significant portions of their foreign exchange earnings to debt payments, making them unavailable for consumption or investment. And, despite this, many countries ended the 1980s with significantly larger external debts than they had in 1982; this increase is 62 per cent for all debtor countries, but stands at 113 per cent for sub-Saharan African countries (George, 1992: xvi).

The social and political implications of the debt crisis and the ensuing IMF restructuring plans have been widely documented (Thomas, 1987: 39–64 and 146–97; George, 1988; George, 1992; Onimode, 1992). Here, two points are important. One is that debt appears itself to have been a precipitating factor in much of the deforestation of highly forested developing countries such as Brazil, Indonesia, Colombia and Malaysia. While most of this book has been concerned with reductions in fossil CO_2 emissions, deforestation remains an important, although disputed, source of CO_2 in the atmosphere.[13] The IPCC put the contribution of deforestation at 18 per cent of total greenhouse forcing in the 1980s, with an uncertainty range of between 9 and 26 per cent (IPCC, 1990b: xxx).[14] Figures for carbon emissions from deforestation are put in the range of 1 billion tonnes, plus or minus 0.6 billion, while those for fossil carbon emissions are 6 billion (Grubb, 1989: 6).

Thus, deforestation is a significant source of CO_2 emissions. Susan George has found significant correlations between rates of indebtedness and deforestation (1992: ch. 1); as countries have had to pay increased debts, they have been forced to increase export earnings, which has stimulated the need to bring more land under cultivation for cash cropping. Debt may thus have helped to cause increased CO_2 emissions, through deforestation, from some large developing countries.

The second important point here about the impact of debt is that the levels of indebtedness clearly inhibit, to a very great extent, what is possible in developing countries in terms of investment in energy efficiency, alternative energy sources, and so on, which could foster less carbon-intensive development. These constraints have been exacerbated by the response from the Northern dominated IMF, whose structural adjustment programmes have stressed currency devaluations, limiting imports, and curbs on public expenditure. These objectives, in particular the last one, are contradictory to the aim of introducing climate policies in those countries. Finally, the constraints imposed by high levels of indebtedness have been exacerbated by, and have in turn exacerbated, the low administrative and political ability of developing countries to implement programmes such as a set of climate policies. Developing countries in the climate negotiations were acutely aware of these constraints in a way in which the negotiators from industrialised countries were not, an awareness which is clearly reflected in the position that all developing country commitments must be dependent on finance and technology from the North. Hyder has emphasised that 'debt write-off and relief would free all those resources in the developing countries for more economic, environmentally friendly, and increasingly sustainable development' (1992: 334). Given this background, the level of North–South conflict over global warming, illustrated in Chapter 4, is not particularly surprising.

With regard to the division between countries concerning their vulnerability to climate impacts, historical materialism can also play a significant role in explaining this split. The most assertive proponents of *reductions* in CO_2 emissions (rather than simply stabilisation) were the AOSIS states. These were clearly threatened by potential climate impacts, some with their very survival. Other countries were also disproportionately concerned about potential climate impacts – mainly those countries with significant low-lying areas (e.g. Bangladesh, the Netherlands) and those countries which were already experiencing, and were threatened with further, desertification. Others, such as the US (under the Bush Administration) and Russia, have seemed relatively unconcerned about potential impacts.

However, much of this division is clearly social rather than the result of some 'natural' division. While climatological factors have been involved, states have been more or less concerned about climate impacts primarily because of questions of wealth. A simple comparison between the Netherlands and Bangladesh illustrates the point. While the Netherlands has been noticeably more in favour of reductions in CO_2 emissions than most other industrialised countries, the level of threat due to sea-level rise is insignificant when compared to the threat to Bangladesh, due to the position of the Netherlands in the world economy and its ensuing financial and technological capacity. This division, therefore, can be explained within the North–South rubric given above for historical materialism.

One final point here relates back to the shift to flexible accumulation. The shift from price competition to product innovation competition, with its corresponding reduction in product cycles, has meant that firms have had to be more responsive to consumer tastes. This has meant that, during the 1980s, after a substantial industrialisation in many developing countries in 'world market factories' during the 1970s (Froebel, 1980), firms moved plant back closer to the main markets (Kaplinsky, 1991). Thus, developing countries' share of world Foreign Direct Investment declined substantially during the 1980s, from a high of 25 per cent in the 1970s to a low of 17 per cent in the 1980s (Kegley and Wittkopf, 1993: 197). This, of course, had implications in terms of the debt crisis, but it can be used here to help locate historically the intensity of the North–South conflict over global warming. It clearly rested on the back of much resentment over how the North had been able during the 1980s, due to the debt crisis and the decline of investment in developing countries, to increase its power over developing countries. Many developing countries saw global warming as an opportunity to redress this balance, and to exercise some leverage over the North (Paterson, 1992).

CONCLUSIONS

This chapter has tried to show how a political economy approach, rooted largely in historical materialism, can offer a significantly more comprehensive account of the international politics of global warming than can either neorealism or liberal institutionalism. Such an approach is able to locate the politics of global warming historically, while the other positions are noticeably weak in this respect. It is able to explain the underlying factors influencing states' positions in the negotiations, through the assumption of the state's relationship to capital accumulation. It shows how those domestic bases are themselves globally constituted through the workings of a globalised capitalism. It is able to give significant explanations for the North–South conflict in the negotiations.

This seems to me to place state sovereignty and international anarchy in their proper context. The structure of anarchy is a secondary consideration to that of the structural constraints imposed by world capitalism. That is because it is largely the latter which constitutes the states' outlook onto the world, particularly regarding questions which (potentially) impose economic costs on states and the fractions of capital they respond to, and which require collective action for their resolution. Global warming is a prime example of both of these.

This analysis also, of course, has significant normative implications for those interested in developing political responses to climate change. It means, first and foremost, that it is to be expected that proposals for emissions reductions will be resisted by powerful fractions of capital with substantial capacity to exert power over state decision-makers. In the context of globalisation, it means that responses will have to be sought even more at the global level, since, as reductions in emissions are developed, countries will have increasingly great incentives to avoid actions with significant costs in terms of lost investment. It also, perhaps, in the context of environmentalist debates over the nature of economic growth, adds weight to the argument that growth must be sacrificed in the search for sustainability, since it is the pursuit of economic growth by states (to fund welfare programmes and other projects, and to maintain legitimacy) which is a significant source of the structural power of capital.

It suggests that any response which is likely to have significant effects on greenhouse gas emissions will need to be rooted in a broader counter-hegemonic project (in the Gramscian sense), mobilising political forces around ideas which can legitimate broader social changes, as these may be required to overcome political objections from entrenched parts of capital. Such a project would need to incorporate the (global) environ-mental movement, much of the labour movement, and parts of capital which would benefit from greenhouse gas abatement, such as the energy efficiency industries, renewables, and perhaps parts of the financial sector, especially the insurance industry worried about the costs of insurance claims in a warming world.

Chapter 9

Conclusions

The argument of the book has traversed a series of debates. I suggested how, within a neorealist–liberal institutionalist debate, institutionalism provides a significantly more adequate account of interstate cooperation over global warming. Neither realist analyses based purely on power, or those based on anarchy, are adequate as an explanation for outcomes. While the assumption of anarchy yields a useful basic assumption about why cooperation may be difficult, liberal institutionalists also hold this assumption. Further, institutionalists' emphasis on how institutions themselves become important in terms of affecting outcomes was clearly demonstrated in relation to global warming.

The next debate, however, is between rationalist and constructivist theories of international relations. Here, I suggested that a constructivist account gives more plausible interpretations of global warming. When examining states' actions, an interpretation which suggests that they are rational actors in the sense outlined by rational choice theory is less plausible than an interpretation which suggests they are role-players and reflexive about their goals. This argument was then developed concerning the politics of science, where I suggested that the 'discursive practices' argument adopted by Litfin gives a more plausible interpretation of this than does the 'epistemic communities' approach of Haas and others. Peter Haas's approach, while useful, still operates with an assumption that scientific consensus is a prerequisite for interstate cooperation, rather than science providing a set of resources for various actors which could just as easily produce as resolve conflict. This perspective also usefully supplements a more general constructivist approach by providing plausible explanations of agenda-setting, and of the constitution of state interests and identities.

Finally, however, historical materialism was introduced. This introduces political economy into the analysis. It enables us to explain the depth of the North–South rift over global warming in a way that no other perspective can. And it allows us to explain the particular ways in which the state's role in promoting capital accumulation has provided the most important context within which the development of climate policies within industrialised states has operated; this has depended primarily on the way in which fossil energy is inserted into the national economy.

Both historical materialism and a discourse-theoretic approach can provide fruitful interpretations of climate politics. Historical materialism allows us to place climate politics in a broader political-economic context, which transcends the division between the domestic and the international. It also allows us, like some of the constructivist writers do, to integrate normative and explanatory concerns. And the discourse-theoretic approach allows us both to explain the deployment of scientific (and other) knowledge in the negotiations, and to explore in more convincing ways the manner in which state interests are constituted.

However, it would be fair to say that this still leaves some room for analysing interstate processes in terms of collective action problems, which liberal institutionalism (and realism) does. The point, however, is that we need to understand how state positions concerning global warming are constituted before it makes sense to analyse the interstate negotiations. Furthermore, it seems clear that those negotiations are not primarily guided by rational unitary states instrumentally pursuing their predefined national interest. It has been more a case of state representatives trying to develop norms to guide their action in relation to global warming, reflecting their sense of belonging to a system in which they have some rudimentary responsibilities to the other members of that system. Thus, state interests are constituted by both domestic pressures and international processes and structures. So the value of rational choice approaches which focus on collective action problems is in their ability to model the strategic situation(s) which state decision-makers face, rather than to *explain* why a particular outcome occurs.

The central problem here is how to integrate the constructivist position on interstate relations with an understanding of the state's position within a global capitalist system. This has both an explanatory and a normative/critical aspect: it seeks to explain how global climate politics works; and to identify potential transformative processes within those politics. There are a number of clear tensions between the constructivist position, outlined here, on interstate relations and the historical materialist position. One of these concerns a foundational question. Constructivist approaches, particularly those coming from poststructuralism, are wary of the foundational claims about the nature of capitalist society which historical materialists make, seeing in them the universalistic, totalising claims which are both inadequate to understanding the complexity and contradictions of politics, and can create oppressive political projects. Some work has been done to try to reformulate them, to create a constructivist political economy which has, however, much in common with Marxism (e.g. Daly, 1991), but this is an area which is underdeveloped.

However, the most important problem is that constructivists in IR, such as Wendt, while writing about the structure–agency debate, have as their ontology of the structure of international relations the anarchic international system of neorealism. The theoretical problems for them are to show that state interests and practices are constituted both by systemic and domestic forces, that state practices are more guided by norms than by the rational choice of realists and liberal institutionalists, and that international systems can change over time. However, if a central feature of international relations is that the system is capitalist, and that this has certain effects, a completely different set of questions comes up for investigation within a constructivist framework. The nature of the power of global capital in curtailing the possibilities for interstate cooperation, or the emergence of norms to govern particular issues, such as global warming, becomes crucial in any analysis.

For example, Wendt, despite discussing world systems theory in 'The agent–structure problem' (1987), emerges with a fairly strong realist ontology about the nature of the international system. 'I will not dispute here the neorealist description of contemporary state system as a competitive, self-help world', he writes later (1992: 396). Elsewhere in the later article, he states that 'I also believe, with realists, that in the medium run sovereign states will remain the dominant political actors in the international system' (1992: 424).

That states are the dominant actors is not necessarily the problematic point here. The important point is the way in which we conceive the structure which states constitute and are constituted by. Wendt and Duvall do consider some aspects of capitalism and its effects on constituting state identities and interests – for example, the monetary regime makes certain practices possible, such as monitoring the exchange rate, and engaging in particular employment or price policies (1989: 61–2). This considers the effects of global capitalism on the constitution of state identities and interests purely at the level of regimes created by states and their unintended consequences. However, global capitalism operates at a deeper level, structuring states in certain ways – in particular by making promotion of capital accumulation central to their identity, something which they cannot avoid in decisions and still maintain their legitimacy either domestically (to electorates) or internationally (with international financial institutions). As shown in Chapter 8, this has had clear impacts on the possibilities for states to respond to global warming. Thus, an important question for future research is integrating this with the approach developed by Wendt – how to reorient the structure–agency debate with a globalised capitalism as a key feature of the structure. The argument given by Hay (1994), outlined in Chapter 8, would seem like the most appropriate starting point for this enquiry. Environmental crises are seen as causing political crises because of the contradiction they throw up between the state's structural responsibility for promoting capital accumulation and its need to legitimate itself. The politics of global environmental problems is seen as a combination of these crises, the location of particular economies within the global economy, and the interstate politics of 'global environmental diplomacy'.

POLICY DEBATES

What do these conclusions imply in terms of the policy debates mentioned in the introduction to this book? Hopefully, some implications are reasonably clear, although this is more obvious in some cases than in others. The introduction mentioned three key policy debates: one about the role and importance of organisations set up by the Climate Convention; one about the merits or otherwise of tradeable permits for carbon emissions; and one about considerations of equity or justice in the negotiations with respect primarily to North–South relations.

One obvious implication is that this analysis would support claims about the importance of institutions made by many writing about UNCED. However, the focus of much of the policy debate on these institutions has tended to associate institutions with organisations *per se*; much of this debate has been over the 'strength' of the Commission on Sustainable Development. The institutionalist analysis given in Chapter 6 suggests a different conclusion with regard to institutions. What matters is the way in which institutions are inserted into, and relate to, the states who will be implementing any agreements; how they confer roles on states. Chapter 6 outlined how a number of theorists conceive of these institutional effects. This section will follow Levy, Keohane and Haas's suggested framework. Institutions function effectively by 'increasing governmental concern, enhancing the contractual environment, and increasing national political and administrative capacity' (Levy, Keohane and Haas, 1993: 424).

In the case of global warming, the first of these implies that ongoing processes to build scientific and, in particular, techno-economic consensus will be crucial in developing the cognitive base for future negotiations. These will make it more possible for states' positions to converge, and make future agreements easier to reach and more robust, since the cognitive base on which they rest will be more uniform across countries. States are unlikely to undertake strong action without agreement about the costs of various policies and strategies. This may well also involve an increased role for epistemic communities (scientific, technological and economic) within state structures, which, in turn, may mean that any consensus reached within those communities is more likely to result in stronger political action.

Second, institutions stabilise expectations about others' actions, so that states know their cooperation will be reciprocated. This involves both building ongoing negotiations to develop trust and mutual learning, and monitoring or 'verification' functions which institutions can fulfil (Greene and Salt, 1992). The game-theoretic language becomes more viable here, perhaps, as defined criteria for cooperation and defection now exist.[1]

On the third point, the Climate Convention has produced a set of procedures designed in part to increase capacity, especially in developing countries. This is in two forms, the first and most familiar of which consists of the clauses on 'financial resources and technology transfer', designed to facilitate data collection and, possibly, policy implementation (see Chapter 3 for details). But the second is designed to enable developing countries to increase capacity, by fostering the development of knowledge about emissions and sinks, which – if the analyses in the volume edited by Haas, Keohane and Levy (1993), as well as in many other works, are any guide – should help those countries identify areas for possible cost-free or low-cost options for limiting emissions. It is, of course, too early to identify whether such an institutional effect has operated successfully.

In addition to these three institutional functions, and possibly the most important point, the above analysis highlights how important the *informal* development and the intersubjective development of norms will be. States will not enact policies or sign up to commitments without greater mutual understanding of why it is they are acting, without those norms being internalised by decision-makers. With respect to these conclusions, the bodies set up by the Climate Convention are likely to be of significantly greater importance than the Commission for Sustainable Development. These will be where states share information about the effectiveness of various policies to reduce emissions, or gain a sense of trust (if that happens) about each others' intentions to carry out obligations. As emphasised by constructivists, this entails a transformation of state *identities* over global warming, not merely an adjustment to the incentives they face to behave in particular ways.

Regarding tradeable permits, it might seem that the analysis has little to say since, while it would, in general, support conclusions which emphasise the importance of international institutions, of which tradeable permits would clearly be an example, it is underspecific with regard to what form those institutions could take. It suggests that institutions are important in that they stabilise expectations about the actions of others, but it is not clear that tradeable permits would achieve this any more than would multilaterally negotiated fixed targets.

It does, however, suggest an important corrective to the analyses of most writing about tradeable permits. As mentioned in Chapter 1, the primary concern in that literature is with economically optimal outcomes. The analysis here emphasises the importance of politics. However, it seems to me still to be unclear whether Grubb's argument (1989) about the political advantages of tradeable permits – that they separate decisions about global targets from ones about each country's contribution, and reduce the costs of abatement – is convincing. States will always be able to calculate the costs to themselves of any particular allocation arrangement or trading procedure. Two important arguments from institutionalist writers remain. One is Oran Young's assertion that 'there is a sense of fairness that everyone can relate to in across-the-board percentage cuts which is hard to match in more complex arrangements featuring charges or transferable production permits' (Young, 1989a: 369; see also Ostrom, 1990: 16). This remains debatable, given differing conceptions of equity. Possibly more important is Levy, Keohane and Haas's statement that 'the great political virtue of such rules (across-the-board cuts) is that the severity of required reductions is likely to correlate with the intensity of domestic support for action to protect the environment' (1993: 414).

Another substantive political point which might come out is that a problem with tradeable permits is that they reduce much of the politics of reducing emissions to bilateral relations between states, and almost always between developing and industrialised states.[2] I suggested that one of the reasons why neorealism cannot offer an adequate account for the politics of global warming is that the interdependence involved makes calculations of the relative power of states in the negotiations very difficult to engage in, while realist analyses require us to know where power lies in order to claim that power determines outcomes. Thus, in the politics of global warming, it has been difficult for traditionally powerful states to get their own way. The problem with tradeable permits derived from the analysis in this book (there are other problems which do not derive from these conclusions) is that they disengage the ecological interdependence involved in global warming, which makes power assessments difficult, from the economic/political aspects of reducing emissions at the practical level. While power is still difficult to assess at the multilateral level, where overall global targets are negotiated, it becomes much more prominent at the bilateral level in negotiations about the value of a permit between, for example, the US and the Sudan. Thus, tradeable permits may enable the traditionally powerful countries to regain predominance, which the multilateral processes in the climate negotiations, combined with the particular characteristics of global warming, have denied them. For those who are normatively concerned with the interests of the South, therefore, tradeable permits may be problematic. The ability of the South to defend its perceived interests is likely to be enhanced by keeping as much of the politics of global warming as possible at the multilateral level.

On the question of equity, this analysis is ambiguous with regard to claims made by those writers who assert that equity considerations are essential to the practical success of agreements on global warming. This claim was made more difficult on the basis of the analysis here, since I argued that the rational choice approach to analysing how the politics of global warming worked before UNCED is highly problematic. Many (but not all) claims about the importance of equity are based on assumptions about rational action on the behalf of states, and on equity becoming important as a result of states' strategic interactions. But, possibly more important, it suggests ways in which particular conceptions of equity might be advanced or hindered. Some of the writers use the term as if it had commonly-understood meanings and implications, apparently without any sense that the term might be problematic (Young, 1989a: 368–9). However, a variety of positions are possible on what an equitable agreement would look like, ranging from a 'status quo' position to an equal *per capita* emissions position (Grubb, Sebenius, Magalhaes and Subak, 1991; Paterson, 1996). The point here is that the institutional analysis above implies that particular conceptions of equity could be furthered by particular strategies within institutions. In particular, conceptions of equity favourable to the South (at the extreme, an equal *per capita* emissions position, but there are others less strong than this) are most likely to be furthered through making sure that as much of the cognitive and normative development as possible occurs at the international level. To the extent that industrialised states are left to their own devices with regard to developing the positions and rationales for their climate policies, they are less likely to come to accept conceptions of equity which specifically challenge North/South inequalities. The more that climate policies can be formulated and developed within international organisations, the more the developing countries can make use of their 'organizationally dependent capabilities' (Keohane and Nye, 1977: 55) – such as the universal membership of the UN, and the general sympathy of UN Secretariat officials (especially those in the environmental field) to developing countries' needs – to further their aims.

On the other hand, it is here, perhaps, where both a constructivist perspective in IR and the historical materialist perspective have similar things to say. Both would be able to emphasise the question of justice, although from different positions. For constructivists such as Wendt, certain normative structures necessarily underlie international relations. These also necessarily contain some elements which relate to questions of justice.[3] These have given space to those seeking just outcomes to make their claims. And many historical materialists share a core normative concern for (a particular conception of) social justice, and also have an explanation for the exacerbation of distributive injustice under capitalism.

Both, however, would emphasise that achieving just outcomes would involve significantly greater transformations than can be contained in particular allocation systems for permits to emit CO_2, or provisions for finance and technology transfer. Constructivists could suggest that existing failures to achieve just outcomes are rooted in the existing normative structure of international relations which constitutes states as self-regarding entities; in other words, which makes it possible for states to ignore the effects of their actions on others beyond their borders. In an analogous way, historical materialists could suggest that just outcomes require broad transformations away from capitalism, as capitalist reproduction depends on intensifying existing inequalities. Therefore, to the extent that resolution of the problem of global warming requires justice to be taken seriously, it would also require broad transformations in global politics.

Notes

1 INTRODUCTION

1 Chapter 7 discusses the politics of the terms in more detail. Three main terms have been used – 'climate change', 'the greenhouse effect', and 'global warming'. I will use 'global warming' for largely arbitrary reasons.

2 This book will not deal with the whole range of issues discussed at UNCED. For assessments of the UNCED conference as a whole, see for example Thomas (1992a); Grubb *et al.* (1993); Holmberg *et al.* (1993); Islam (1993); Freestone (1994). For critiques, see Doran (1993), or Chatterjee and Finger (1994).

3 See for example Grubb (1989) on tradeable permits and their advantages over other schemes, and UNCTAD (1992) for a fully fledged account.

4 The size of this literature is considerable. For a selection, see Krause, Koomey and Bach (1989); Weiss (1989); Agarwal and Narain (1991); Bergesen (1991); Young (1991); Grubb, Sebenius, Magalhaes and Subak (1992); Grubb (1995a); *Global Environmental Change,* June 1992. Arguably the most sophisticated writings are the series of pieces by Henry Shue (1992; 1993a; 1993b; 1993c; 1994a; 1994b). I have tried elsewhere to analyse how the positions identified in the text here could be justified by reference to broader traditions of international ethics (Paterson 1996).

5 This is, as will hopefully become obvious, only one way to frame the question in relation to climate change.

6 Many of the main arguments in this debate have been reproduced in Baldwin (1993).

7 Transnational historical materialism is the term adopted by Gill and Law (1988), open Marxism is used by Drainville (1994) and Burnham (1994). Gramscian IPE is in more widespread use.

8 The exception is Karen Litfin's very useful contribution, *Ozone Discourses* (1994), which uses a poststructuralist approach to discuss the politics of science in the ozone negotiations. Litfin takes issue with Haas's epistemic community approach, suggesting the politics of knowledge is less straightforward than he claims. Her approach will be developed in Chapter 7.

9 For an account of this body, and the politics of its report, see Chapter 2.

10   Note that not all of these gases are part of the naturally occurring greenhouse effect. In particular, CFCs do not occur naturally.

11   For details of these impacts, see McTegart (1990); for fuller summaries, see Wirth (1989); Paterson (1992a).

12   The widely noted regressive distributional effect of carbon taxes is one obvious example of this. See Johnson *et al.* (1990) for a discussion.

13   I say undeniably, because it became a matter of political contention, with the US and the oil producing states trying to downplay its centrality.

2   THE HISTORICAL DEVELOPMENT OF CLIMATE ON THE INTERNATIONAL AGENDA

1   Fourier (1827). On his importance in the history of climate science see, for example, Kellogg (1987: 115); Boyle and Ardill (1989: 12); Pearce (1989: 97); Gribbin (1990: 30); Lyman (1990: 9); Lunde (1991: 58). Pearce (and, following him, Lunde), also erroneously asserts that he referred to the role of CO_2 in this process. Fourier's article is, however, simply concerned to establish that the atmosphere is an important determinant of the earth's temperature, independent of heat from the sun and from the earth's core (Fourier, 1827: 580).

2   Pearce notes that his interest in heat became obsessive, and suggests that this lead him to his death, as he stumbled down stairs having 'heated his home to absurd temperatures and swathed himself in layer upon layer of clothing' (Pearce, 1989: 97).

3   Again, Kellogg wrongly states that in his 1863 article, Tyndall suggested that CO_2 acts in a similar fashion, but he only mentioned water vapour there. Gribbin (1990: 31) says that Tyndall had calculated the greenhouse properties of CO_2, but does not state if or where these calculations were published.

4   Arrhenius is also often cited as providing a historical rationale for using the arbitrary figure of a doubling of CO_2 concentrations in contemporary models and scenarios. In fact, Arrhenius calculated the temperature changes for a change in CO_2 concentration of 0.67, 1.5, 2, 2.5, and 3 times the original concentration. See Arrhenius (1896: 266).

5   Revelle (1985: 3) also quotes this passage (without a reference) but completely changes the order of the sentences (although not the meaning) and adds one phrase at the beginning which is not in the original.

6   Who gets the most credit depends on who you read. Atwood (1959) gives ICSU the primary role, while WMO publications usually emphasise the role of WMO. Atwood was Director of the Office of International Relations of the National Academy of Sciences – National Research Council (the US member body of ICSU).

7   A more detailed account of the scientific developments following the IGY than is produced here can be found in Victor and Clark (1991).

8   According to Hart and Victor (1993: 648–50), Revelle and Suess's article was stimulated by ideas in two earlier papers by Suess (1955) and Plass (1956).

9   Bolin, Jaeger and Doos's summary at the conference of the then consensus was worded even more strongly. Summarising the background papers to the Villach Conference, they wrote that 'This assessment concludes that a

doubling of the CO_2 concentration would lead to an increase of the globally averaged surface temperature by 1.5–5.5 degrees Celsius. The uncertainty is considerable, but there is almost unanimous agreement that a substantial warming would occur.... The observed increase of mean global surface temperature during the last hundred years is ... in general accord with model results' (Bolin *et al.*, 1986: 27).

10   This would mean that any potential global warming due to human activities would occur significantly earlier than was previously thought likely or possible, since the effective doubling of CO_2-equivalent concentration in the atmosphere would be advanced.

11   The conference didn't advocate anything like radical reductions in CO_2 emissions. But it did suggest that over-reliance on coal was unwise, that energy supply should be diversified, and that efforts should be made to reduce energy demand (Williams, 1978: 316–18).

12   The story here is told primarily at the international level. National level analyses telling a similar tale both for scientific development, and the issue becoming political, have been conducted for Germany by Cavender and Jaeger (1993: 4–12), for the US by Hatch (1993), and for the EC Commission by Liberatore (1994).

13   Rowlands (1994: 73) cites an article in *Nature* which claims the hot weather was much more important than the science in influencing politicians, but it seems to me more plausible that it was the conjunction of the two. Mazur and Lee (1993: 697–8) show how the US media's coverage of the drought and of Hansen's statement intertwined to produce this effect.

14   For a review of the conference statement which regards a 20 per cent reduction as 'woefully inadequate to stabilize the atmosphere', see Usher (1989). Usher works for UNEP.

15   Later, once the UK had established its stabilisation target, but only for the year 2005 rahter than 2000 as others had done, Trippier again produced high-quality rhetoric. 'We could go for 2000, if we wanted to close down half the coal mines in Britain and go for no economic growth', he stated (quoted in the *Independent* 21 September 1990; Rowlands, 1994: 142–3).

16   At the time the IPCC was set up both men worked for the US State Department.

17   It was also decided that the working groups would be chaired by the UK, Soviet Union and the US respectively (IPCC, 1988: Annex V).

18   The Working Groups met throughout 1989 and the first half of 1990. Their meetings interspersed with full plenary meetings, the second in Nairobi in June 1989, then in Washington DC in February 1990, and the final one in Sundsvall, Sweden in August 1990, where the IPCC's First Assessment Report was adopted.

19   There were of course less extreme objections. One of the most prominent was Robert Balling's *The Heated Debate* (1992). Hempel's review essay (1993) gives a useful overview to this debate.

20   It should also be noted that, of these, only thirty-seven responded, a low number for a survey of a highly motivated group.

21   The US in particular took a lot of persuading of the need for formal negotiations at that point. See Bodansky (1993: 471–3) for an account of how they were persuaded.

3 BEFORE AND AFTER RIO: INTERSTATE NEGOTIATIONS

1 In all, five sessions were held over eighteen months, between February 1991 and May 1992. They were held in Chantilly near Washington DC, Geneva, Nairobi, and New York. The fifth session in New York was resumed between 30 April and 8 May. This session was called the 'resumed Fifth Session', rather than the sixth session, largely for tactical reasons. One member of the secretariat commented that referring to the sixth session during the fifth session would be likely to give delegates the impression that they had more time than in fact they had. The normative beliefs among most members of the secretariat about the desirability of reaching a strong agreement were never far from the surface (Personal notes, INC Fifth Session, New York, February 1992). Then, following Rio, there were a further six sessions before the first Conference of the Parties, all held either in Geneva or New York.

2 The Chair was Jean Ripert of France, and the Vice-Chairs were Ahmed Djoghlaf (Algeria), Ion Draghici (Romania), Raul Estrada-Oyuela (Argentina) and T. Prabhakar Menon (India). Later in the session, Mr Menon was replaced by Chandrashekhar Dasgupta, also of India. (See INC, 8 March 1991.)

3 See *ECO* (7 February 1991: 2–5), for a summary of these statements. *ECO* is a daily journal produced by environmental NGOs at many international environmental negotiations (originally at the Stockholm Conference in 1972). It is an invaluable source of information on the negotiations, as well as of wit and critique.

4 These Co-Chairs and Vice-Chairs were, however, not elected until the Second Session in June 1991.

5 Bodansky (1993: 482) suggests that much of the disappointment was because the perception was widespread that a number of adequate draft texts already existed which could be quickly used and built upon.

6 The use of the term 'greenhouse gases' here itself masks a significant political argument. Its use in the negotiations would imply a position that all greenhouse gases should be controlled (primarily carbon dioxide, methane, nitrous oxide, CFCs). The general position, even accepted by the US by the end of the negotiations, was that this blanket use was inadequate. In particular, it would allow reductions in CFC emissions to be offset against carbon dioxide growth. CFCs are, of course, controlled for their ozone-depleting properties under the Montreal Protocol on Substances That Deplete the Ozone Layer and its amendments. There was also much debate throughout the negotiations about whether it was possible and/or desirable to include all gases, or deal with them on an individual basis. This was the US's so-called 'Comprehensive Approach'. See US Department of Justice (1991); for a critique, see Grubb, Victor and Hope (1991).

7 For example, by US Senate Majority Leader George J. Mitchell; *ECO* (7 February 1991: 1).

8 Dan Bodansky has suggested that India was isolated within the G77 on this point. Personal communication, 1993.

9 INC, (19 August 1991: 13). The term 'specific commitments' in this context referred to quantitative limits imposed on the emissions of industrialised

countries. They were specific, both in the sense that they were quantified, and that they applied only to some countries.

10　The Climate Action Network called it 'Hedge and retreat' (cited in Bodansky, 1993: 486).

11　The Bureau is a name used in the negotiations to refer to the co-chairs and vice-chair of the Working Group. There was also a Bureau of the entire INC, which consisted of the Bureaux from both Working Groups and the Chair and Vice-Chairs of the Committee as a whole. Its role was to engage in such work as producing compiled texts in between sessions, and helping the Chair to guide the negotiations. Texts 'produced by the Bureau' were in reality produced by the Secretariat, with the Bureau amending and approving them.

12　See Bodansky (1993: 488–9) for an account of this. Also, see *ECO* (19 December 1991). For the G24 text, see INC (18 December 1991). Djoghlaf (1994: 106) suggests that this text was highly influential on the course of the negotiations on commitments.

13　Technically, in UN terminology, an 'informal' simply means meetings which are not recorded or where a verbatim record is taken, but here it was used more generically. In effect, a hierarchy of exclusiveness of the meetings was established. Dasgupta (1994: 142) attributes the final success of the negotiations to this new procedure.

14　The pages of *ECO* are littered with examples of this conflict between the US and other industrialised countries. For examples, see 'US Rejects Compromise plan' (19 June 1991); 'EC Raises Climate Stakes' (12 September 1991); 'Industrial World v. US – Round 1' (13 September 1991); 'Log-jam on Commitments' (17 September 1991); 'Ripert Points the Finger' (5 May 1992).

15　Nitze (1994: 188), in his detailed account of the emergence of the US position, claims that the US achieved its major goals. While this is perhaps broadly true, it still shifted its position significantly.

16　For an excellent insider's account of how this occurred, which emphasises the emergence of personal understandings between negotiators, see Kjellen (1994: 157–65).

17　There were no Working Group meetings during the resumed Fifth Session, but the meeting operated through three 'clusters' of delegations interested in particular parts of the convention text. See *ECO* from throughout that session.

18　An additional spur was that the OECD countries began to coordinate themselves as a group and, in essence, negotiated the text on commitments between themselves. Kjellen (1994: 157) reports that they had been reluctant to do this to avoid looking like they were 'ganging up' on the G77, but the G77 pushed them into it at the December 1991 session with their text which left the industrialised countries' commitments blank. Kjellen headed the Swedish delegation to the INC.

19　These are on Floor 39 of the UN building, while the main conference rooms are in the basement. The point was deliberately to isolate other delegations from the 'main' group.

20　Djoghlaf (1994: 103) and Dowdeswell and Kinley (1994: 118–19) both suggest that the timing of Ripert's intervention was crucial and a useful piece of leadership. Like Dowdeswell, Kinley was on the Canadian delegation.

21 See, for example, Berreen and Meyer (1992); Grubb (1992); Hanisch (1992); Kelly and Granich (1992); Pachauri (1992); Paterson (1992b); Bodansky (1993). The most detailed account, written from a legal perspective, is in Rowbotham (1996).

22 This, of course, is a different question to the structural constraints imposed by the world economy. Those constraints will be discussed in the next chapter; they are more adequate to explain why countries adopted no more ambitious CO_2 reduction policies than they did, and, to an extent, why countries' positions differed. But given those differing positions, the structure of anarchy then becomes important in explaining why it was difficult to reach agreement at any other level than that of the lowest common denominator.

23 See the reports of the various INC meetings in the bibliography. Dasgupta (1994: 132) also states there were no votes on substantive issues, but suggests that the existence of a voting procedure made states moderate their positions to reach consensus decisions.

24 In the Working Group I meetings which I attended in Nairobi (about three-quarters of the total), the Saudis made fifteen out of a total of 274 interventions, i.e. just over 5 per cent of all speeches. Kuwait also made a significant number (Personal notes, INC III, Nairobi, September 1991). The commentary column in *ECO*, known (for the sessions held in Geneva) as Léman, illustrates this nicely in one column: 'Léman was, as usual, being lulled to sleep by the gentle drone of Saudi intervention . . . '. (*ECO*, 26 August 1994: 4). Kjellen (1994: 156) is not alone in claiming the Saudis were simply 'obstructionist'.

25 Another change in working practices was that, after Rio, the secretariat was given significantly more autonomy. Instead of simply producing summaries of interventions made by delegations, it was now being given requests to come up with ideas for text on particular parts of the convention on which the COP would have to decide. For example, at the February–March 1993 meeting, the secretariat was asked to prepare documents on the meaning of 'agreed full incremental costs', a controversial element in deciding the criteria which developing countries would have to meet to get money from the financial mechanism. See INC (27 April 1993: paragraph 32 (g)).

26 The new Chair of the INC was Raul Estrada-Oyuela of Argentina. The new Co-Chairs of Working Group I were Mahmoud Ould El Ghaouth (Mauritania) and Cornelia Quennet (Germany), and those of Working Group II were Nobutoshi Akao (Japan) and Robert Van Lierop (Vanuatu). See INC (27 April 1993: 4).

27 One of the issues which some in the INC, including Estrada-Oyuela, the Chair, saw as a hindrance was that the IPCC refused to adjust the timetables for their next report to those of the INC, giving a resource for some delegations to suggest delaying a decision until the next report was out. See Pearce (1994a).

28 The proposal also amended the existing commitment to a firm stabilisation target. Articles 4.2 (a) and (b) say that emissions need only return to 1990 levels by the year 2000, but specify nothing about what is to happen after 2000.

29 *Climate Watch*, from where this quote is taken, is 'The Bulletin of the Global Climate Coalition', one of the main industry lobby groups involved in climate

change politics. The thinly veiled interests of coal and oil companies are fairly clear to see in its pages, behind attacks on the IPCC, or in apparent defence of developing countries' interests.

30   Oil-producing states also continued to try simply to slow negotiations down, again taking the floor more than other delegations, and introducing objections to particular texts even when they had no clear interest in them (see, for example, *ECO*, 25 August 1993: 2). One clear example was to try to use scientific uncertainty to its limit, often in the most blatant manner. For example, at the Berlin COP, Kuwait produced a climatologist, working for the *Oil Ministry*, who argued that if global warming was occurring, then oil and coal could not be blamed for it (*Guardian*, 29 March 1995).

31   An additional factor was the splintering of industrial interests. The Global Climate Coalition and the Climate Council had been the main industry participants in the INC, representing mainly coal and oil interests. However, a development within INC 10 was the emergence of an industry lobby in favour of the convention and further CO_2 reductions (*ECO*, 24 August 1994: 4; 26 August 1994: 1). There was now a wide coalition of industrial interests favouring action on climate change. One consisted of parts of the insurance industry, scared of losses from freak weather (and whose interests have been forwarded, interestingly, by Greenpeace). Another was the 'sunrise industries' of renewables and energy efficiency. Yet another was the gas industry, which has come to see itself as the immediate beneficiary of responses to climate change, as the fossil fuel with the lowest carbon content. The gas industry's interest has also split the oil industry, as there are considerable links between the two (Grubb, 1995: 3–4). While the International Chamber of Commerce (ICC), industry's main overarching global organisation, opposed strengthening the commitments in the convention until existing ones had been assessed, and 'dangerous interference with the climate system' (United Nations, 1992: Article 2) had been defined, the tone of their address to the Berlin COP was considerably less hostile to CO_2 than coal or oil interests would have wanted (ICC, 1995). The World Energy Council, an umbrella body representing energy industries and governments around the world, was also very favourable to the Berlin outcome (WEC, 1995b).

32   See, for example, the selection reproduced in Climate Network Europe (1995).

4   THE POLITICS BEHIND THE NEGOTIATIONS

1   This chapter draws on and builds from an earlier work by myself and Michael Grubb (Paterson and Grubb, 1992).

2   The term 'limit' had a specific meaning in the climate negotiations which I follow here. It was used as an umbrella term to describe any action which would negatively affect future ghg emissions. This could therefore include actions which simply limited the rate of future growth of emissions.

3   There were, of course, differences within this group on a number of issues. For example, there were disagreements: about whether emissions should be counted on a gross or net (emissions minus absorption through sinks) basis; over whether to count CO_2 only or also other greenhouse gases; and

concerning whether states should be allowed to implement commitments 'jointly'. For a fuller discussion of these questions, see Bodansky (1993).

4   This is not necessarily to suggest that the South acted as a bloc. Bodansky (1992: 7) points out that, at the December 1991 session, the G77 broke down almost completely. Several writers have focused on the groups which have emerged within the developing countries, a focus which will be followed up here (see Nitze (1990), Ramakrishna (1990), Bodansky (1992), and Paterson and Grubb (1992)). However, around the issue of financial resources and technology transfer, the focus of much of this section, developing countries remained united.

5   For a useful discussion of how the usage of sovereignty as a principle has changed in environmental negotiations from Stockholm to UNCED, see Pallemaerts (1993).

6   This occurred only very late on in the negotiations. The draft drawn up in the middle of the resumed Fifth Session still included the sovereignty principle, with the words 'Not Fully Agreed' put in brackets in front of it. But by the time of the full convention text drawn up at the end of the session, it had simply been withdrawn. See INC (5 May 1992 and 27 May 1992).

7   I have no direct evidence as to why this was. The most plausible explanation is simply that the developing countries realised they were not going to have the demand met, although presumably it is possible they were persuaded to drop it while other issues were accepted by the North.

8   Some estimates put the figure as up to US $100bn annually. See Brown *et al.* (1988).

9   The GEF was a body set up in November 1990 to finance projects to deal with four areas of global environmental concern – climate change, biodiversity, international water pollution, and ozone depletion. It is organised jointly by the World Bank, UNEP and the UN Development Programme, although it is administered on a day-to-day basis by the World Bank, and – in particular before Rio – the Bank was assumed by most observers to dominate its operations (*Tiempo* No.4, February 1992: 21; Thomas, 1992: 87–91). For a general review of how the GEF has worked in relation to the climate treaty, see Mott (1993). Mott also suggests that GEF activities related to global warming have become much more under the control of the convention's bodies, following its restructuring after UNCED. See also Rowlands (1994: 196–200).

10 In the initial submissions to the INC Secretariat, only Norway mentioned the GEF by name (INC, 26 June 1991: 63); however, throughout the negotiations, it became clear that industrialised countries would insist on the GEF being used.

11 INC (26 June 1991: 58–9). On the arrangements for the Montreal Protocol as amended at London in 1990, see Benedick (1991: chs 12–13). After Rio, the GEF was in fact restructured along similar lines, although slightly more in donor countries' favour. The voting procedure became one where decisions have to be taken by double majority, as in the Montreal Protocol, but where the first majority is of donor countries, voting weighted by financial contributions, and the second majority is in a committee, made up of half industrialised and half developing countries. See Rowlands (1994: 204).

12   Mohamed T. El-Ashry was Chair of the GEF, and Environment Director of the World Bank.

13   The range of critiques is huge. A classic critique of its whole operations is Hancock's *Lords of Poverty* (1991). Thomas (1992: 79–91) provides a good overview of the main points regarding environmental questions and how the World Bank has tried to respond. On developing country and NGO positions on the GEF, see Inter Press Service (1991), or Kuroda (1992).

14   Other analyses, although not making the point explicitly, support this claim. For example, Fish and South (1994) give eight criteria to account for the climate policies of industrialised countries, five of which are energy/economic in nature. Rowland's (1994) useful comparison of climate politics in the US and Germany also focuses largely on the political economy of energy, as does Beuermann and Jaeger's (1996: 26) discussion of Germany.

15   Of course, these latter two are largely contradictory since, in practice, humans can significantly affect sinks only for CO_2.

16   It should be noted, however, that at least the Saudi position was different early on. Saudi Arabia took a leading role in the IPCC (occupying one of the Vice-Chair positions). As late as the Noordwijk Conference in November 1989, the Saudis were stating that global warming was 'a life and death issue for considerable areas of the earth', acknowledged that CO_2 was clearly the 'main culprit', and that greenhouse gas emissions should be stabilised or reduced (statement of Prince Fahad Bin Abdullah Al Saud, quoted in Bodansky, 1993: 467, note 100). Bodansky (1993: 467) states that the Saudi position had reverted to the one outlined in the main text by the end of 1990.

17   Figures calculated from BP (1993: 4–8). The figures for natural gas and coal are less extreme. However, excluding the major producers (UK and Germany for coal, UK, the Netherlands and Norway for gas), Western European countries remain dependent on imports for about 75 per cent of their consumption of gas, and 56 per cent of their coal (BP, 1993: 20–2 [for gas], 28–9 [for coal]).

18   It is worth noting also that this effect has varied according to the character of the existing balance of payments. It is certainly reasonable to explain Japan's slightly weaker commitment to CO_2 stabilisation (see Chapter 2, Table 1) than that of the EC countries in terms of Japan's already huge balance-of-payments surplus. The climate negotiations coincided with wider pressure on Japan (from the US in particular) to reduce this surplus.

19   The Netherlands is a significant (for its size) natural gas exporter. Gas is the fossil fuel expected to be used more in the short term in response to global warming, having the lowest carbon intensity of the fossil fuels.

20   This is not to suggest that this factor is the only one at play. Others, such as taxes and world prices, are also important.

21   Figures measured are Total Fuel Consumption (measured in million tons of oil equivalent) per US $1000 at 1985 prices. See IEA (1992b: 28).

22   This is not meant to be a technological determinist argument that the strength of the oil and coal lobbies is solely due to the abundance of fossil fuels in the US. The US polity is in general one dominated by interest group politics (Cigler and Loomis, 1991). In addition, it should be remembered that, as for developing countries, financial constraints, in this case in the form of the huge budget deficit, have acted as a strong constraint on politically

feasible options for US politicians, even those who wished to act. The gross US Federal Government debt in 1992 was $1tn, while the deficit on the 1992 budget alone was $399.7bn (US Bureau of the Censuses, 1992: 315). However, looking after Rio, the Clinton Administration has clearly been unable to move anywhere near as far as proclamations before the election might have suggested he would, primarily because of the power of the energy lobbies.

23   The upper limit of this range rapidly became the figure commonly cited in economic discussions of global warming (e.g. *Economist*, 19 May 1990: 94).

24   See, for example, Mors (1991: 93–5). Mors shows figures similar to those given by US writers, with GDP losses of 0.5–1.5 per cent for a 20 per cent reduction in CO_2 emissions (1991: 95), but clearly has a greater sense that this is not a particular problem. At the time of that publication, Mors was Head of Sector in the Directorate-General for Economic and Financial Affairs in the European Commission. Skjaerseth (1994: 27–8) also suggests that the Commission believed 15–20 per cent cuts could be achieved without 'major macroeconomic costs'.

25   This also reflects another factor not related to energy dependence: that is the differing strengths of neoliberal ideology within governments in the US and Europe. Certainly much of their opposition was to the rigidity imposed by targets on individual countries, although it is certainly reasonable to argue that some of this at least masked a hostility to any strong political response in general. The dominance of neoliberal ideology in the US throughout the 1980s made it more easy for them to identify a targets-based approach as economically inefficient, which – if neoliberal assumptions hold – strictly speaking it is. Other states, particularly the Europeans and Japanese, held more pragmatic or different ideological positions on the merits of what remains an arbitrary politically determined target.

26   The personal hostility of Bush's Chief of Staff, John Sununu, to any climate action was also widely noted by observers. One suggested that Sununu's 'impatience [with environmentalists] stops just short of contempt' (Andresen, 1991: 20). Himself a former university scientist, he was famed for running Global Climate Models on his own personal computer to demonstrate their uselessness. Sununu's departure was widely held to herald a change in US policy.

27   Developing countries have approximately 75 per cent of the world's population.

28   Hyder was head of the Pakistani delegation to the climate negotiations, and Pakistan held the Chair of the G77 during a crucial period of the negotiations, during the fourth (Geneva, December 1991) and fifth (New York, February 1992) sessions, taking over from Ghana.

29   India did propose a text at the resumed fifth session in May 1992, which included reductions in emissions after 2000 (Dasgupta, 1994: 143), but this was not a prominent part of the Indian position.

30   IPCC figures give a projected sea level rise of between 30 and 100 cm by 2100, with a mean of 65cm, in business-as-usual scenarios (Houghton *et al.*, 1990: xi).

31   Many of these islands, especially those in the Pacific, also have quasi-colonial relationships with the United States. Joni Seager (1993: 68) reports that, in

the Marshall Islands, proposals have been made to import 34 billion pounds of household waste from the US which, according to the Marshall Islands President, in addition to generating much needed income, would help protect the islands against future sea-level rise.

32   Skjaerseth (1994: 36) suggests that only in the Netherlands were concerns about climate impacts important. But his analysis is conducted purely at the immediate level of government policy and its considerations, whereas at the broader level of political culture, this factor seems to have been important.

33   See Warren (1992), or Grubb and Hope (1992). For the most comprehensive overview of climate politics in the EC, see Haigh (1996).

34   OPEC and the Gulf Cooperation Council also threatened to retaliate should the tax be introduced (*European Environment*, 1992: 1; *Financial Times*, 4 March 1992; Skjaerseth, 1994: 31).

35   This distrust was, however, successfully circumvented by Northern NGOs as they provided great assistance to many developing country delegations (especially AOSIS states) and to developing country NGOs, and generally supported the developing countries' position on financial resources and technology transfer.

5   ANARCHY, THE STATE AND POWER

1   Strange (1987: especially 559–64). See also Isabel Grunberg (1990: 476), who examines the 'paradox of the enduring popularity of hegemonic stability theory in the face of convincing challenges to its validity'.

2   Of course, a Gramscian notion of hegemony differs greatly and, in Chapter 8, I argue that it is much more useful.

3   This is leaving aside for the moment more general problems with neorealists' particular use of the concept of power.

4   It also then becomes more problematic to make Waltz's distinction between capabilities and the distribution of capabilities, a distinction he requires himself to make in order to avoid reintroducing 'unit-level' factors to his theory. However, the more complex a measure of power in an issue-area we are forced to try to use, the more difficult it becomes to maintain that distinction. When power has to be measured, rather than being something we can simply gauge in terms of the states' relative positions, we cannot avoid unit-level factors.

5   This is equivalent to Putnam's statement that 'the larger the perceived win-set [domestic coalition supporting a measure] of a negotiator, the more [s]he can be "pushed around" by the other level 1 [international] negotiators'. See Putnam (1988: 440).

6   This argument is elaborated in detail, and with some objections, by myself in Paterson (1992). I am no longer as convinced of the argument as I was when that article was written (in 1991).

7   This section largely ignores the game-theoretic work undertaken on global warming by economists. A number of studies of this sort have been done (Hoel, 1991; Barrett, 1992a, 1992b; Fankhauser and Kverndokk, 1992; Kverndokk, 1992). However, the focus of their work is on what an economically optimal (i.e. cost-efficient) agreement, and level of CO_2 reductions,

would look like, rather than on how game theory helps us to predict or explain cooperation. What some of the studies do tell us about (notwithstanding problems associated with some of the assumptions used), is the distribution of economic gains under various types of agreement, which will affect the political likelihood of cooperation, and the incentives for some actors which need to be generated.

I am also ignoring the broader literature on collective action problems with respect to the environment – a literature which often refers to the 'tragedy of the commons' or, less apocalyptically, to 'common property resources' (CPRs) (Hardin, 1968; Berkes, 1989; Ostrom, 1990; Keohane and Ostrom, 1995). Many of the features in those studies are similar to global environmental problems, and it would clearly be possible to apply the ideas of that literature (often contradictory, as Ostrom points out [1990: 8–13]) to global environmental problems. However, I have chosen not to focus on that literature and instead stick to IR works, for two reasons. One is that most of its current attention is on small-scale CPRs, for example local fisheries or forests. The actors in those situations are individuals. To translate this to the international arena where states are (usually regarded to be) the central actors would require a significant modification of the theory. The other is that the focus of the literature on CPRs is usually on those situations where the actors are 'heavily dependent on the CPR for economic returns' (Ostrom, 1990: 26). This is clearly not the case for global warming, at least not in the same way as fisheries are for individual fishers.

8 Most importantly regarding neorealism, there is a much less clear sense that the overall structure of the international system determines outcomes. It is the focus on anarchy which leads me to place them in this chapter.

9 Taylor (1987: ch. 1), however, argues that this feature is unimportant. I am grateful to Hugh Ward for pointing this out to me.

10 The notion of structure here is very different to that in Waltz. For Waltz, structure in international relations refers to the anarchic nature of the system, the like-nature of the units, and the distribution of capabilities among the units. For game theorists, structure refers to the structure of the incentives of different actors to behave in particular ways in a specific context (the 'pay-off matrix').

11 A wider debate also exists about the extent to which Waltz's neorealism depends on a rationality assumption. Waltz denies that it does but, as Keohane suggests, it is required if his theory of the balance of power is to work; see Keohane (1989d: 41, 46).

12 For an introduction to rational choice theory, see Elster (1986).

13 Fankhauser and Kverndokk (1992) modelled the global warming as a five-person game, the groups being the US, other OECDs, the USSR, China, and the rest of the world.

14 An additional problem here is that game-theoretic formulations such as that of Snidal (1985), based on the notion of a 'k-group' (the smallest group of actors which can collectively provide a public good), suffer from a similar problem to that experienced by hegemonic stability theory. That is to say, by focusing on the size of actors and examining the implications of differing distributions of size within the major states (as Snidal does schematically for the US, West Germany and Japan [1985: 598–612]), there is an assumption

that the bigger the state, the larger its interest is in the provision of the public good. As we saw for hegemonic stability theory, this does not hold in relation to global warming.

15   Certainly, many were aware of this problem during the negotiations, and suggested that their establishment under the UN General Assembly, rather than within UNEP, was a mistake (Ramakrishna, 1990; Sebenius, 1991). However, an institutionalist response would focus on the increased legitimacy of an UNGA treaty rather than a UNEP one. Thus Michael Zammit Cutajar, Executive Secretary of the INC, states that the fact that it became a *United Nations* convention is important. (Cutajar, personal communication, 5 August 1992.)

16   But see below for a possible qualification to this regarding the US.

17   Kverndokk (1992: 20–1) also assesses which groups of countries will be most likely to support differing methods of allocating reductions between states (tradeable permits allocated on a number of differing bases, or uniform percentage reductions).

18   The Bush administration repeatedly asserted that, in its view, the targets set by the EC and other countries were paper targets alone, not backed up by policy change or action. This could support an interpretation that they felt unconvinced that other states were themselves committed to cooperating.

19   This is described by Hugh Ward as 'Testing the Waters'. See Ward (1989).

20   The targets of Australia, Sweden and the UK all contain these qualifications. See IEA (1992b).

21   Another way of expressing this point is that Waltz's (1959) objections to 'Second Image' explanations of state behaviour do not apply, since these were aimed at internal explanations of state behaviour in matters of peace and war.

22   Such an objection would also apply to reformulations of the agent-structure problem from a structurationist perspective, since it remains dependent on a reasonably precise account of the structure, which cannot be given. Structuration theory would, however, give more latitude for the ambiguity of state interests and their co-determination by both internal and international factors. See Wendt (1987).

23   cf. Thomas (1987); Thomas (1992: ch. 4). See also Brown (1989); Mathews (1989); Imber (1991); Prins (1993); for a critique of the 'environmental security' approach, see Deudney (1990).

6   COOPERATION AND INSTITUTIONS

1   The account I am giving will focus on what both Keohane (1989) and Grieco (1988) have termed neoliberal institutionalism. For convenience, however, I shall in general simply use the term 'institutionalism' to refer to it, except when it is being contrasted with an earlier version of institutionalist theory.

2   See Snidal (1991) for the centrality of the 'relative gains debate' in debates between realists and institutionalists about the likelihood of international cooperation. Snidal makes some modifications, however, arguing that, if the game structure is not PD, and if there are large numbers of actors, relative gains become a less important constraint on cooperation.

3   Bull (1977). However, Bull's focus on rules and the institutions required to uphold them was relatively limited. His discussion of institutions in international society is limited to those of 'the balance of power, international law, the diplomatic mechanism, the managerial system, the managerial system of the great powers, and war' (1977: 74). These are certainly institutions in the sense in which Oran Young uses the term. However, a wider focus, such as that of Young, might generate the conclusion that institutions are even more prevalent in international society than Bull suggests.

4   This could be the case, even if such an international system emerged on the basis of a world of such actors, in the manner outlined by Axelrod (1984). He shows spontaneous cooperation to be clearly possible in a world of egoistic actors without central authority, and that, over time, such cooperation serves to generate norms for behaviour which alter the nature of the actors' preferences and perceived self-interest.

5   Arguably, this is not inconsistent with assumptions about utility maximising behaviour. Axelrod's (1984) discussion of the 'live and let live' system in the trenches during the First World War showed how utility maximising could lead to the emergence of norms. In a later article (1986), he showed this in more general terms, although it is important to note that there he explicitly states he has only a very limited rationality assumption (actors keep doing what seems to work and only change if a strategy fails). The important point here seems to me to be that, once instituted, norms can serve to affect strongly how actors define utility maximising within a particular context.

6   Another tension is between Young's and Keohane's definitions of institutions. Predominantly, however, this is simply a matter of emphasis. Young's focus is on institutions as *social practices* while, for Keohane, it is on *sets of rules*, which simply constrain practices. For Young, rules are simply connected with roles, while for Keohane, rules prescribe roles. These differences of emphasis are not greatly significant, but possibly indicate differing assumptions about the force of institutions.

7   The other approach is the rationalistic approach, suggesting institutions come from absolute gains maximising self-interested states.

8   An additional advantage of the third of these positions is that it does not need to rely on a prior assumption that it is reasonable to ascribe the characteristics of an individual to the state. The problem of making this projection of utility maximising behaviour on to organisations is familiar within rational choice theory. See Elster (1986a: 3–4). See also Wendt (1992: 397) on problems with this state–individual isomorphism. I am grateful to John Barry for reminding me of the importance of this.

9   It is of course hard to make such a rigid distinction, which may be why writers from the institutionalist and epistemic community perspectives see their work as compatible (Haas, Keohane and Levy, 1993).

10 Compare, for example, the Montreal Protocol negotiations, where small numbers of delegations met in a relatively informal setting, enabling much more flexible and imaginative bargaining. See Benedick (1991).

11 A similar objection applies, although less strongly, to Ward's interpretation (1993: 203–4) of the strategy of the US and China as one of establishing a reputation for toughness within a Chicken game. (Bodansky [1993: 489] also, although more colloquially, uses a Chicken metaphor to describe the

negotiations.) This seems to me to be more convincing if a common under-standing between states of the game structure (and, by implication, of state preferences) can be presumed, which I have suggested here cannot be done.

12 Indeed, an analogy with the oft-quoted statement about the former Soviet Union seems appropriate: 'It is only part in jest that one says "The United States may *have* a military–industrial complex, but the Soviet Union *is* a military–industrial complex"' (Bialer, 1976: 37). Similarly, Saudi Arabia does not have an oil industry because it is one. I am indebted to Neil Robinson for this citation.

13 Against the initial plans of the EC, the tax proposal finally included significant exemptions for some industries, and was made conditional on similar measures being implemented by the EC's main competitors.

7   SCIENCE, POLITICS AND GLOBAL WARMING

1 Adler does not define 'consummatory values', which is a rather vague term. I would interpret it to mean values or norms which are guides to actions, i.e. those which can be 'consummated'.

2 This is leaving aside for the moment any normative considerations which may be associated with the dominant influence of scientists and technicians, such as problems of technocracy and democracy. See, for example, Ellul (1964); Marcuse (1964); Habermas (1968), especially 'The Scientization of Politics and Public Opinion' and 'Science and Technology as "Ideology"'.

3 The position adopted by most writers using this approach has emphasised the social construction of knowledge. See *International Organization* (1992: passim).

4 There is clearly a tension in this intention. When epistemic communities are analysed there is a clear recognition that a hard fact/value distinction collapses. The communities have normative goals which imbue the *science*; they are not simply add-on extras. This ambiguity is that, while the writers – by and large explicitly – adopt such a constructionist position when analysing the relationship between science and politics, they still construe them as separate spheres of life, with science as embodying rationality, and politics as being messy and irrational.

5 It should also be noted that the approach is more specific than the more general literature on the relationship between science and political decision-making, which specifies a number of broad conditions for scientific advice to contribute to decision-making. See Underdal (1989).

6 I mean by this either that they have secured positions in official state bureaucracies, or that they have access to channels of information dissem-ination which policy-makers use but which are outside the formal channels of state bureaucracies; e.g. regular NGO briefings and seminars, and so on.

7 For other such normative statements in the declaration, see SWCC, 1990: Part IA para. 9, Part II paras 1.2, 2.3, 3.3, and 4.2.

8 Wynne (1994), and O'Riordan and Jordan (1996), both suggest that the IPCC made discussion of these sorts of political features of global warming invisible by turning it into a techno-scientific discourse. While I would agree that, if societies rely purely on scientists for their sources of knowledge about global warming, this may have the effect of de-politicising it in undesirable

ways, this seems unfair as a direct criticism of the IPCC. The quotes given in the text show how they were clearly aware of such aspects of global warming.

9   It is also inconsistent with his application of the model to ozone depletion in the same article in *Millennium*. At the equivalent point in those negotiations (c.1984), the epistemic community had even vaguer ideas about the implications of ozone depletion than does the one for global warming.

10   For example, through the IPCC Update (Houghton *et al.*, 1992). Bert Bolin, Chair of the IPCC, delivered the main conclusions of this to the negotiators directly, in plenary time, at the negotiating session in New York in February 1992.

11   It is also obvious from what follows that there is a significant overlap between this account, generated by institutionalist analysis, as given in Chapter 6. However, it seems to me that both are needed to do justice to each theory, and hopefully I have made clear the differing theoretical positions through the emphasis and interpretation of each event.

12   This is not to suggest that the scientific consensus is merely a construct of the members of the epistemic community's own preferences. It is merely to suggest that the fact that members of the epistemic community held beliefs that global warming was a possible occurrence affected the direction of scientific research and subsequent knowledge.

13   Or at least, what became widely perceived to be a scientific consensus. For discussions on this see Lunde (1991). On the way in which WMO actively fostered a consensus, see also Boehmer-Christiansen (1994a: 153–5).

14   For example, an analysis of the delegates to the 5th Session of the INC in New York in February 1992 reveals the following: from industrialised countries, 45 per cent of heads of delegations were from Foreign Offices, and only 34 per cent were from Environment or Meteorology Departments (and of these latter, all the *meteorologists* were from Eastern Europe, including the Russian Federation). By contrast, only 22 per cent of heads of delegations from developing countries were from Foreign Offices, while 47 per cent were from Environment or Meteorology Departments, and a much greater proportion of these were meteorologists (note: this is an approximate analysis). A certain amount of judgement has to be used in some cases as to who was the head of delegation, since UN Ambassadors were always cited first although they hardly ever participated in the negotiations. Calculated from INC (24 February 1992).

15   For other interventions by Bolin in the negotiations, see, for example, *ECO*, 10 December 1992: 1; 9 February 1994: 1; 24 August 1994: 2; Bolin (1994).

16   For example, the SWCC Declaration states that 'industrialised countries *must* implement reductions even greater than those required, on average, for the globe as a whole' in order to allow developing countries' emissions to grow. This is worded significantly more strongly than the convention. See SWCC (1990: Part II, para. 4.1).

17   The epistemic communities approach avoids the former of these problems to an extent, being consistent with the notion that scientists can be entrepreneurs in relation to policymakers, and also that they often advance clear, normative positions. But despite some social constructionist statements, it still implicitly assumes that the knowledge which scientists produce is as it is in the conventional notion of science – value-free, objective, and so on.

18   This does not necessarily sound particularly conspiratorial. However, she claims in an earlier piece (1994a), for example, while discussing WMO: 'Have they been "taken over" by the managers of Big Science to advance national research agendas in the name of global problem solving...?'. She suggests that this process of being 'taken over' has meant that WMO has become involved in research coordination, rather than policymaking. Yet WMO, as we saw in Chapter 2, has been involved in coordinating research since at least 1882!

19   This is perhaps unfair to some of these writers, in that they do try to distance themselves from positivism. However, the 'political whirl' quote does seem to indicate that the project is about identifying in a clear way *causes* of particular pieces of international cooperation.

8   A POLITICAL ECONOMY OF GLOBAL WARMING

1   I should perhaps offer a caveat here that, for many, I may be too cavalier and imprecise in using the term historical materialism to describe some of the arguments in this chapter. Certainly, some of the themes, such as globalisation, are by no means unique to this approach. However, I do think that this framework provides the best overall one for developing these ideas. 'Political economy' would be an alternative description of the focus of the chapter, but this is rather imprecise, and I wanted to avoid the ambiguity of leaving out liberal and realist positions in the discussion. I should also perhaps add that the discussion here does not mean that I accept Marxist arguments wholesale. Many problems remain within that framework, in particular its class reductionism, its universalistic pretensions, determinism (not entirely resolved by Gramsci) and so on. See Barrett (1991: 52–7) among others, for a review of these problems.

2   Jessop remains ambiguous on whether this is a central feature of the capitalist state. On the previous page of *State Theory* (1990: 359) he contradicts the quote given in the main text here. He asserts that the capitalist state operates 'in terms of prevailing state projects and definitions of "illusory community"', and denies that the capitalist has a necessary task 'to create, maintain and restore the conditions of capital accumulation'. The point here, perhaps, is that much of the ambiguity derives from the fact that, although state managers, for Jessop, necessarily aim to promote accumulation, this does not specify the strategies they follow, since these depend on their understandings of the conditions for successful accumulation, which will change over time, and it also of course does not mean that the strategies they adopt will be successful (1990: 354).

3   One important point here is that this need not be a determinist position, since the state may be influenced by only fractions of capital rather than by capital as a whole, and policies will necessarily benefit some parts of capital more than others (Jessop, 1990: 357).

4   This increased in 1992, as the IPCC downgraded the role of CFCs (Houghton *et al.*, 1992). For a review of arguments for focusing on CO_2 in responding to global warming, see Paterson (1992a).

5   The terms used vary. Fordism and organised capitalism are commonly used to describe the earlier period. Post-Fordism, disorganised capitalism and flexible accumulation have all been used to describe the latter period.

6   Different writers obviously emphasise different features and give more extensive lists of Fordism's features. See, for example, Harvey (1990: Part II), and Lash and Urry (1987), among others. I give this simple list for brevity.

7   This list is condensed from Harvey's third table outlining the nature of these shifts, which derives from Swyngedouw (1986). See Harvey (1990: 177–9).

8   Perhaps the most comprehensive study within a Gramscian framework is Overbeek (1993). For a detailed study of the UK, see Gamble (1988).

9   Of course, a debate raged about whether dependency theory was Marxist or not, centred around the focus of many dependency theorists on relations of exchange (e.g. Emmanuel, 1972) rather than relations of production (Laclau, 1977; Warren, 1980).

10   Works by Jesse Ribot on regulation of charcoal markets in Senegal, and by Nancy Lee Peluso on forestry policy in Kenya and Indonesia, graphically illustrate this point in relation to environmental problems. See Ribot (1993) and Peluso (1993), and the book in which they are contained more generally; Lipschutz and Conca (1993).

11   She gives this as a conservative estimate, excluding South–North flows such as repatriated profits or dividends for Northern investors.

12   The figures for Latin American countries are for 1988; those for African ones for 1987.

13   This is both in the sense that deforestation directly releases CO_2 and CH_4 into the atmosphere, and that forests act as CO_2 sinks, lost through deforestation.

14   'Greenhouse forcing' refers to a measure which includes all greenhouse gases but allows for factors such as how powerful a greenhouse gas is in heating the atmosphere, and how long it stays in the atmosphere.

9   CONCLUSIONS

1   Although the wording in the convention about states' obligations with regard to CO_2 emissions are notoriously vague, some basic criteria on whether states comply with them or not exist. While the claim made by David Fisk (head of the UK delegation), that the final negotiated text was 'virtually indistinguishable' from an absolute guarantee to stabilise emissions, is unduly optimistic, Bill Hare of the Australian Conservation Foundation is right to point out that industrialised states are committed under the Climate Convention to adopting policies which, in theory, are capable of stabilising their emissions (Hare, 1992). Thus a basic yardstick against which to evaluate states' actions exists.

2   Most of the proposed schemes appear to assume bilateral trading. The nearest to a multilateral system is a 'clearing-house mechanism' which would provide information to participants about the 'going rates' for permits, and thereby reduce transaction costs. See UNCTAD (1992).

3   This would, of course, primarily be to do with procedural justice, such as norms of non-aggression or non-intervention.

Bibliography

AALCC (1991) *Framework Convention on Climate Change: An Overview*, Nairobi: African–Asian Legal Consultative Committee, 24 October.

Adler, E. (1992) 'The emergence of cooperation: national epistemic communities and the international evolution of the idea of nuclear arms control', *International Organization*, 46, 1: 101–46.

African Centre for Technology Studies (1990) *The Nairobi Declaration on Climatic Change, International Conference on Global Warming and Climatic Change: African Perspectives, 2–4 May 1990*, Nairobi: Acts Press.

Agarwal, A. and Narain, S. (1990) *Global Warming in an Unequal World – a Case of Environmental Colonialism*, New Delhi: Centre for Science and Environment.

Aglietta, M. (1979) *A theory of capitalist regulation*, London: New Left Books.

Al-Sabban, M. S. (1991) 'The impact of response measures by industrialized countries on the world economy', in B. Flannery and R. Clarke (eds) *Global Climate Change: A Petroleum Industry Perspective*, London: International Petroleum Industry Environmental Conservation Association.

Andresen, Steinar (1991) 'US greenhouse policy: reactionary or realistic?', *International Challenges*, 11, 1: 17–24.

Andresen, S. and Ostreng, W. (eds) (1989) *International Resource Management: the role of science and politics*, London: Belhaven.

AOSIS (1992) *The Status of Negotiations on a Framework Convention on Climate Change*, New York: Alliance of Small Island States.

Arrhenius, Svante (1896) 'On the Influence of Carbonic Acid in the Air on the Temperature of the Ground', *Philosophical Magazine*, 41, 251: 236–76.

—— (1908) *Worlds in the Making: The Evolution of the Universe*, New York: Harper.

Ashley, Richard (1986) 'The Poverty of Neorealism', in Robert O. Keohane (ed.) *Neorealism and Its Critics*, New York: Columbia University Press.

Athanasiou, Tom (1991) *US Politics and Global Warming*, Westfield NJ: Open Magazine Pamphlet Series, Pamphlet 14.

Atwood, Wallace W. Jr. (1959) 'The International Geophysical Year in Retrospect', *Department of State Bulletin*, 40, May: 682–9.

Augelli, E. and Murphy, C. N. (1988) *America's Quest for Supremacy and the Third World*, London: Pinter.

Axelrod, Robert (1984) *The Evolution of Cooperation*, New York: Basic Books.

—— (1986) 'An evolutionary approach to norms', *American Political Science Review*, 80, 4: 1095–111.

Axelrod, Robert and Keohane, Robert O. (1986) 'Achieving Cooperation under Anarchy: Strategies and Institutions', in Kenneth A. Oye (ed.) *Cooperation under Anarchy*, Princeton: Princeton University Press.

Baldwin, D. A. (1993) *Neorealism and Neoliberalism: The Contemporary Debate*, New York: Columbia University Press.

Balling, R. (1992) *The Heated Debate: Greenhouse Predictions versus Climate Reality*, San Francisco: Pacific Research Institute.

Barrett, Michèle (1991) *The Politics of Truth: From Marx to Foucault*, Cambridge: Polity.

Barrett, Scott (1992a) 'Side-payments in a Global Warming Treaty', in OECD *Convention on Climate change: Economic Aspects of Negotiations*, Paris: OECD.

—— (1992b) 'Freerider deterrence in a Global Warming Treaty', in OECD *Convention on Climate change: Economic Aspects of Negotiations*, Paris: OECD.

Baumgartner, T. and Midttun, A. (1987) *The Politics of Energy Forecasting*, Oxford: Clarendon Press.

Beardsley, Tim (1990) 'Profile: Dr. Greenhouse', *Scientific American*, December: 16–17.

Benedick, Richard Elliot (1991) *Ozone Diplomacy: New Directions in Safeguarding the Planet*, Cambridge MA: Harvard University Press.

Bergesen, H. O. (1991) 'A Legitimate Social Order in a "Greenhouse" World: Some Basic Requirements', *International Challenges*, 11, 2: 21–9.

Bergesen, H. O. and Estrada, Javier (1994) *Environmental Issues and how they affect Oil Companies*, Oslo: Fridtjof Nansen Institute.

Berkes, Fikrit (ed.) (1989) *Common Property Resources: Ecology and Community-Based Sustainable Development*, London: Belhaven.

Berreen, Jim and Meyer, Aubrey (1992) 'A Package Marked "Return to Sender": Some Problems with the Climate Convention', *Network 92*, 18: 6–7.

Beuermann, Christine and Jaeger, Jill (1996) 'Climate Change Politics in Germany: how long will any double dividend last?', in T. O'Riordan (ed.) *The Politics of Climate Change in Europe*, London: Routledge.

Bialer, Seweryn (1976) 'Soviet political elite and internal developments in the USSR', in William Griffiths (ed.) *The Soviet Empire: Expansion and Detente*, Lexington MA: Lexington Books.

Bodansky, Daniel (1991) 'Report on the Third Session of the Intergovernmental Negotiating Committee for a Framework Convention on Climate Change', School of Law, University of Washington, November 19.

—— (1992) 'Draft Convention on Climate Change', *Environmental Policy and Law*, 22, 1: 5–15.

—— (1993) 'The United Nations Framework Convention on Climate Change: A Commentary', *Yale Journal of International Law*, 18, 2: 451–558.

Boehmer-Christiansen, S. (1993) 'Science Policy, the IPCC and the Climate Convention: The Codification of a Global Research Agenda', *Energy and Environment*, 4, 4: 362–407.

—— (1994a) 'Global Climate Protection Policy: the Limits of Scientific Advice – Part 1', *Global Environmental Change*, 4, 2: 140–59.

—— (1994b) 'Global Climate Protection Policy: the Limits of Scientific Advice – Part 2', *Global Environmental Change*, 4, 3: 185–200.

—— (1995a) 'Britain and the International Panel on Climate Change: The Impacts of Scientific Advice on Global Warming. Part I: Integrated Policy Analysis and the Global Dimension', *Environmental Politics*, 4, 1: 1–18.

—— (1995b) 'Britain and the International Panel on Climate Change: The Impacts of Scientific Advice on Global Warming. Part II: The Domestic Story of the British Response to Climate Change', *Environmental Politics*, 4, 2: 175–96.

Boehmer-Christiansen, Sonja and Skea, Jim (1991) *Acid Politics*, London: Belhaven.

Bolin, Bert (1994) 'Statement to the First Session of the Conference of the Parties to the UN Framework Convention on Climate Change', Berlin 28 March, Geneva: Intergovernmental Panel on Climate Change.

Bolin, Bert *et al.* (1986) *The greenhouse effect, climatic change and ecosystems*, Chichester: John Wiley & Sons.

Borione, Delphine and Ripert, Jean (1994) 'Exercising Common but Differentiated Responsibility', in I. M. Mintzer and J. A. Leonard (eds) *Negotiating Climate Change*, Cambridge: Cambridge University Press.

Boyle, Stewart and Ardill, John (1989) *The Greenhouse Effect: A Practical Guide to the World's Changing Climate*, London: Hodder & Stoughton.

BP (1993) *BP Statistical Review of World Energy*, London: British Petroleum.

Brookes, Warren (1989) 'The Global Warming Panic', *Forbes*, December 25: 96–102.

Brown, Chris (1992) *International Political Theory: New Normative Approaches*, Hemel Hempstead: Harvester Wheatsheaf.

Brown, Lester *et al.* (1988) *State of the World 1988*, New York: Norton.

Brown, Neville (1989) 'Climate, Ecology and Security', *Survival*, XXXI, 6: 519–32.

Bruce, J. P. (1990) *The Atmosphere of the Living Planet Earth*, Geneva: World Meteorological Organization.

—— (1991) 'The World Climate Programme: Achievements and Challenges', in J. Jaeger and H. L. Ferguson (eds) *Climate Change: Science, Impacts and Policy – Proceedings of the Second World Climate Conference*, Cambridge: Cambridge University Press.

Bull, Hedley (1977) *The Anarchical Society: A Study of Order in World Politics*, London: Macmillan.

Burnham, Peter (1994) 'Open Marxism and vulgar international political economy', *Review of International Political Economy*, 1, 2: 221–31.

Cain, Melinda L. (1983) 'Carbon dioxide and climate: Monitoring and the Search for Understanding', in D. Kay and K. Jacobson (eds) *Environmental Protection: The International Dimension*, Osmun: Allanheld.

Callendar, G. D. (1938) 'The artificial production of carbon dioxide and its influence on temperature', *Quarterly Journal of the Royal Meteorological Society*, 64: 223–40.

Cammack, P., Pool, D. and Tordoff, W. (1988) *Third World Politics: A Comparative Introduction*, London: Macmillan.

Cavender, J. and Jaeger, J. (1993) 'The History of Germany's Response to Climate Change', *International Environmental Affairs*, 5, 1: 3–18.

Cerny, Philip G. (1990) *The Changing Architecture of Politics: Structure, Agency, and the Future of the State*, London: Sage.

Chamberlain, T. C. (1899) 'An Attempt to Frame a Working Hypothesis of the Cause of Glacial Periods on an Atmospheric Basis', *Journal of Geology*, 7: 545–61.

Charles, Dan (1991) '"Petty" politics mars global warming conference', *New Scientist*, 23 February: 16.

✓ Chatterjee, Pratap and Finger, Matthias (1994) *The Earth Brokers: power, politics and world development*, London: Routledge.

Churchill, R. and Freestone, D. (1991) *International Law of Global Climate Change*, London: Graham & Trotman.

Cigler, Allan J. and Loomis, Burdett A. (1991) *Interest Group Politics*, Washington DC: Congressional Quarterly Press.

Clark, William C. (ed.) (1990) *Usable Knowledge For Managing Global Climatic Change*, Stockholm: Stockholm Environment Institute.

Clegg, Stewart (1989) *Frameworks of Power*, London: Sage.

Climate Network Europe (1995) *International Press Cuttings from the Berlin Summit, 28th March – 7th April 1995*, Brussels: Climate Network Europe.

Commonwealth Heads of Government (1989) *The Langkawi Declaration on the Environment*, Kuala Lumpur, Malaysia, October.

Cox, Robert W. (1986) 'Social Forces, States and World Orders: Beyond International Relations Theory', in Robert O. Keohane (ed.) *Neorealism and Its Critics*, New York: Columbia University Press.

Daly, Glyn (1991) 'The discursive construction of economic space: logics of organization and disorganization', *Economy and Society*, 20, 1: 79–102.

Daniel, Howard (1973) *One Hundred Years of International Cooperation in Meteorology, 1873–1973*, Geneva: World Meteorological Organization.

Dasgupta, Chandreshekhar (1994) 'The Climate Change Negotiations', in I. M. Mintzer and J. A. Leonard (eds) *Negotiating Climate Change*, Cambridge: Cambridge University Press.

Davies, David A. (1972) 'The role of the WMO in Environmental Issues', *International Organization*, 26, 2: 327–36.

—— (1979) 'Foreword', in WMO *Proceedings of the World Climate Conference – A Conference of Experts on Climate and Mankind, 12–23 February 1979*, WMO Publication no. 537, Geneva: World Meteorological Organization.

Declaration of the Hague (1989), The Hague, the Netherlands.

Dessler, David (1989) 'What's at Stake in the Agent-Structure Debate?' *International Organization*, 43: 441–74.

Deudney, Daniel (1990) 'The Case Against Linking Environmental Degradation and National Security', *Millennium*, 19, 3: 461–76.

Djoghlaf, Ahmed (1994) 'The Beginnings of an International Climate Law', in I. M. Mintzer and J. A. Leonard (eds) *Negotiating Climate Change*, Cambridge: Cambridge University Press.

Doniger, David (1992) 'US Wall About to Crumble?', *ECO*, 19 February.

Doran, Peter (1993) 'The Earth Summit (UNCED): Ecology as Spectacle', *Paradigms*, 7, 1: 55–65.

Dorfman, Robert (1991) 'Protecting the Global Environment: An Immodest Proposal', *World Development*, 19, 1: 103–10.

Dowdeswell, Elizabeth and Kinley, Richard J. (1994) 'Constructive Damage to the Status Quo', in I. M. Mintzer and J. A. Leonard (eds) *Negotiating Climate Change*, Cambridge: Cambridge University Press.

Drainville, André C. (1994) 'International political economy in the age of open Marxism', *Review of International Political Economy*, 1, 1: 105–32.

Earth Negotiations Bulletin (1995) 'A Summary Report on the First Conference of the Parties to the Framework Convention on Climate Change', *Earth Negotiations Bulletin*, 12, 21, 10 April.

Eden, Sally E. (1994) 'Using sustainable development: the business case', *Global Environmental Change*, 4, 2: 160–7.

Eikeland, P. O. (1993) 'The shaping of US Energy Policy', *International Challenges*, 13, 4: 3–16.

El-Ashry, Mohamed T. (1992) 'The GEF and its Future', *Network 92*, 14: 5.

Ellul, Jacques (1964) *The Technological Society*, New York: Alfred A. Knopf.

Elster, Jon (ed.) (1986) *Rational Choice*, Oxford: Basil Blackwell.

—— (1986a) 'Introduction', in Jon Elster (ed.) (1986) *Rational Choice*, Oxford: Basil Blackwell.

Emmanuel, A. (1972) *Unequal Exchange: A Study in the Imperialism of Trade*, New York: Monthly Review Press.

Enloe, Cynthia (1989) *Bananas, Beaches and Bases: Making Feminist Sense of International Relations*, Berkeley: University of California Press.

European Environment (1992) Editorial, 2, 4: 1.

Fankhauser, Samuel and Kverndokk, Snorre (1992) *The Global Warming Game – Simulations of a CO_2 Reduction Agreement*, CSERGE GEC Working Paper 92–01, University of East Anglia, Norwich.

Faulks, John (1991), 'Small island states strengthen their position', *Tiempo: Global Warming and the Third World*, 2, July.

Fish, A. and South, D. (1994) 'Industrialized Countries and Greenhouse Gas Emissions', *International Environmental Affairs*, 6, 1: 14–43.

Fisher, Diane (ed.) (1990) *Options For Reducing Greenhouse Gas Emissions*, Stockholm: Stockholm Environment Institute.

Flannery, B. and Clarke, R. (1991) *Global Climate Change: A Petroleum Industry Perspective*, London: International Petroleum Industry Environmental Conservation Association.

Fourier, J. (1827) 'Memoire sur Les Temperatures du Globe Terrestre et des Espace Planetaires', *Memoires de l'academie Royal des Sciences de l'Institut de France*, VII: 659–704.

Freestone, D. (1994) 'The Road from Rio: International Environmental Law after the Earth Summit', *Journal of Environmental Law*, 6, 2: 193–218.

French, Hilary (1992) *After the Earth Summit: The Future of Environmental Governance*, Worldwatch Paper 107, Washington DC: Worldwatch Institute.

Froebel, F., Heinrichs, J. and Kreye, O. (1980) *The new international division of labour*, Cambridge: Cambridge University Press.

Gamble, Andrew (1988) *The free economy and the strong state*, London: Macmillan.

Gardner, Richard N (1992) *Negotiating Survival: Four Priorities After Rio*, New York: Council on Foreign Relations Press.

GARP (1975) *The Physical Basis of Climate and Climate Modelling – Reports of the International Study Conference in Stockholm, 29 July – 10 August 1974*, Geneva: World Meteorological Organization/ International Council of Scientific Unions, GARP No. 16.

George, Susan (1988) *A Fate Worse Than Debt*, London: Penguin.

—— (1992) *The Debt Boomerang: How Third World Debt Harms Us All*, London: Pluto Press.

Gill, Stephen and Law, David (1988) *The Global Political Economy: Perspectives, Problems and Policies*, Brighton: Wheatsheaf.

—— (1993) 'Global hegemony and the structural power of capital', in Stephen Gill (ed.) *Gramsci, historical materialism and international relations*, Cambridge: Cambridge University Press.

Gilpin, Robert (1987) *The Political Economy of International Relations*, Princeton NJ: Princeton University Press.

Gramsci, Antonio (1971) 'Fordism and Americanism', in *Selections from the Prison Notebooks*, London: Lawrence & Wishart.

Gray, C. Boyden and Rivkin Jr., David B. (1991) 'A "no regrets" environmental policy', *Foreign Policy* 83: 47–65.

Greene, Owen and Salt, Julian (1992) 'Verification and Information Exchange in the Development of an Effective Climate Change Convention: The Agenda after UNCED', paper presented to IRNES Conference on Perspectives on the Environment: Research and Action in the 1990s, Leeds University, September 14–15.

Greenpeace International (1992) *International Environmental Issues: President Bush's Irresponsible Actions*, Washington DC: Greenpeace International, February.

Gribbin, John (1990) *Hothouse Earth: The Greenhouse Effect and Gaia*, London: Bantam Press.

Grieco, Joseph M. (1988) 'Anarchy and the limits of cooperation: a realist critique of the newest liberal institutionalism', *International Organization*, 42, 3, 485–507.

Grubb, Michael (1989) *The Greenhouse Effect: Negotiating Targets*, London: Royal Institute of International Affairs.

—— (1990) *Energy Policies and the Greenhouse Effect: Volume One*, London: Dartmouth/ Royal Institute of International Affairs.

—— (1992) 'The heat is on', *The Higher*, June 5: 16.

—— (1995) 'The Berlin Climate Conference: Outcome and Implications', Briefing Paper No.21, London: Royal Institute of International Affairs.

—— (1995a) 'Seeking fair weather: ethics and the international debate on climate change', *International Affairs*, 71, 3: 463–96.

Grubb, Michael and Hope, Chris (1992) 'EC climate policy: where there's a will . . .', *Energy Policy*, November: 1110–14.

Grubb, Michael and Steen, Nicola (1991) *Pledge and Review Processes: Possible Components of a Climate Convention, Report of a Workshop held 2 August 1991*, London: Royal Institute of International Affairs.

Grubb, M., Koch, M., Munson, A., Sullivan, F. and Thomson, K. (1993) *The Earth Summit Agreements: A Guide and Assessment*, London: Earthscan.

Grubb, M., Sebenius, J. K., Magalhaes, A. and Subak, S. (1992) 'Sharing the Burden', in Irving Mintzer (ed.) *Confronting Climate Change: Risks, Implications and Responses*, Cambridge: Cambridge University Press.

Grubb, M. J., Victor, D. G. and Hope, C. (1991) 'Pragmatics in the Greenhouse', *Nature*, 5 December: 348–50.

Grunberg, Isabelle (1990) 'Exploring the "myth" of hegemonic stability', *International Organization*, 44, 4: 431–77.

Haas, Ernst B. (1980) 'Why Collaborate? Issue-Linkage and International Regimes', *World Politics*, 32, 3: 356–405.

Haas, Peter M. (1989) 'Do regimes matter? Epistemic communities and Mediterranean pollution control', *International Organization*, 43, 3: 377–403.

—— (1990) *Saving the Mediterranean: The Politics of International Environmental Cooperation*, New York: Columbia University Press.

—— (1990a) 'Obtaining International Environmental Protection through Epistemic Consensus', *Millennium*, 19, 3: 347–64.

—— (1992) 'Introduction: epistemic communities and international policy coordination', *International Organization*, 46, 1: 1–36.

Haas, P. M., Keohane, R. O. and Levy, M. A., (1993) *Institutions for the Earth: Sources of Effective Environmental Protection*, Cambridge MA: MIT Press.

Habermas, Jurgen (1968) *Toward A Rational Society*, London: Heinemann.

—— (1975) *Legitimation Crisis*, London: Heinemann.

Haigh, Nigel (1993) 'EC Implementation: Options and Constraints', in Pier Vellinga and Michael Grubb (eds) *Climate Change Policy in the European Community, Report of a Workshop held October 1992*, London: Royal Institute of International Affairs.

—— (1996) 'Climate Change Policies and Politics in the European Community', in T. O'Riordan (ed.) *The Politics of Climate Change in Europe*, London: Routledge.

Hamer, Mick (1987) *Wheels within Wheels*, London: Routledge & Kegan Paul.

Hancock, G. (1991) *Lords of Poverty*, London: Mandarin.

Hanisch, Ted (ed.) (1991) *A Comprehensive Approach to Climate Change: Additional Elements from an Inter-disciplinary Perspective, Report of a Workshop, Oslo July 1–3 1991*, Oslo: CICERO.

Hanisch, Ted (1992) 'The Rio Climate Convention: real solutions or political rhetoric?', *Security Dialogue*, 23, 4: 63–73.

Hansen, James E. (1989) 'The Greenhouse Effect: Impacts on Current Global Temperature and Regional Heatwaves', in Dean Edwin Abrahamson (ed.) *The Challenge of Global Warming*, Washington: Island Press.

Hardin, Garrett (1968) 'The Tragedy of the Commons', *Science*, 162: 1243–8.

Hare, Bill (1992) 'The Climate Convention – What Does It Mean?', *ECO*, UNCED Issue, June.

Hare, F. Kenneth (1988) 'Jumping the greenhouse gun?', *Nature*, 25 August 1988: 646.

Hart, David M. and Victor, David G. (1993) 'Scientific Elites and the Making of US Policy for Climate Change Research, 1957–74', *Social Studies of Science*, 23: 643–80.

Harvey, David (1990) *The Condition of Postmodernity*, Oxford: Blackwell.

Hatch, Michael T. (1993) 'Domestic Politics and International Negotiations: the Politics of Global Warming in the United States', *Journal of Environment and Development*, 2, 2: 1–39.

—— (1995) 'The Politics of Global Warming in Germany', *Environmental Politics*, 4, 3.

Hay, C. (1994) 'Environmental Security and State Legitimacy', in M. O'Connor (ed.) *Is Capitalism Sustainable? Political Economy and the Politics of Ecology*, New York: Guilford Press.

Hempel, L. C. (1993) 'Greenhouse Warming: The Changing Climate in Science and Politics', *Political Research Quarterly*, 46, 1: 213–40.

Holloway, Marguerite (1992) 'Still Negotiating', *Scientific American*, June: 8–9.

Holmberg, Johan, Thomson, Koy and Timberlake, Lloyd (1993) *Facing the Future: Beyond the Earth Summit*, London: Earthscan.

Hoel, Michael (1991) 'Efficient International Agreements for Reducing Emissions of CO_2', *The Energy Journal*, 12, 2: 93–108.

Houghton, J. T. (1990) 'World Needs Concerted Climate Action', *Financial Times*, 11 November.

Houghton J. T., Callander B. A. and Varney, S. A. (eds) (1992) *Climate Change 1992: The Supplementary Report to the IPCC Scientific Assessment*, Cambridge: Cambridge University Press.

Houghton, J. T., Jenkins, G. J. and Ephraums, J. J. (1990) *Climate Change: The IPCC Scientific Assessment*, Cambridge: Cambridge University Press for the Inter-governmental Panel on Climate Change.

Houghton, R. A. and Woodwell, G. M. (1989) 'Global climate change', *Scientific American*, April: 18–26.

House of Commons Energy Committee (1989) *Energy Policies and the Greenhouse Effect*, Sixth Report, Session 1988–89, HC192, London: HMSO.

Hunt, John (1991) 'UK backs voluntary greenhouse gas targets', *Financial Times*, 26 June.

Hyder, Tariq Osman (1992) 'Climate Negotiations: The North/South Perspective', in Irving Mintzer (ed.) *Confronting Climate Change: Risks, Implications and Responses*, Cambridge: Cambridge University Press.

ICC (1995) 'Statement by the International Chamber of Commerce to the United Nations Framework Convention on climate change, First Meeting of the Conference of the Parties', Berlin, March 29.

Idso, Sherwood B. (1989) *Carbon Dioxide and Global Change: Earth in Transition*, Tempe AZ: IBR Press.

IEA (1991) *Climate Change Policy Initiatives: Update*, Paris: International Energy Agency, 15 July.

—— (1992a) *Climate Change Policy Initiatives: Update*, Paris: International Energy Agency, 9 March.

—— (1992b) *Climate Change Policy Initiatives*, Paris: International Energy Agency.

Imber, Mark (1991) 'Environmental security: a task for the UN system', *Review of International Studies*, 17: 201–12.

—— (1993) 'Too many cooks? The post-Rio reform of the UN', *International Affairs*, 69, 1: 55–70.

INC (1991, 11 February) *Rules of Procedure*, UN Document A/AC.237/5.

—— (1991, 8 March) *Report of the Intergovernmental Negotiating Committee for a Framework Convention on Climate Change on the Work of its First Session, held at Washington, D.C., from 4 to 14 February 1991*, UN Document A/AC.237/6.

—— (1991, 24 June) *Beijing Ministerial Declaration on Environment and Development*, Geneva.

—— (1991, 26 June) *Compilation of Possible Elements for a Framework Convention on Climate Change Submitted by Delegations*, UN Document A/AC.237/Misc.5/Add.2.

—— (1991, 19 August) *Report of the Intergovernmental Negotiating Committee for a Framework Convention on Climate Change on the Work of its Second Session, held at Geneva from 19 to 28 June 1991*, UN Document A/AC.237/9.

—— (1991, 25 October) *Elements related to the Preamble, Principles and Commitments, Text submitted by the Bureau of Working Group I*, UN Document A/AC.237/Misc.12.

—— (1991, 18 December) *Proposal on the entire section on commitments*, UN Document A/AC.237/WG.1/L.7.

—— (1991, 19 December) *Consolidated Working Document, Addendum IV, Commitments,* UN Document A/AC.237/Misc.17/Add.1.

—— (1992, 29 January) *Report of the Intergovernmental Negotiating Committee for a Framework Convention on Climate Change on the Work of its Fourth Session, held at Geneva from 9 to 20 December 1991,* UN Document A/AC.237/15.

—— (1992, 24 February) *Provisional List of Participants,* UN Document A/AC.237/Misc.19.

—— (1992, 28 February) *Draft Report of the Intergovernmental Negotiating Committee for a Framework Convention on Climate Change on the Work of its Fifth Session, held at New York from 18 to 28 February 1992,* UN Document A/AC.237/L.7.

—— (1992, 5 May) *Draft United Nations Convention on Climate Change, 1992,* UN Document A/AC.237/CRP.1/Rev.1.

—— (1992, 27 May) *Report of the Intergovernmental Negotiating Committee for a Framework Convention on Climate Change on the Work of its Fifth Session, held at New York from 30 April to 9 May 1992, Annex 1: United Nations Convention on Climate Change, 1992,* UN Document A/AC.237/18 (Part II) Add.1.

—— (1992, 24 August) *Note by the Executive Secretary,* UN Document A/AC.237/21.

—— (1992, 16 October) *Report of the Intergovernmental Negotiating Committee for a Framework Convention on Climate Change on the Work of the Second Part of its Fifth Session, held at New York from 30 April to 9 May 1992,* UN Document A/Ac.237/18 (Part II).

—— (1992, 30 October) *Note by the Executive Secretary, Addendum,* UN Document A/AC.237/21/Corr.1.

—— (1993, 6 January) *Report of the Intergovernmental Negotiating Committee for a Framework Convention on Climate Change on the Work of its Sixth Session, held at Geneva from 7 to 10 December 1992,* UN Document A/AC.237/24.

—— (1993, 27 April) *Report of the Intergovernmental Negotiating Committee for a Framework Convention on Climate Change on the Work of its Seventh Session, held at New York from 15 to 20 March 1993,* UN Document, A/AC.237/31.

—— (1993, 20 October) *Report of the Intergovernmental Negotiating Committee for a Framework Convention on Climate Change on the Work of its Eighth Session, held at Geneva from 16 to 27 August 1993,* UN Document A/AC.237/41.

—— (1993, 16 December) *Review of Adequacy of Commitments in Article 4.2(A) and (B),* UN Document A/AC.237/47.

—— (1994, 15 February) *Revised Proposal by the Co-Chairs of Working Group I,* UN Document A/AC.237/WG.1/L.15/Rev.1.

—— (1994, 16 February) *Revised draft conclusions proposed by the Co-Chairs of Working Group I,* UN Document A/AC/237/WG.1/L.17/Rev.1.

—— (1994, 27 September) *Letter dated 22 September 1994 from the Permanent Representative of Trinidad and Tobago to the United Nations in New York to the Executive Secretary of the interim secretariat, transmitting a draft protocol to the United Nations Framework Convention on Climate Change on Greenhouse Gas Emissions Reduction,* UN Document A/AC.237/L.23.

—— (1994, 10 October) *Report of the Intergovernmental Negotiating Committee for a Framework Convention on Climate Change on the Work of its Tenth Session held at Geneva from 22 August to 2 September 1994,* UN Document A/AC.237/76.

—— (1995, 8 March) *Report of the Intergovernmental Negotiating Committee for a Framework Convention on Climate Change on the Work of its Eleventh Session, held at New York from 6 to 17 February 1995,* UN Document A/AC.237/91/Add.1.

—— (1995, 24 May) *Report of the Conference of the Parties on its First Session, held at Berlin from 28 March to 7 April 1995*, UN Document FCCC/CP/1995/7.

—— (1995, 6 June) *Report of the Conference of the Parties on its First Session, held at Berlin from 28 March to 7 April 1995*, Addendum, UN Document FCCC/CP/1995/7/Add.1.

Ince, J. (1990) *The Rising Seas*, London: Earthscan.

International Organization (1992) Special Issue on 'Knowledge, Power and International Policy Coordination', edited by P.M. Haas, 46, 1.

Inter Press Service (1992) 'Third World suspicious of "green fund" in World Bank', *Third World Resurgence*, No 14/15: 28–44.

IPCC (1988) *Report of the First Session of the WMO/UNEP Intergovernmental Panel on Climate Change, Geneva, 9–11 November*, World Climate Programme Publications Series, TD - No. 267, Geneva: World Meteorological Organization.

—— (1989) *Report of the Second Session of the WMO/UNEP Intergovernmental Panel on Climate Change, Nairobi, 28–30 June*, World Climate Publications Series, IPCC-3, Geneva: World Meteorological Organization.

—— (1990) *IPCC First Assessment Report, Volume I*, Geneva: WMO/UNEP, August, Overview.

—— (1990a) 'Policymakers Summary, Prepared by Working Group I', in J. T. Houghton, G. J. Jenkins and J. J. Ephraums (eds) *Climate Change: The IPCC Scientific Assessment*, Cambridge: Cambridge University Press for the Intergovernmental Panel on Climate Change.

—— (1990b) *Climate Change: The IPCC Response Strategies*, Geneva: World Meteorological Organization.

Islam, N. (1993) 'An UNCED Overview', *International Environmental Affairs*, 5, 3: 173–99.

Jackson, Robert H. (1990) *Quasi-states: sovereignty, international relations and the Third World*, Cambridge: Cambridge University Press.

Jaeger, Jill (1988) *Developing Policies for Responding to Climate Change, A summary of the discussions and recommendations of the Workshops held in Villach (28 September – 2 October 1987) and Bellagio (9–13 November 1987), under the auspices of the Beijer Institute*, Stockholm, WMO/TD-No.225, Geneva: World Meteorological Organization.

—— (ed.) (1990) *Responding to Climate Change: Tools For Policy Development*, Stockholm: Stockholm Environment Institute.

—— (1996) 'The History and Politics of Climate Change Science', in T. O'Riordan (ed.) *The Politics of Climate Change in Europe*, London: Routledge.

Jaeger, J. and Ferguson, H. L. (eds) (1991) *Climate Change: Science, Impacts and Policy – Proceedings of the Second World Climate Conference*, Cambridge: Cambridge University Press.

Jessop, Bob (1977) 'Recent theories of the capitalist state', *Cambridge Journal of Economics*, 1: 353–73.

—— (1990) *State Theory: Putting Capitalist States in their Place*, Cambridge: Polity Press.

Johnson, P., McKay, B. and Smith, S. (1990) 'The Distributional Consequences of Environmental Taxes', *IFS Commentary No.24*, London: Institute for Fiscal Studies.

Johnson, Rachel, (1991) 'US shrugs off pressure on greenhouse gas emissions', *Financial Times*, 18 July.

Jones, P. D., Wigley, T. M. L. and Wright, P. B. (1986) 'Global Temperature Variations Between 1861 and 1984', *Nature*, 31 July: 430–4.

Kaplinsky, Raphael (1991) 'TNCs in the Third World: Stability or Discontinuity', *Millennium*, 20, 2: 257–67.

Kegley, Charles and Wittkopf, Eugene (1993) *World Politics: Trend and Transformation*, fourth edition, New York: St Martins Press.

Kellogg, William W. (1987) 'Mankind's Impact on Climate: The Evolution of an Awareness', *Climatic Change*, 10: 113–36.

Kelly, M. and Granich, S. (1992) 'A step in the right direction?', *Tiempo*, 6, September: 1–3.

Keohane, Robert O. (1980) 'The Theory of Hegemonic Stability and Changes in International Economic Regimes, 1967–1977', in R. O. Keohane (ed.) *International Institutions and State Power: Essays in International Relations Theory*, Boulder CO: Westview Press.

—— (1984) *After Hegemony: Cooperation and Discord in the World Political Economy*, Princeton NJ: Princeton University Press.

—— (1989) *International Institutions and State Power: Essays in International Relations Theory*, Boulder CO: Westview Press.

—— (1989a) 'Neoliberal institutionalism: A Perspective on World Politics', in R. O. Keohane (ed.) *International Institutions and State Power: Essays in International Relations Theory*, Boulder CO: Westview Press.

—— (1989b) 'International Institutions: Two Approaches', in R. O. Keohane (ed.) *International Institutions and State Power: Essays in International Relations Theory*, Boulder CO: Westview Press.

—— (1989c) 'Reciprocity in International Relations', in R. O. Keohane (ed.) *International Institutions and State Power: Essays in International Relations Theory*, Boulder CO: Westview Press.

—— (1989d) 'Theory of World Politics: Structural Realism and Beyond', in R. O. Keohane (ed.) *International Institutions and State Power: Essays in International Relations Theory*, Boulder CO: Westview Press.

Keohane, Robert O. and Nye, Joseph S. (1974) 'Transgovernmental relations and International Organizations', in Michael Smith, Richard Little, and Michael Shackleton (eds) *Perspectives on World Politics*, London: Croom Helm/Open University Press.

—— (1977) *Power and Interdependence: World Politics in Transition*, Boston: Little Brown & Company.

Keohane, Robert O. and Ostrom, Elinor (1995) *Local Commons and Global Interdependence: heterogeneity and cooperation in two domains*, London: Sage.

Kindleberger, Charles P. (1973) *The World in Depression, 1929–1939*, Berkeley: University of California Press.

Kjellen, Bo (1994) 'A Personal Assessment', in I. M. Mintzer, and J. A. Leonard (eds) *Negotiating Climate Change*, Cambridge: Cambridge University Press.

Krasner, Stephen D. (1983a) *International Regimes*, Ithaca NY: Cornell University Press.

—— (1983b) 'Structural causes and regime consequences: Regimes as intervening variables', in Stephen D. Krasner (ed.) *International Regimes*, Ithaca NY: Cornell University Press.

—— (1983c) 'Regimes and the limits of realism: Regimes as autonomous variables', in Stephen D. Krasner (ed.) *International Regimes*, Ithaca NY: Cornell University Press.

Kratochwil, F. and Ruggie, J. G. (1986) 'International organization: a state of the art on an art of the state', *International Organization*, 40, 4: 753–75.

Krause, F., Koomey, J. and Bach, B. (1989) *Energy Policy in the Greenhouse: From Warming Fate to Warming Limit*, El Cerrito: International Project for Sustainable Energy Paths.

Kuroda Yoichi (1992) 'Japan and the World Bank', *AMPO Japan–Asia Quarterly Review*, 23, 3: 37–41.

Kverndokk, Snorre (1992) *Global CO_2 Agreements: A Cost Efficient Approach*, CSERGE GEC Working Paper 92–01, University of East Anglia, Norwich.

Laclau, Ernesto (1977) *Politics and Ideology in Marxist Theory*, London: New Left Books.

Lapid, Y. (1989) 'The Third Debate: On the Prospects of International Theory in a Post-Positivist Era', *International Studies Quarterly*, 33, 3: 235–54.

Lash, Scott and Urry, John (1987) *The End of Organized Capitalism*, Cambridge: Polity.

Lashof, D. and Tirpak, D. (1989) *Policy Options for Stabilizing Global Climate*, Washington: US EPA.

Lees, A. (1992) *Earth Matters* (UK Friends of the Earth magazine), 16: 1.

Leggett, Jeremy (ed.) (1990) *Global Warming: The Greenpeace Report*, Oxford: Oxford University Press.

—— (1990a) 'The Nature of the Greenhouse Threat', in Jeremy Leggett (ed.) *Global Warming: The Greenpeace Report*, Oxford: Oxford University Press.

—— (1995) 'Climate change and the financial sector', *Journal of the Society of Fellows, Chartered Insurance Institute*: 9, 2: 119–41.

Levy, M., Keohane, R. and Haas, P. (1993) 'Improving the Effectiveness of International Environmental Institutions', in P. M. Haas, R. O. Keohane and M. A. Levy *Institutions for the Earth: Sources of Effective Environmental Protection*, Cambridge MA: MIT Press.

Liberatore, A. (1994) 'Facing Global Warming: The Interactions between Science and Policy-Making in the European Community', in M. Redclift and T. Benton (eds) *Social Theory and the Global Environment*, London: Routledge.

Lipietz, Alain (1992) *Towards a New Economic Order*, Cambridge: Polity.

Lipschutz, Ronnie D. and Conca, Ken (eds) (1993) *The State and Social Power in Global Environmental Politics*, New York: Columbia University Press.

Litfin, Karen (1994) *Ozone Discourses: Science and Politics in Global Environmental Cooperation*, New York: Columbia University Press.

Lovins, A. B., Lovins, L. H., Krause, K. and Bach, B. (1981) *Least-Cost Energy: Solving the CO_2 Problem*, Andover: Brick House.

Lunde, Leiv (1991), *Science or Politics in the Global Greenhouse? A Study of the Development towards Scientific Consensus on Climate Change*, Oslo: Fridtjof Nansens Institute.

Lyman, Francesca (1990) *The Greenhouse Trap – What We're Doing to the Atmosphere and How We Can Slow Global Warming*, Boston: Beacon Press.

McCormick, John (1991) *British Politics and the Environment*, London: Earthscan.

Mackenzie, Debora (1991) 'America creates cold climate for greenhouse talks . . . ', *New Scientist*, 22 June: 16.

McKibben, Bill (n.d.) *The End of Nature*, New York: Doubleday, Anchor Books.

McTegart W. J., Sheldon G. W. and Griffith D. C. (eds) (1990) *Climate Change: The IPCC Impacts Assessment*, Canberra: Australian Government Publishing Service.

Malone, Thomas F. (1986) 'The CO_2 problem revisited', in WMO *Report of the International Conference on the Assessment of the role of carbon dioxide and of other greenhouse gases in climate variations and associated impacts, Villach, Austria, 9–15 October 1985*, WMO Publication no. 661, Geneva: World Meteorological Organization.

Manne, Alan and Richels, Richard (1990) 'CO_2 emission limits: an economic cost analysis for the USA', *Energy Journal*, 11, 2: 51–74.

Marcuse, Herbert (1964) *One Dimensional Man*, London: Sphere.

Marx, Karl and Engels, Friedrich (1970) *The German Ideology*, London: Lawrence & Wishart.

Mathews, Jessica Tuchman (1989) 'Redefining Security', *Foreign Affairs*, 68, 2: 162–77.

Matthews W. H., Kellogg W. W. and Robinson G. D. (eds) (1971) *Man's Impact on the Climate*, Cambridge MA: Massachusetts Institute of Technology.

Maunder, W. J. (1990) *The Climate Change Lexicon*, Stockholm: Stockholm Environment Institute.

Mazur, Allan and Lee, Jinling (1993) 'Sounding the Global Alarm: Environmental in the US National News', *Social Studies of Science*, 23: 681–720.

Milner, Helen (1991) 'The assumption of anarchy in international relations theory: a critique', *Review of International Studies*, 17: 67–85.

MIT (1970) *Man's Impact on the Global Environment – Report of the Study of Critical Environmental Problems*, Cambridge MA: Massachusetts Institute of Technology.

Mors, Matthias (1991) *The Economics of Policies to Stabilize or Reduce Greenhouse Gas Emissions: the Case of CO_2*, Commission of the European Communities Economic Papers, No. 87, Brussels, October.

Moss, Norman (1991), *The Politics of Global Warming*, London: Centre for Defence Studies.

Moss, R. H. (1995) 'Avoiding "dangerous interference in the climate system"', *Global Environmental Change*, 5, 1: 3–6.

Mott, Richard N. (1991), 'Looking Through "America's Climate Change Strategy"', *ECO*, 5 February.

—— (1993) 'The GEF and the Conventions on Climate Change and Biological Diversity', *International Environmental Affairs*, 5, 4: 299–312.

NAS (1979) *Carbon Dioxide and Climate: A Scientific Assessment*, Washington DC: Climate Research Board, National Academy of Sciences.

New Delhi Conference (1989) *International conference on Global Warming and Climate change: Perspectives from Developing Countries, New Delhi, 21–23 February*, New Delhi: Tata Energy Research Institute.

Nierenberg, W. A., Jastrow, R., and Seitz, F. (1989) *Scientific Perspectives on the Greenhouse Problem*, Washington DC: Marshall Institute.

Nitze, William (1989) 'The Intergovernmental Panel on Climate Change', *Environment*, 31, 9: 44–5.

—— (1990) *The Greenhouse Effect: Formulating a Convention*, London: Royal Institute of International Affairs.

—— (1994) 'A Failure of Presidential Leadership', in I. M. Mintzer and J. A. Leonard (eds) *Negotiating Climate Change*, Cambridge: Cambridge University Press.

Noordwijk Declaration (1989) *Declaration for the Ministerial Conference on Atmospheric Pollution and Climatic Change*, Noordwijk, the Netherlands, November.

Nusser, Richard (1992) 'US may be less rigid on key environmental issues', *Earth Summit Times*, 24 February.

Obasi, G. O. P., Tolba, M. K., Mayor, F., Saouma, E. and Menon, M. G. K. (1991) 'Foreword', in J. Jaeger and H. L. Ferguson (eds) *Climate Change: Science, Impacts and Policy – Proceedings of the Second World Climate Conference*, Cambridge: Cambridge University Press.

Onimode, Bade (1992) *A future for Africa: Beyond the politics of adjustment*, London: Earthscan.

Oppenheimer, M. and Boyle, R. (1990) *Dead Heat: The Race Against the Greenhouse Effect*, New York: Basic Books.

O'Riordan, Timothy and Jordan, Andrew (1996) 'Social Institutions and Climate Change: An Introduction', in T. O'Riordan (ed.) *The Politics of Climate Change in Europe*, London: Routledge.

Ostrom, Elinor (1990) *Governing the Commons: The evolution of institutions for collective action*, Cambridge: Cambridge University Press.

Ottawa Meeting (1989) *Meeting statement of the International Meeting of Legal and Policy Experts on the Protection of the Atmosphere*, Ottawa, Canada, February 20–22.

Overbeek, Henk (1993) *Restructuring Hegemony in the Global Political Economy: The Rise of Transnational Neo-Liberalism in the 1980s*, London: Routledge.

Oye, Kenneth A. (1986) 'Explaining Cooperation under Anarchy: Hypotheses and Strategies', in Kenneth A. Oye (ed.) *Cooperation under Anarchy*, Princeton: Princeton University Press.

—— (ed.) (1986) *Cooperation under Anarchy*, Princeton: Princeton University Press.

Pachauri, R. K. (1992) 'The Climate Change Convention ... What it may mean for the poor', *Network 92*, 19: 14–15.

Palan, Ronen (1993) *Underconsumption and widening income inequalities: the dynamics of globalization*, Newcastle discussion papers in politics No. 4, University of Newcastle upon Tyne.

Pallemaerts, Marc (1993) 'From Stockholm to Rio: Back to the Future?', in Phillipe Sands (ed.) *Greening International Law*, London: Earthscan.

Paterson, Matthew (1992) 'Global Warming: The Great Equaliser?', *Journal für Entwicklungspolitik*, VIII, 3: 217–28.

—— (1992a) 'Global Warming', in Caroline Thomas (1992) The Environment in International Relations, London: Royal Institute of International Affairs.

—— (1992b) 'The Convention on Climate Change Agreed at the Rio Conference', Environmental Politics, 1, 4: 267–72.

—— (1993) 'The politics of global warming after the Earth Summit', *Environmental Politics*, 2, 4: 174–90.

—— (1996) 'International Justice and Global Warming', in Barry Holden (ed.) *The Ethical Dimensions of Global Change*, London: Macmillan.

Paterson, Matthew and Grubb, Michael (1992) 'The international politics of climate change', *International Affairs*, 68, 2: 293–310.

Pearce, Fred (1989) *Turning Up The Heat*, London: Paladin.

—— (1994a) 'Frankenstein syndrome hits climate treaty', *New Scientist*, 11 June: 5.

—— (1994b) 'All gas and guesswork', *New Scientist*, 30 July: 14.

—— (1994c) 'Greenhouse targets beyond 2000', *New Scientist*, 3 September: 7.

—— (1995) 'Climate treaty heads for trouble', *New Scientist*, 18 March 1995: 4.

Peluso, Nancy Lee (1993) 'Coercing Conservation: The Politics of State Resource Control', in Ronnie D. Lipschutz and Ken Conca (eds) *The State and Social Power in Global Environmental Politics*, New York: Columbia University Press.

Picciotto, Sol (1991) 'The Internationalisation of Capital and the International State System', in Simon Clarke (ed.) *The State Debate*, London: Macmillan.

Plass, G. N. (1956) 'The Carbon Dioxide Theory of Climatic Change', *Tellus*, 8: 140–54.

Pool, Robert (1991) 'Stalemate in Nairobi', *Nature*, 26 September: 1.

Porter, Gareth and Brown, Janet Welsh (1991) *Global Environmental Politics*, Boulder CO: Westview.

Prins, Gwyn (ed.) (1993) *Threats without enemies: facing environmental insecurity*, London: Earthscan.

Putnam, Robert D. (1988) 'Diplomacy and domestic policy: the logic of two-level games', *International Organization*, 42, 3: 427–60.

Ramakrishna, Kilaparti (1990) 'Third World Countries in the Policy Response to Global Warming', in Jeremy Leggett (ed.) *Global Warming: The Greenpeace Report*, Oxford: Oxford University Press.

Ramanathan, V. (1975) 'Greenhouse effect due to chlorofluorocarbons: climatic implications', *Science*, 190, 50–2.

Rawls, John (1973) *A Theory of Justice*, Oxford: Oxford University Press.

Rayner, S. (1991) 'The greenhouse effect in the US: the legacy of energy abundance', in Michael Grubb (ed.) *Energy Policies and the Greenhouse Effect, volume II: country studies and technical options*, Aldershot: Royal Institute of International Affairs/Dartmouth.

Reinstein, Robert (1992) *U.S. Statement on Commitments*, INC V, February 27 1992, New York, mimeo.

Revelle, Roger (1985) 'Introduction: The Scientific History of Carbon Dioxide', in E. T. Sundquist and W. S. Broecker (eds) *The Carbon Cycle and Atmospheric CO_2: Natural Variations Archean to Present*, Geophysical Monograph 32, Washington: American Geophysical Union.

Revelle, R. and Suess, H. (1957) 'Carbon dioxide exchange between atmosphere and ocean, and the question of an increase of atmospheric CO_2 during the past decades', *Tellus*, 9, 18: 18–27.

Ribot, Jesse C. (1993) 'Market–State Relations and Environmental Policy: Limits of State Capacity in Senegal', in Ronnie D. Lipschutz and Ken Conca (eds) *The State and Social Power in Global Environmental Politics*, New York: Columbia University Press.

Rijsbern, F. R. and Swart, R. J. (eds) (1990) *Targets and Indicators For Climatic Change*, Stockholm: Stockholm Environment Institute.

Ross, Andrew (1991) *Strange Weather: Culture, Science and Technology in the Age of Limits*, London: Verso.

Rothstein, Robert L. (1984) 'Consensual knowledge and international collaboration: some lessons from the commodity negotiations', *International Organization*, 38, 4: 733–62.

Rowbotham, Elizabeth (1996) 'The Legal Obligations and Uncertainties in the Climate Change Convention', in T. O'Riordan (ed.) *The Politics of Climate Change in Europe*, London: Routledge.

Rowlands, I. H. (1994) *The politics of global atmospheric change*, Manchester: Manchester University Press.

Sand, Peter (1990) *Lessons Learned in Global Environmental Governance*, Washington DC: World Resources Institute.

Saurin, Julian (1995) 'The end of International Relations? the state and international theory in the age of globalization', in John MacMillan and Andrew Linklater (eds) *Boundaries in Question: New Directions in International Relations*, London: Pinter.

Schevardnadze, Eduard (1988) *Address to the United Nations General Assembly*, UN Document A/43/PV.6.

Schmidheiny, Stephan (ed.) (1992) *Changing Course*, Cambridge MA: MIT Press.

Schmidt, Karen (1991) *Industrial Countries' Responses To Global Climate Change*, Washington DC: Environmental And Energy Study Institute.

Schneider, Stephen H. (1976) *The Genesis Strategy: Climate and Global Survival*, New York: Plenum.

—— (1991) 'Three Reports of the Intergovernmental Panel on Climate Change', *Environment*, 33, 1: 25–30.

Scholte, J. A. (1993) 'From power politics to social change: an alternative focus for international studies', *Review of International Studies*, 19, 1: 3–23.

Seager, Joni (1993) *Earth Follies: Feminism, politics and the environment*, London: Earthscan.

Sebenius, James K. (1991) 'Negotiating a Regime to Control Global Warming', in Richard Elliot Benedick (ed.) *Greenhouse Warming: Negotiating A Global Regime*, Washington DC: World Resources Institute.

Shackley, S. (1994) 'Global Climate Science and Policy Making: Multiple Studies, Reduced Realities', CSEC Working Paper 94.27, Lancaster: Centre for the Study of Environmental Change.

—— (n.d.) *'Reducing the uncertainties': sinking a currency for the emerging constitution of the global environment, science and policy*, Lancaster: Centre for the Study of Environmental Change.

Shackley, S., Parkinson, S., Young, P. and Wynne, B. (n.d.) *Uncertainty, Complexity and Concepts of Good Science in Climate Change Modelling: Are GCMs the Best Tools?*, Lancaster: Centre for the Study of Environmental Change.

Shlaes, John (1995) 'Debate Heats up for Berlin Conference', *Climate Watch*, 3, 2: 5.

Shue, Henry (1992) 'The Unavoidability of Justice', in Andrew Hurrell and Benedict Kingsbury (eds) *The International Politics of the Environment*, Oxford: Oxford University Press.

—— (1993a) 'Subsistence Emissions and Luxury Emissions', *Law and Policy*, 15, 1: 39–59.

—— (1993b) 'Environmental Change and the Varieties of justice: An Agenda for Normative and Political Analysis', paper for conference on Global Environmental Change and Social Justice, Cornell University, Ithaca NY, Sept 1993.

—— (1993c) 'Avoidable Necessity: Global Warming, International Fairness, and Alternative Energy', prepared for *Theory and Practice*, *NOMOS XXXVII*, draft.

—— (1994a) 'Equity in an International Agreement on Climate Change', paper for IPCC Working Group II Workshop on *Equity and Social Considerations related to Climate Change*, Nairobi, July 1994.

—— (1994b) 'After You: May Action by the Rich be Contingent on Action by the Poor?', *Indiana Journal of Global Legal Studies*, 1, 2: 343–66.

Singer, S. Fred (1990) 'Global Climate Change: Facts and Fiction', *World Climate Change Report*, December: 19–23.

—— (1991) 'No Scientific Consensus on Greenhouse Warming', *Wall Street Journal*, 23 September.

—— (ed.) (1991a) *The Greenhouse Debate Continued: An Analysis and Critique of the IPCC Climate Assessment*, Arlington VA: Science and Environmental Policy Project.

—— (1992) 'Warming Theories Need Warning Label', *The Bulletin of the Atomic Scientists*, June: 34–9.

—— (1992b) 'Earth Summit Will Shackle the Planet, Not Save It', *Wall Street Journal*, 19 February.

Skjaerseth, J. B. (1994) 'The Climate Policy of the EC: Too Hot to Handle?', *Journal of Common Market Studies*, 32, 1: 25–45.

SMMT (1990) *The Motor Industry and the Greenhouse Effect*, London: Society of Motor Manufacturers and Traders.

—— (1993) *Road Transport and Climate Change*, London: Society of Motor Manufacturers and Traders.

Snidal, Duncan (1985) 'The limits to hegemonic stability theory', *International Organization*, 39: 479–614.

—— (1986) 'The Game Theory of International Politics', in Kenneth A. Oye (ed.) *Cooperation under Anarchy*, Princeton: Princeton University Press.

—— (1991) 'Relative Gains and the Pattern of International Cooperation', *American Political Science Review*, 85, 3: 701–26.

Solow, A. and Broadus, J. (1990) 'Global Warming Quo Vadis?, *Fletcher Forum of World Affairs*, 14: 262–9.

Sontheimer, Sally (ed.) (1991) *Women and the Environment: A Reader*, London: Earthscan.

Soroos, Marvin S. (1991) 'The Atmosphere as an International Common Property Resource', in S. S. Nagel (ed.) *Global Policy Studies: International Interaction Towards Improving Public Policy*, London: Macmillan.

Stewart, P. J. (1990) 'Life Between Greenhouse and Icebox', in H. Bradby (ed.) *Dirty Words*, London: Earthscan.

Stopford, J. and Strange, S., with Henley, J. S. (1991) *Rival states, rival firms: Competition for world market shares*, Cambridge: Cambridge University Press.

Strange, Susan (1983) 'Cave! hic dragones: A critique of regime analysis', in Stephen D. Krasner *International Regimes*, Ithaca NY: Cornell University Press.

—— (1986) *Casino Capitalism*, Oxford: Blackwell.

—— (1987) 'The persistent myth of lost hegemony', *International Organization*, 41: 551–74.

Suess, H. E. (1955) 'Radiocarbon Concentration in Modern Wood', *Science*, 122: 415–17.

SWCC (1990) 'Declaration of the Scientific and Technical Sessions of the Second World Climate Conference', in J. Jaeger and H. L. Ferguson (1991) *Climate Change: Science, Impacts and Policy – Proceedings of the Second World Climate Conference*, Cambridge: Cambridge University Press.

Swoboda, G. (1950) L'Organisation Meteorologique Mondiale', *Revue des Transports et des Communications*, April–June.

Swyngedouw, E. (1986) 'The socio-spatial implications of innovations in industrial organisation', Working paper no.20, Lille: Johns Hopkins European Center for Regional Planning and Research.

Tanabe, Akira, and Grubb, Michael (1991) 'The Greenhouse Effect in Japan: Burden or Opportunity', in Michael Grubb *et al. Energy Policies and the Greenhouse*

Effect, Volume Two: country studies and technical options, Aldershot: Royal Institute of International Affairs/Dartmouth.

Tanzer, Michael (1992) 'After Rio', *Monthly Review*, November: 1–11.

Taylor, Michael (1976) *Anarchy and Cooperation*, New York: John Wiley & Sons.

—— (1987) *The Possibility of Cooperation*, Cambridge: Cambridge University Press.

Thatcher, Margaret (1988) *Speech given at the Royal Society Annual Dinner*, Oxford, Tuesday 27 September.

Thomas, Caroline (1987) *In Search of Security: The Third World in International Relations*, Hemel Hempstead: Wheatsheaf.

—— (1992) *The Environment in International Relations*, London: Royal Institute of International Affairs.

—— (1992a) 'The United Nations Conference on Environment and Development (UNCED) of 1992 in context', *Environmental Politics*, 1, 4: 250–61.

Thomas, David (1990) 'The cracks in the greenhouse theory', *Financial Times*, 3 November.

Tickell, Crispin (1977) *Climatic Change and World Affairs*, Cambridge MA: Harvard Studies in International Affairs.

Toronto Conference (1988) 'The Changing Atmosphere: Implications for Global Security', in Dean Edwin Abrahamson (ed.) (1989) *The Challenge of Global Warming*, Washington: Island Press.

Tyndall, J. (1863) 'On Radiation Through the Earth's Atmosphere', *Philosophical Magazine*, 4, 200–7.

UK Government (1989) *The greenhouse effect – The UK Government View*, London.

UNCTAD (1992) *Tradeable Entitlements for Carbon Emissions Abatement*, Geneva: United Nations Conference on Trade and Development, INT/91 A29.

UNCTC (1992) *Climate Change and Transnational Corporations: Analysis and Trends*, New York: United Nations Center on Transnational Corporations.

Underdal, Arild (1989) 'The politics of science in international resource management: a summary', in D. Andresen and W. Ostreng (eds) *International Resource Management*, London: Belhaven.

UNECE (1990) *Report on the Regional Conference at Ministerial Level on the follow-up to the report of the World Commission on Environment and Development in the ECE region – Action for a Common Future*, Bergen, May 8–16, UN Economic Commission for Europe.

United Nations (1992) *Framework Convention on Climate Change*, New York: United Nations.

UN General Assembly (1990) 'Protection of global climate for present and future generations', *Resolution 45/212*, 21 December.

—— (1992) 'Protection of global climate for present and future generations of mankind', Draft Resolution, 25 November, Document A/C.2/47/L.58.

Universidade de Sao Paolo (1990) *Regional Conference on Global Warming and Sustainable Development, June 18–20*, Sao Paolo: University of Sao Paolo.

US Bureau of the Censuses (1992) *Statistical Abstract of the United States: 1992*, 112th Edition, Washington DC.

US CAN/CNE (1995) *Independent NGO Evaluations of National Plans for Climate Change Mitigation: OECD Countries, Third Review, January 1995*, Brussels: Climate Action Network.

US Department of Justice (1991) *A Comprehensive Approach to Addressing Potential Climate Change*, Washington DC: US Task Force on the Comprehensive Approach to Climate Change, February.

Usher, Peter (1989) 'World Conference on the changing Atmosphere: Implications for Global Security – The Conference Statement Reviewed by Peter Usher', *Environment*, 31, 1: 25–7.

Van Miegham, J. (1968) 'International Cooperation in Meteorology: An Historical Review', *Report of Proceedings of Symposium on International Cooperation in Meteorology, International Association of Meteorology and Atmospheric Physics*, Toronto: International Association of Meteorology and Atmospheric Physics.

Vasquez, John A. (1995) 'The Post-Positivist Debate: Reconstructing Scientific Enquiry and International Relations Theory After Enlightenment's Fall', in Ken Booth and Steve Smith (eds) *International Relations Theory Today*, Cambridge: Polity.

✓ Victor, David and Clark, William (1991) 'The Greenhouse Effect in the U.S.: A history of the Science up to 1985', draft paper, January.

Vogel, D. (1986) *National Styles of Regulation: Environmental Policy in Great Britain and the United States*, London: Cornell University Press.

Waltz, Kenneth (1959) *Man, the State and War*, New York: Columbia University Press.

—— (1979) *Theory of International Politics*, Reading MA: Addison-Wesley.

Ward, Hugh (1989) 'Testing the Waters: Taking Risks to Gain Reassurance in Public Goods Games', *Journal of Conflict Resolution*, 33, 2: 274–308.

—— (1992) 'Game Theory and the Politics of the Global Commons', *Journal of Conflict Resolution*, 37, 2: 203–35.

Warren, Andrew (1992) 'Brussels spout', *Evening Standard*, Monday 28 September.

Warren, B. (1980) *Imperialism, Pioneer of Capitalism*, London: Verso.

Waterstone, M. (1993) 'Adrift on a Sea of Platitudes: Why we will not solve the Greenhouse Problem', *Environmental Management*, 17, 2: 141–52.

Weale, Albert (1992) *The new politics of pollution*, Manchester: Manchester University Press.

WCED (1987) *Our Common Future – Report of the World Commission on Environment and Development*, Oxford: Oxford University Press.

WEC (1995a) 'Post-Rio '92 – Developments Relating to Climate Change', Report No.2, London: World Energy Council, April.

—— (1995b) 'Post-Rio '92 – Developments Relating to Climate Change', Report No.3, London: World Energy Council, April.

✓ Weiss, Edith Brown (1975) 'International Responses to weather modification', *International Organization*, 29: 805–26.

—— (1989) 'Climate Change, Intergenerational Equity and International Law: An Introductory Note', *Climatic Change*, 15: 327–35.

Wendt, Alexander (1987) 'The agent-structure problem in international relations theory', *International Organization*, 41: 335–70.

—— (1992) 'Anarchy is what states make of it: the social construction of power politics', *International Organization*, 46, 2: 391–425.

Wendt, Alexander and Duvall, Raymond (1989) 'Institutions and International Order', in E. O. Czempiel and J. N. Rosenau (eds) *Global Changes and Theoretical Challenges: Approaches to World Politics for the 1990s*, Lexington MA: Lexington Books.

White, Robert M. (1979) 'Climate at the Millennium', in WMO (1979) *Proceedings of the World Climate Conference – A Conference of Experts on Climate and Mankind, 12–23*

February 1979, WMO Publication no. 537, Geneva: World Meteorological Organization.

—— (1990) 'The great climate debate', *Scientific American*, July: 18–25.

White House (1990) 'Remarks by the President in the opening address to the White House conference on science and economics related to global change', Washington DC, 17 April.

Williams, J. (ed.) (1978) *Carbon Dioxide, Climate and Society*, Oxford: Pergamon Press/ International Institute for Applied Systems Analysis.

Wirth, D.A. (1989) 'Climate chaos', *Foreign Policy*, Spring: 3–22.

WMO (1979a) *Proceedings of the World Climate Conference – A Conference of Experts on Climate and Mankind, 12–23 February 1979*, WMO Publication no. 537, Geneva: World Meteorological Organization.

—— (1979b) 'The Declaration of the World Climate Conference', in WMO (1979) *Proceedings of the World Climate Conference – A Conference of Experts on Climate and Mankind, 12–23 February 1979*, WMO Publication no. 537, Geneva: World Meteorological Organization.

—— (1986) *Report of the International Conference on the Assessment of the role of carbon dioxide and of other greenhouse gases in climate variations and associated impacts, Villach, Austria, 9–15 October 1985*, WMO Publication no. 661, Geneva: World Meteorological Organization.

World Resources Institute (1991) *World Resources 1990–91*, Washington DC: World Resources Institute.

World Sustainable Energy Coalition (1993) *Global Energy Charter for Sustainable Energy Development*, Zurich: World Sustainable Energy Coalition.

Wynne, Brian (1994) 'Scientific Knowledge and the Global Environment', in M. Redclift and T. Benton (eds) *Social Theory and the Global Environment*, London: Routledge.

Young, H. P. (1991) *Sharing the Burden of Global Warming*, University of Maryland.

Young, Oran (1989a) 'The politics of international regime formation: managing natural resources and the environment', *International Organization*, 43: 349–75.

—— (1989b) *International Cooperation: Building Regimes for Natural Resources and the Environment*, Ithaca NY: Cornell University Press.

—— (1994) *International Governance: Protecting the Environment in a Stateless Society*, Ithaca NY: Cornell University Press.

Index